Emotion and Social Change

Emotion and Social Change

TOWARD A NEW PSYCHOHISTORY

EDITED BY

Carol Z. Stearns

and

Peter N. Stearns

HM

HOLMES & MEIER

New York London

Published in the United States of America 1988 by
Holmes & Meier Publishers, Inc.
30 Irving Place
New York, NY 10003

Book design by Dale Cotton

The paper used in this publication meets the requirements
of the American National Standard for Permanence of Paper
for printed Library Materials, Z39.48-1984.

Library of Congress Cataloging-in-Publication Data

Emotion and social change: toward a new psychohistory

  Bibliography: p.
  Includes index.
  1. Emotions—History. I. Stearns, Carol Zisowitz.
II. Stearns, Peter N.
BF531.H56 1988   152.4   87-28912
ISBN 0-8419-1048-0 (alk. paper)

Manufactured in the United States of America

To the memory of our colleague
Shula Sommers

Contents

Introduction
    Carol Z. Stearns and
    Peter N. Stearns   *1*

1   Understanding Emotions:
    Some Interdisciplinary Considerations
    Shula Sommers   *23*

2   "Lord Help Me Walk Humbly":
    Anger and Sadness in England and America, 1570–1750
    Carol Z. Stearns   *39*

3   Shame and Guilt in Early New England
    John Demos   *69*

4   From Ritual to Romance:
    Toward an Alternative History of Love
    John R. Gillis   *87*

5   Anger and American Work:
    A Twentieth-Century Turning Point
    Peter N. Stearns   *123*

6   Meanings of Love:
    Adoption Literature and Dr. Spock, 1946–1985
    Judith Modell   *151*

7   The Rise of Sibling Jealousy
    in the Twentieth Century
    Peter N. Stearns   *193*

Bibliography   *223*

Notes on Contributors   *225*

Index   *227*

Introduction

C a r o l   Z .   S t e a r n s
a n d
P e t e r   N .   S t e a r n s

The historical study of emotion, though a relatively new field of inquiry, has already produced considerable debate within the discipline of history, while providing a vital temporal framework for sociological discussion of love, anger, grief, and other feelings.[1] The subject, in other words, promises to add considerably to our grasp of the texture of the past and to contribute to the reviving interdisciplinary inquiry into what emotions are all about, now as well as before.

It is more than conceivable, indeed, that historical study of emotion will finally link concern with the psyche with a broader understanding of social change, a linkage promised, but not on the whole delivered, by psycho-history per se.[2] A focus on emotional change, grasped through models of emotionality sufficiently flexible to take both change and variety into account, and aimed at group patterns more than individual biography, is beginning to yield some sense of periods, trends, and even causation in emotional behavior and perception. Further exploration, of the sort represented in and encouraged by essays in this collection, may allow still further connection between emotional repertoires and other aspects of the human experience.

This volume, featuring essays on various emotions and several time periods, seeks to introduce a wider readership to the findings and issues in emotions history. It presents some intrinsically interesting aspects of the West European and American past. Individual essays deal with distinctive early modern combinations of anger and sadness; with a New England transition from inculcation of shame to the quite different emotion of guilt; with the experience and expression of love in courtship; with work-based anger; with parental love as applied to adoptive as well as biological parents in recent American history; and with some recent changes in jealousy. The essays in combination show a variety of emotional ranges in the past and a series of significant shifts over time.

The collection also presents something of a second generation of research that benefits from some of the pioneering studies, particularly of romantic love, and also from some characteristic mistakes or distortions of earlier

1

research. Although still imperfect, the developing maturity in this field is involved with widening the range of relevant sources. Many initial researchers, such as David Hunt or Lawrence Stone,[3] were content to rely on a small number of commentaries or hortatory tracts—materials still regarded as relevant, but now supplemented by a wider array of diary documentation and, as John Gillis particularly suggests, evidence derived from accounts of ritual. The quest for appropriate sources is hardly completed in the selections that follow. As items of research on the past, emotions leave a particularly obscure trace as they do even in our own time and in our own experience. But there are clear signs of innovation and extension in emotions history in the choice and manipulation of materials.

Greater maturity in the historical study of emotion shows in the willingness explicitly to address emotions themselves, rather than treating the subject somewhat indirectly as part of an inquiry into family relations or attitudes toward death. Distinctions here need not be forced. Many classic historical works—such as Johan Huizinga's *Waning of the Middle Ages*—focus extensively on the emotional tenor of the time.[4] Important models of change in romantic or parental love have been developed as part of family history, and if they are flawed in some respects, as we will argue later, it is not simply because emotions have been subsumed under larger headings.[5] Grief, to be sure, has been less coherently treated than is possible from more explicit attention to the emotion itself, but again a plausible pattern of evolution has already emerged.[6] But direct inquiry into the histories of major individual emotions, and links among emotions, is a vital next step, among other things in order to interrelate historical and other findings in emotions research. Aspects of such an interrelationship are sketched in the initial essay, by social psychologist Shula Sommers. Other essays in this volume that treat emotions such as shame, or jealousy, or sadness, as well as love of several sorts, perform a service in bringing emotions toward the center of historical attention as subjects in their own right. From this step it will be desirable to return to the wider impact of emotional styles, but the isolation of emotion in historical analysis is an essential way station.

There are two corollaries to the explicit treatment of past emotionality and emotional change, again illustrated in this collection and to be encouraged in a growing body of research. First, an increasing array of emotions is subject to historical scrutiny. While there is some recent precedent for systematic treatment of fear and of anger,[7] rather than asides based on assumptions about, say, an inverse love-anger correlation, the most prominent historical work has focused on parental and romantic love. These subjects are far from exhausted, as the Gillis and Modell essays suggest. But it is vital to probe other key emotions, and several essays here add momentum to this effort.

Especially noteworthy are John Demos's examination of shame and guilt and Peter Stearns's exploration of jealousy in recent American history.

Second, in addition to expanding the range of emotions considered, it is essential to explore emotion outside as well as within family context. Much initial work on emotions history assumed, understandably enough, what is in fact a modern artifact: that emotions rivet on family settings and that a substantial distinction exists between "private" and "public" emotional display. And without question the family remains crucial to an understanding of emotions and emotional standards, in premodern as well as modern periods. But the history of emotion can also apply to work relationships, to leisure expressions, to community relations, and to courtroom dramas. These and other settings contribute to our understanding of how emotions operate and change, often to be sure in some correspondence to standards emphasized within families. While hardly exploring all the extrafamilial avenues through which emotions history can be approached, the essays in this volume definitely and deliberately contest the notion that emotions are a province of family history alone.

Along with a wider array of sources, greater explicitness, and a growing list of emotions and their settings, the essays in this volume also signal an effort toward greater subtlety and sophistication in the crucial interpretive debate that has already taken shape in this historical field—a debate that in fact mirrors, although usually unwittingly, some of the basic contentions in emotions research more generally.

The first historians to deal very directly with emotions as part of an essentially social (as opposed to biographical) history sought to emphasize change.[8] Their impulse was both understandable and correct. It was understandable because at least superficial soundings of the premodern Western experience do suggest an emotional world quite different from our own. Traditional peasant insults and contentiousness among neighbors, for example, suggest a level, or at least an articulation, of anger with which most modern Western people would feel uneasy.[9] Standards of discipline of children hardly connote the kind of love that modern Westerners have been taught (however imperfectly) their offspring deserve. Thus a host of early histories of child rearing, and also of courtship and marriage, were inclined to emphasize the contrasts between a then and a now, and some developed challenging hypotheses also about the causation of change.[10] Besides being understandable, given apparent differences between past and present, the attempt to stress change also correctly identified the historian's chief task in this field. Rejecting some versions of psychohistory, which assumed an essentially static psyche such that the past becomes a simple illustration of a human reality derived from contemporary or near-contemporary (typically

Freudian) theory, the social historians who initially treated emotion viewed it as a variable. They saw that if history is seriously to contribute to understanding this human expression, it will be through examining the ways it has changed and by dealing with change as a process that cannot be mechanically derived from a smattering of evidence combined with theory.[11]

The most widely noted attempts to contrast modern and premodern focused of course on family relations. Edward Shorter and Lawrence Stone painted a bleak picture of low emotional levels in premodern times. Randolph Trumbach, Jean Flandrin, and to an extent John Demos, though in different ways, called attention to fierce levels of anger in premodern households or communities, as against a reduction of anger associated with the rise of modern love.[12] Philippe Ariès suggested changes in the conception of children that could be emotion related, and Lloyd deMause, hailing our own century as the first in which children have been appropriately regarded emotionally, carried this theme further.[13] Studies of death attitudes, though not without their complications, suggested a far different level of grief at the death of many family members, particularly but not exclusively young children and the elderly, before the late eighteenth century, from that which would characterize Victorian culture.[14]

The historical emphasis on change in emotions, and particularly on a crucial modern transition, has begun to exercise a fascination for other students of the social expression of emotions, particularly in sociology. History provides badly needed perspective for sociological inquiry on emotion—if nothing else, a baseline against which to assess current data—and a number of practitioners have quite properly seized upon this framework. Some, however, have taken up and even exaggerated only the initial historical approach, thus stressing a stark premodern/modern contrast. A few even misread this contrast into the twentieth century, lumping the nineteenth century and its own antecedents into an undifferentiated traditional category—which means that they are not taking seriously even the simplest historical findings. Some, finally, measure emotional change according to dubious, or at least premature, criteria of modernization, though here they correctly build on implications of the early historiography. Thus in one formulation, emotional expressiveness in family life is modern, while all other approaches, though identifiable as recently as the 1960s, become throwbacks to a rather unexamined traditionalism.[15] Here, surely, what was an understandable but oversimple impulse in the pioneering historical analysis is carried to misleading lengths.

Among historians, however, the effort to describe and explain a simple premodern/modern divide has come under increasing challenge. Earlier scholars painted a starker differentiation between the premodern and the modern than the facts sustain. They misconstrued certain evidence: harsh or sporadic physical discipline for children does not, whatever our own sensibilities, prove lack of intense and often reciprocal affection. They erred on certain practices: parentally arranged marriages without courtship were less common than was once assumed.[16] And they forgot, partly because their attention to emotion was somewhat tangential, that emotions have some biological determinants and corollaries that are unlikely to change completely. As against one French popularization, for example, which sought to demonstrate that mother love is simply a fabrication of the eighteenth century and after,[17] there are some "natural," hormonal ingredients in the mother-child dyad, though most definitely not a single "natural" expression in all times and places.

In reaction to the early contrast theme, a number of recent historical studies have sought to emphasize continuity. Renouncing an earlier evolutionary model, Philip Greven portrayed a trinity of American personality styles that, while not necessarily timeless, spanned a long sweep of time.[18] Variation within any period, not change from one period to the next, receives pride of place in his masterful study of the colonial temperament. Linda Pollock, using diary evidence that purports to run from the sixteenth into the nineteenth centuries, found that parents loved their children all along; the heralded modern-premodern break, at least in this crucial emotional relationship, is mere smokescreen. A grief theorist, using nineteenth-century materials, similarly finds no significant emotional difference between that era and our own—contemporary models fit without serious qualification.[19] And so a picture begins to emerge of unchanging Western emotion—a picture that could effectively put emotions history out of business as a serious contributor to understanding the phenomenon of emotion unless as historians return to a role of applying theories developed in other contemporary disciplines to their own concerns with the past.

The essays in this volume show, however, that the emphases on continuity, though a welcome corrective to excessive claims of change, are as exaggerated in their way as the approach they attacked. Too much insistence on basic continuity involves misreading the sources involved or in fact relying on sources that for the most part postdate the change the study seeks to deny. Linda Pollock, for example, relies mainly on late seventeenth- and eighteenth-century materials that stem from the early decades of revision of parental outlook.

The essays that follow, though diverse in focus, and occasionally indeed in disagreement on specific points, almost uniformly fall between the everything changed and nothing changed schools. They see love before the modern centuries, or hesitancies about expressing anger, but they also see shifts in the nature, intensity, and modes of expression of these and other emotions. They illustrate, in other words, a second-generation approach to the problem of change that gets beyond the oversimple terms of existing debate. The resultant indications of ways that emotions history can be grasped in terms of partial change constitute the most important collective contribution of this volume. As against some historians eager to dismiss emotions history on grounds that people are people (and so uncritically receptive to the revisionist school); and as against some sociologists lured by the beguiling simplicity of the modernization approach, in which the present moves dramatically away from the past in bold, unidirectional trends, the historical picture now grows more nuanced, and more realistic. Change remains the subject, but it now must be grasped in specific contexts and amid some continuities deriving in part from the nature of the human animal.[20]

Exploration of the complexity of change in emotions has several specific facets, besides the key effort to skate between the poles of much prior historiography. First, teleological implications may be challenged. The seventeenth and eighteenth centuries remain a break in emotional experience in some respects, but the resultant changes do not flow neatly in a single direction. Unlike Flandrin, for example, who painted an eighteenth-century precursor to the twentieth-century love without even bothering to explore the intervening period,[21] historians can now suggest that not all fundamental changes move lockstep toward what we regard as modern standards. Nor are they all benign. Because of our involvement with cherished ideals, there was a tendency in early work on the history of emotion to adopt a present-centered evaluation of emotional change. Loving families in the modern mode were good families; families that had different emotional standards were bad. But even apart from the need to note greater subtleties and oscillations in change, and the existence of various emotional approaches both then and now as opposed to a single standard, the fact is that emotional change has often brought loss as well as possible gain. Lessened spontaneity, overreliance on the family, increasing manipulation[22]—these are serious interpretive themes in the history of emotion now, along with some ongoing progressive motifs.

Understanding emotional change also involves examination of emotions history as a persisting subject, not simply defined by what admittedly remains a seventeenth–eighteenth century watershed. There is still, to be sure, a concentration on the centuries of transition. Carol Stearns, John Demos, and John Gillis all move, however, to the later eighteenth and early nineteenth centuries, though with some fleshing out still desirable in the characterizations of later emotionality. Judith Modell and Peter Stearns turn directly to the phenomenon of twentieth-century change. Shifts within the past half-century, perhaps slightly less crucial than those of the Enlightenment era, are nevertheless substantial. Even the translation of disapproval of anger to the workplace, though in some sense applying an emotional standard developed two centuries earlier, represents a crucial change in actual emotional range.

The possibility of further emotional change just developing, explored in Judith Modell's research on the potential significance of new emotional criteria for adoptive parents, reminds us that emotions history must be an ongoing concern, not simply a subject defined by a single break. And while this volume does not deal directly with centuries before the early modern, the same lesson translates backward as well: where permitted by sources, an exploration of emotional change before the compelling early-modern transition will be vitally important and significantly revealing about emotional variety and the causes and timing of emotional shifts. Given the tendency (reflected in the Gillis and Carol Stearns articles in this volume and also in work by David Sabean) to push back the dates of significant early-modern emotional change, a firmer handle on medieval or pre-transition patterns in Western Europe becomes increasingly essential.[23] And this, of course, expands the theoretical potential of having a wider array of historical cases considered. This volume is intended, certainly, to encourage and to facilitate attention to the subject of emotions change beyond the early modern transition alone.

The attempt to handle change accurately involves, finally, an increasing willingness to recognize some distinction, though not necessarily a complete distinction, between emotional standards and emotional experience. It becomes increasingly obvious that emotional standards—what the editors have urged be labeled "emotionology"[24]—change more rapidly and completely than emotional experience does. This historical distinction replicates differentiation made in other emotions research between basic (often biological) experience and influential standards—and like this differentiation it involves some blurry lines. Emotionology constitutes more than the theorizing of intellectuals about the nature of emotion or desirable emotional behavior. There is, of course, the potential for a history of this subject as well, but it has sometimes been confused with inquiry into actual, widely popularized, and deeply held standards.[25] Emotionology, like other aspects of a group's or a society's mentality, is not simply the province of the intelligentsia, and it is much more than theory; it affects behavior as well as judgment, and enters into the cognition by which individuals evaluate their emotional experience. In this sense, by producing affect about emotion—judgment, for example, that fear is pleasurable (as on a scary amusement park ride) or objectionable—it enters into emotional experience directly. But emotionology does not describe the whole of emotional experience. A society or even an individual may disapprove of romantic love, find its actual occurrence troubling—in other words, have an antiromantic emotionology—but still experience something akin to romantic love on occasion. The assumption is that an emotionology, once established, will affect the incidence of emotion and reactions to it, as well as building appropriate social institutions in courtship, or child rearing, or other emotionally salient areas. But without much question, changing standards are not entirely paralleled by equivalent change in experience. One of the reasons historians at first exaggerated change was quite simply because they took emotionology to mean emotion: thus when love came to be mentioned, in diaries or family manuals, with greater approval, they assumed that a new emotion had been born.

The distinctions among various levels of emotions history parallel those that have developed, though not always sufficiently explicitly, in the history of sex. There is an interesting history of formal, intellectual ideas about sex. There is another history of sexual mentalities—that is, deeply held personal and group attitudes about sexual goals and methods. And there is a third area, of actual sexual behavior. All three of these segments may dovetail. But they may also diverge substantially and seldom will mesh completely. All three are, furthermore, significant, though social historians are likely to be primarily interested in actual standards and behaviors rather than in formal ideas alone. Only by making distinctions among categories—so that Victorian standards, for example, are examined seriously but not taken as a full description of actual sexuality, while actual sexuality is not assumed to make possibly discordant standards meaningless—can the interrelationships among ideas, mentalities, and biological behaviors be put back together.[26] So too in the emotions area, where, however, the biological evidence is still more elusive.

The essays in this volume all reflect, though in somewhat diverse ways, awareness of the distinction between standards and experience. Some deal with emotionology pure and simple, correctly stressing the importance of deeply held standards in describing ways that people function and evaluate. Thus, for example, the comparison of standards for biological and adoptive parents, in Judith Modell's essay, where the power of mainstream emotionology long produced an effort to persuade adoptive parents to generate unusual intensity to compensate for what "nature" had not automatically provided in parent-child emotional bonds. Other essays try to show how standards and experience interrelate, using ritual or other behavioral evidence, as in the Gillis or Peter Stearns essays, or an analysis of diarists' experiential implications, or (with John Demos) the emotional cues provided by social punishments and child-rearing styles. None of the essays offers a definitive resolution of the relationship between changing emotionology and "real" emotion. They do show that emotionological shifts alter the location, targets, modes, and comfort or discomfort of emotions themselves, even as they resist the temptation to claim that standards describe the whole subject. In this way, the essays fit the issue of change—the central historical contribution of emotions research—into a set of problems inherent even in contemporary study of socially expressed emotion.[27]

In sum: the essays in this volume advance the study of emotions history by expanding its chronological range; by focusing more explicit attention on a growing array of emotions; by examining a widening number of sources; by distinguishing more carefully among ideas, standards, and direct expression or experience; and above all by sketching a more subtle rendering of emotional and emotionological change while preserving the issue of change at the forefront of the historical agenda.

There are, to be sure, other tasks for historical research on emotion that this collection fulfills more sporadically or not at all. The subject remains confined to Western history, which is a serious limitation. Ultimately, the issue of emotional change in non-Western cultures must be addressed, just as differences in contemporary experience and standards have been treated. This need is evoked in Shula Sommers's essay, but deserves much wider exploration. The question of social class, raised in earlier studies,[28] remains tricky. Several essays deal quite frankly with middle-class standards and experience, while assuming some wider impact. The discussion of anger at work involves direct interaction between standard-setters and various occupational groups, thus dealing in part with class distinctions; and John Gillis shows the autonomy, in important cases, of lower-class or age-group standards, as well as experience. But a general model of the impact of class on emotions history, or of the social levels at which influential standards develop, has yet to emerge—again, an important agenda item for the future.

Relationships among emotions in cases of change constitute another topic suggested in several essays but not systematically treated. Ultimately, along with analyses of change in specific emotion areas, we need to construct a larger picture in which interactions among emotions, or an overall history of emotionality receives pride of place. Earlier historians of emotion have suggested some relationships, such as an assumption that, in modern Western history, rising attention to familial love brought a corresponding reduction of anger (or at least growing emotionological disapproval of anger).[29] Several essays in this volume work more extensively with this subject, notably in Carol Stearns's exploration of changes in a linkage between anger and sadness. So the challenge is beginning to be perceived, but it remains to be fully addressed.[30] Nor is there systematic attention to the question of the impact of the results of emotional change. In some treatments, emotional life is viewed as a subject in itself or at most an ingredient of immediate personal relationships. Other essays, dealing with anger at work or the implications of a shift from shame to guilt, show in contrast a tentative reaching out toward a claim that emotional change might impact on phenomena such as protest or law. Surely it is wise to remain cautious. Lacking general theories about the relationship between emotion and public behaviors such as politics or entrepreneurship or diplomatic contention, and with an undeniable potential for balderdash in premature or sweeping assertions ("how new childhood fears caused the Civil War"), it is sensible to keep the focus on emotions themselves, at least for a time. But ultimately, as emotional change becomes better understood, it will be essential to work harder on the question of their impact—with the question of how this change relates to more familiar categories of historical change, not only as effect but as cause. And this task, too, remains in large part for future endeavor.

The essays in this volume also collectively hesitate on matters intrinsic to historical emotions research itself. There is an ongoing dispute, in emotions scholarship, between those who argue for a set of "basic" or natural emotions, and those who urge that emotions are simple social constructs. At extremes, this debate pits advocates of biological determinism in our species, producing common basic emotions in all times and cultures even in infants, against those constructivist psychologists and cognitive anthropologists who would deny any biological fixedness in emotions at all, claiming that emotional experience is wholly determined by the cognitive equipment, particularly the language made available within any one culture.[31] Historians have, for the most part, been unaware of this controversy, and those who have searched for theoretical underpinnings have generally embraced one of the more biologically oriented approaches, without explicit recognition that they have stepped into a battlefield. For example, in his work on witchcraft in New England, John Demos has employed Sivlan Tompkins's view that there is a biologically predetermined set of affects and that these same affects can be identified and explored transculturally. Peter Gay and Philip Greven have searched for the Freudian fixities of sexuality and aggression, assuming that these are settled entities, or things, to be found in all people regardless of the context of their cultures.[32]

Some of the essays in this volume serve to bring historians into mainstream awareness of this controversy in the field of emotions. Shula Sommers explores the theoretical importance of examining cultural context in describing emotion. John Gillis and Judith Modell are both conscious that "love," far from being a fixed entity, is an experience which differs widely as historical context changes. Carol Stearns shows that anger and sadness are different experiences for sixteenth- and eighteenth-century Anglo-Americans. Some of the essays, such as John Demos's on shame and guilt, still see a value in talking about basic emotions, and so this volume will not solve the controversy between the relativists and universalists. However, one hopes that it will cause historians to be more aware, in the future, that a controversy exists. In this way, perhaps historians may take their rightful place as equals among social scientists rather than acting as simpleminded empiricists, fit only to dig out the evidence that illustrates the theories of their more sophisticated colleagues in other disciplines. For surely, our explorations of how and to what extent jealousy, anger, love, and sadness both change and remain the same have much to contribute in this dispute. Our colleagues in anthropology, sociology, and psychology do not know to what extent fixed emotions exist. They will be happy to have the historical perspective on this problem, but first, of course, historians themselves must be aware that the problem is there.

A second controversy, related to the first, pertains to the possibility of understanding the emotionality of a foreign culture. Extreme cognitivists, struck by the difficulties of translating terms for emotion, take an almost solipsistic stand. To understand the "anger" of another culture is almost as difficult as to explain "blue" to someone who cannot see. The extremists here argued that cross-cultural comparisons, then, are almost worthless, and that their work is simply to describe, in greater and greater "thick" detail, other cultures, so that by immersing himself in all this information, the reader may in some sense finally understand almost by absorbing the context or categories of the other culture.[33] Some historians who have been aware of these issues have explicitly renounced using present-day categories to understand the past. Examples are Michael MacDonald's view in *Mystical Bedlam* that there is no point to using present concepts of mental illness to think about past phenomena or Charles Cohen's view that it is a mistake to apply present-day psychiatric interpretations to earlier religions, or indeed to try to understand them other than as their adherents themselves understood them.[34] The motivating force behind such arguments is the understandable revulsion, on the part of these historians, stated most explicitly by Stuart Clark, against depicting entire cultures as cognitively inferior or even neurotic. John Gillis, heavily influenced by this sort of thinking, goes so far as to suggest that if early modern people did not think in terms of "inner experiences," then perhaps they did not have such experiences in the sense that we do.[35]

A different point of view in anthropology has been stated by Melford E. Spiro, who argues that as social scientists our job is to at least attempt translation from one culture to the other, and that this includes some investigation of whether our notions of what is universal in the human experience can be applied at all fruitfully to an understanding of other cultures. Spiro has argued that just because other cultures may not think in terms of an inner experience or an unconscious does not mean these entities do not exist.[36] Similarly, in this volume, John Demos uses the psychoanalytic concept of "narcissistic insult" to explore the shame of New England Puritans, and Carol Stearns employs current concepts about defense mechanisms and personality styles to investigate early modern anger and sadness.

Thus, the essays in this volume reveal that historians of emotion face the same theoretical controversies as their colleagues in anthropology and psychology. Although no attempt is made here to put an end to these debates, the essays bear witness to the benefits of pursuing a diversity of approaches, and by adding a historical dimension enhance the empirical and theoretical scope of the key approaches. The essays also bear witness to the common problem, faced by historians and not shared by other social scientists, of the difficulties in ascertaining the emotional experience of dead people. With all the problems our colleagues find, in trying to get to "real" feelings, they at least have access to a host of nonverbal sources that we lack. In the absence of easy data about facial expressions, body language, voice tenor, gait, and all the myriad other cues our colleagues have in evaluating emotion, how are we, solely through the evaluation of texts, to get to inner states? The essays in this volume give some indication of the ingenuity historians may display. John Gillis uses ritual or behavior to get at emotion. John Demos displays great sensitivity to the nuances of language and choice of metaphor, while Peter Stearns suggests how rates of protest may suggest the impact of emotional standards. Carol Stearns displays an interest in what may be discovered by what is not stated about emotion. Without question, efforts to recover the past using such tools can never replicate the sort of certainty achieved by some "hard" scientists, and yet, the desirability of comprehending the total experience, including the emotional experience of the past, is so clear that we must continue to make the effort.

Many historians, to be sure, remain accustomed to dealing with more carefully bounded topics in political history or the history of ideas. One recent comment, deploring trends in recent historiography even before emotions history was explicitly defined, urged that history deal with rational decisions of prominent people, as alone providing proper guidelines for the young and moral example to us all.[37] Even social historians, accustomed to topical expansion of historical inquiry, have a certain tradition of seeking rationality, as in the solid habit of protest history to insist on the careful pursuit of goals by rioters as against the "mad mob" dismissals of conservatives and elitists.[38] Emotions history, of course, does not contradict substantial rationality, particularly given the cognitive element in emotionology and in emotions themselves when experienced. Use of emotions as instruments or tools for manipulation relates emotions history strongly to other social history interests. But there is no question that emotions history not only adds a complex task to history's charge, but calls for a redefinition of subjects and an expansion of the facets of human personality essential to historical inquiry.

Yet once we know, as we now do, that emotions are to an extent historical variables, it is impossible to keep this knowledge from affecting the way we view the past. The study of the family, clearly, must take changes in emotional relations into account, with attention to shifts in key family events such as courtship. So too, although the effort has yet to be extensively made, must the study of changes in neighborhood and community relations. Demographic behavior, as has already been recognized to an extent, is not merely a calculation of costs and economic benefits, but an emotional calculus as well.[39] Aspects of cultural history—examining the role of art, or literature, or sports—must be enriched with a sense of the service of culture in conveying accepted emotionology or providing outlets for emotions not readily tolerated in other spheres—a fascinating subject for twentieth-century history. Without pretending that most of the consequences of emotion or emotionological change are yet known—without contradicting the earlier admission that analysis of impact remains largely an item for future agenda—it is clear that the potential for improving our grasp of past societies through emotions history is considerable.

Two facets of history, in addition to family studies, seem particularly ripe for this kind of extension, and here the essays in this volume do begin to push beyond emotions themselves. Thus it becomes clear (as indeed was already suggested in some previous inquiries into the early modern emotionological transition) that new emotional standards help pick up the human meaning not simply of new intellectual trends, such as Protestantism or the Enlightenment, but of shifts to new economic relationships as well. Growing commercialization and the problem of dealing with strangers commanded, and perhaps in part depended on, emotional standards that had not been traditional in the Western world. This perception elaborates familiar themes about personality changes developed by Max Weber, to be sure. But it also suggests a deeper impact on family and friendship styles and on habits of socialization than has been commonly recognized in sociohistorical work.[40] The weakening of traditional community ties, in favor of greater impersonality and more frequent dealings with strangers, another historical staple, also gains new meaning when juxtaposed with new strictures on anger or love, or the transition from community-based shame to inner guilt. All of this raises the possibility also that emotional identifications can be used as an invitation to inquiry into other structural transformations (such, possibly, as the rise of a service economy in the late twentieth century). Our growing understanding that emotionological or emotional transitions are not glibly or faddishly arrived at, but reflect and interact with some larger shifts in the human experience thus gives fuller human meaning to some of the "big changes" in history than we can arrive at by more conventional historical measurements.

Furthermore, emotionological change is beginning to enhance our knowledge of hierarchical relationships, since emotions are used so regularly to enforce (and perhaps to conceal) such relationships. Emotional inequalities and even differences in rates and directions of change help explain how hierarchies work in human terms, and changes in one area help elucidate changes in the other. Sometimes, indeed, examination of emotional standards and expressions reveals power relationships otherwise partially concealed. Against the impression of workplace democratization,[41] new forms of differentiation in restraint of anger help explain how bosses boss. Inquiry into new sensitivities in the area of disgust help explain the functioning of social inequalities in the nineteenth century.[42] Several essays in this volume also shed light on some easily confused aspects of gender relationships. Both John Gillis and Carol Stearns find a lingering traditionalism in women's emotional standards into the nineteenth century. Despite an imagery that claimed women to be the emotional experts, for better or worse, women may actually have been less open to emotional change than men were. The fact that new economic causation, in the form of greater commercialism and dealings with strangers, bore most heavily on men probably explains this gender gap (which in turn emphasizes the importance of the interaction between emotion and economic framework). The gap, in turn, cautions against making too much of the claims of Victorian women to special lovingness, as against the operation of more dated emotional patterns during the decades of industrialization. Criticisms of female emotionality, correspondingly, were not simply resurrections of sexist classical lore but reflections of newly widening divisions in standards not only in areas where men claimed greater restraint, but also in some aspects of courtship and romance.

In arguing for the importance of emotions history in grasping the precise shape of a number of behaviors more familiar to historians—including ultimately, perhaps, politics and certain aspects of diplomacy—we have no desire to downgrade the fascination or importance of understanding emotional evolutions in their own right. The extent to which emotional changes reflect and define basic conceptions of community and of self, explored in several of the following essays and also in some earlier work,[43] attests to the significance of grasping emotional and emotionological change. The challenge to join with other researchers to try to figure out boundary lines between fixed biology and social construct, which for historians translates into the attempt to balance change against enduring human characteristics, raises vital theoretical and empirical issues and invites historians, as Theodore Zeldin has urged, not simply to apply others' theories, but to contribute to theory directly.[44]

And here, of course, the advantages of the history of emotions to historians easily spill over into the need for historical work from the standpoint of other students of emotion. Despite one interesting, though perhaps somewhat premature, venture in historical theory—the constructivist approach defined particularly by James Averill, which holds that emotions rise and fall depending on social need and therefore, in principle, on historical context[45]—emotions researchers have not been particularly interested in change as a basic condition of the field. Biological research, bent on finding immutable basic emotions and concerned lately with very transient physiological expressions, tends to focus on a discrete set of problems. But even social research has only begun to reflect awareness of the factor of change. Anthropologists in the field, though eager to explore cultural variations, have with rare exceptions not probed the mutations within single cultures, tending at points to suggest almost fixed qualities for certain cultures.[46] Sociological work, already slightly defensive because of an inability firmly to define "basic" emotions in a strictly scientific manner, has sometimes implied change, but rarely has confronted it head-on.[47] Even distinctions drawn in some social psychology, between economic and amical emotional expressions, or between shame and guilt, that have clear potential for historical exploration, have not been pursued over time, in the social science literature, which prefers definitional distinctions in strictly present contexts.[48]

Asking social and behavioral scientists, then, to share in the use of historical findings involves more than an automatic interdisciplinary transfer.[49] Yet the potential benefits are considerable. The fact that change has been demonstrated, at least in deeply held standards, makes attention to the historical dimension essential, however much it complicates existing frameworks. The fact that historians have replicated theoretical dilemmas common in other branches of research, such as the problem of relating standards to experience, adds to the potential benefit of historical inquiry. History provides an additional laboratory for the exploration of issues of this sort. And while the historical laboratory has its limitations, in comparison with strictly contemporary research, it also offers some advantages. More, for example, than cross-cultural comparison, it allows the identification of key variables and so permits analysis of the causation of particular emotional configurations. Examples of the impact of particular emotional styles on family forms or social hierarchies constitute another area where historical inquiry can provide tentative models for contemporary analysis. Outright analogy may be possible at times, as in examining the results of commercialization on emotion in other cultures or the emotional implications of new work patterns of women in our own culture, on the basis of suitably flexible models drawn from earlier Western or industrial history.

Fortunately, the first essay in this volume, by Shula Sommers, directly explores the position of the historical approach in emotions research, showing the importance of considerations of change in the expanding sociological and anthropological literature on emotions as a central subject in understanding human functioning. The role of standards, even apart from direct measures of expression or experience, receives ample treatment in this social perspective, which assumes that emotion as an ingredient of human interaction and as a partial cultural artifact supersedes purely physiological considerations. History, in Sommers's view, participates early in an expanding social science field, integral to key research strategies and not simply introductory backdrop.

While welcoming Sommers's assurance and her insights into how history fits in the conceptual schemes of several other disciplines, it is important also to recognize the subtleties involved. Here, the several essays in this volume provide not only celebration of history's new achievement, but also appropriate caution and complexity—an implicit list of how not to use history as well as how to use it. Social or behavioral scientists who, following the cues of Sommers and others, seek to use historical findings must remember that historical research itself is ongoing; the map of the past is far from completely drawn. They must plan to deal with a mixture of continuity and change, and not just one or the other. They must consider an extensive time frame, and not short-term fads or purely twentieth-century developments— even if their interest is resolutely contemporary. Clearly, some of the key issues in modern emotions history, including aspects of gender styles, took partial shape early in Western history. At the same time, change itself has not been unidirectional; simple modernization formulas, which posit clear, unaltered directions once a basic transition has been completed, do not fit easily with what we know about the history of emotion, though a careful and sophisticated modernization scheme may describe some aspects of the phenomenon. Emotions history has already enlivened an interdisciplinary research agenda, but properly understood it provides some built-in warnings against purely cursory application. Dealing with the real issues involved in the past, including alternating mixtures of continuity and change, or relationships between innovation in standards and innovation in experience, facilitates exploration of conceptual issues in other social approaches as well.

Researchers concerned, then, with emotions as an ingredient of social relations, have a vital and diverse stake in historians' efforts to define patterns of emotional change, to develop models or at least guiding case studies in the timing of fundamental change, to deal with dominant emotionologies and subcultures, and to probe causation and impact. The fact that historians bring the ingredient of significant change to a field already beset with complexity gains some compensation in the additional data base and explanatory apparatus that historians can provide for the field more generally. Historians provide also, of course, a useful reminder that research assumptions are shaped by the standards of a particular time and culture, but they can be more than relativists and perspective givers. The point may be approaching where serious research projects can conjoin historical and contemporary dimensions dealing, for example, with the position of emotionological subcultures in our own society to the benefit of historical and current understanding alike. The possibility that a society, including our own society, encounters its most serious emotional issues in areas where standards are changing, where people grow unsure of appropriate definitions, may suggest the possibility of combining historical perspective even with certain current issues of therapy.

The field of emotions research, after some decades of doldrums and despite some ongoing definitional confusions,[50] is clearly gaining a new lease on life. New experimental procedures, plus some welcome freedom from strictly Darwinian or Freudian approaches in theory,[51] contribute to this renaissance. A contemporary need to assert, in an age of artificial intelligence, the emotional component of humanness may turn out to enter in as well. And certainly, as some research suggests, the perception of some recent or prospective changes in emotional styles has fed the movement, at least to some extent.[52] Historical study of emotions, though the product in part of developments within the discipline, from the general rise of social history to more recent fascination with mentalities and with matters familial, participates in this overall movement. While emotions history brings some daunting complexity, it also represents a frontier of great promise to historian and student of emotions alike. The essays in this volume are designed to signal the historical achievement and to promote further inquiry, toward enhancing our understanding of the human animal in past and present alike.

Notes

1. Steven L. Gordon, "Socialization of Children's Emotions: Toward a Social Constructionist Theory," in Carolyn Saarni and Paul Harris, eds., *Children's Understanding of Emotion* (Cambridge, Eng., 1987); Lynn Lofland, "The Social Shaping of Emotion: The Case of Grief," *Symbolic Interaction* 9 (1985): 171–90.

2. Richard L. Schoenwald, review of Robert J. Brugger, ed., *Our Selves/Our Past: Psychological Approaches to American History,* in *Social Science History* 7 (1983): 345–47; David Stannard, *Shrinking History: Freud and the Failure of Psychohistory* (New York, 1980).

3. David Hunt, *Parents and Children in History: The Psychology of Family Life in Early Modern France* (New York, 1970); Lawrence Stone, *The Family, Sex and Marriage in England, 1500–1800* (New York, 1977).

4. Johan Huizinga, *The Waning of the Middle Ages* (London, 1927); Lucien Febvre, *A New Kind of History* (New York, 1973), p. 9; Norbert Elias, *The History of Manners* (New York, 1982); Max Weber, *The Protestant Ethic and the Spirit of Capitalism* (New York, 1977). See also recent work on the American South: Rhys Isaac, *The Transformation of Virginia, 1740–1790* (Chapel Hill, 1982); Bertram Wyatt Brown, *Southern Honor, Ethics and Behavior in the Old South* (New York, 1982); Elliott J. Gorn, " 'Gouge and Bite, Pull Hair and Scratch': The Social Significance of Fighting in the Southern Backcountry," *American Historical Review* 90 (1985): 18–43.

5. Edward Shorter, *The Making of the Modern Family* (New York, 1975).

6. Philippe Ariès, *The Hour of Our Death* (New York, 1981); Lofland, "Social Shaping."

7. Carol Z. Stearns and Peter N. Stearns, *Anger, The Struggle for Emotional Control in America's History* (Chicago, 1986); Herman W. Roodenburg, "The Autobiography of Isabella de Moerloose: Sex, Childrearing, and Popular Belief in Seventeenth-Century Holland," *Journal of Social History* 18 (1985): 517–40; Jean Delumeau, *La peur en Occident, XIVe–XVIIIe siècles: Une cité assiégée* (Paris, 1978); Jacques LeBrun, *La Peur* (Paris, 1979); Madeleine Laik, *La peur qu'on a* (Paris, 1979).

8. Stone, *Family, Sex and Marriage;* Shorter, *Making of the Modern Family;* Randolph Trumbach, *The Rise of the Egalitarian Family: Aristocratic Kinship and Domestic Relations in 18th Century England* (New York, 1978); Jean Flandrin, *Families in Former Times* (Cambridge, Eng., 1976).

9. *Maledicta: The International Journal of Verbal Aggression* 1 (1977): 7; see also 3 (1979): 2; Lawrence Wylie, *Village in the Vaucluse* (New York, 1964); J. T. Sanders, *Rainbow in the Rock: The People of Rural Greece* (Cambridge, Eng., 1962); Susan Jacoby, *Wild Justice: The Evolution of Revenge* (New York, 1983); Jacob Black-Michaud, *Cohesive Force: Feud in the Mediterranean and the Middle East* (New York, 1975).

10. Philippe Ariès, *Centuries of Childhood: A Social History of Family Life* (New York, 1962); Hunt, *Parents and Children.*

11. An imaginative combination of Freudian theory with stimulating, if somewhat precarious, ideas of change is Christopher Lasch, *Haven in a Heartless World: The Family Besieged* (New York, 1977).

12. John Demos, *A Little Commonwealth: Family Life in Plymouth Colony* (New York, 1970).

13. Lloyd deMause, ed., *History of Childhood* (New York, 1974).

14. Ariès, *Hour of Our Death;* Elisabeth Kubler-Ross, *Death, The Final Stage of Growth* (New York, 1986).

15. Francesca M. Cancian and Steven Gordon, "The Expressive Self: Social Construction of Marital Anger and Love since 1900," paper presented at the Annual Meeting of the American Sociological Association, New York, Sept. 1986.

16. John R. Gillis, *For Better, for Worse: British Marriages 1600 to the Present* (New York, 1985).

17. Elisabeth Badinter, *L'amour en plus: Histoire de l'amour maternel (17e–20e siècles)* (Paris, 1980).

18. Philip J. Greven, Jr., *The Protestant Temperament: Religious Experience and the Self in Early America* (New York, 1977); see also Greven, ed., *Childrearing Concepts, 1628–1861* (Itasca, Ill., 1973), for a rather different approach to change.

19. Linda Pollock, *Forgotten Children: Parent-Child Relations from 1500 to 1900* (Cambridge, 1984); Paul C. Rosenblatt, *Bitter, Bitter Tears: Nineteenth-Century Diarists and Twentieth-Century Grief Theories* (Minneapolis, 1983); *Journal of Social History*, special issue on the history of love, 15, no. 3 (1982); Keith Wrightson, *English Society, 1580–1680* (New Brunswick, N.J., 1982).

20. Cancian and Gordon, "Expressive Self"; Stone, *Family, Sex and Marriage*. As against oversimple renderings of change, the plea for more subtle treatment parallels recommendations for a more complex study of emotionality of late made by anthropologists who see it as a mistake made in their discipline to argue simply that cultures do or do not display "basic" emotions. Robert C. Solomon, "Getting Beyond the Jamesian Theory of Emotion in Anthropology," in Richard A. Shweder and Robert A. LeVine, eds., *Culture Theory: Essays on Mind, Self and Emotion* (Cambridge, Eng., 1984), pp. 252–53.

21. Flandrin, *Families in Former Times*.

22. Arthur Mitzman, "The Civilizing Offensive: Mentalities, High Culture, and Individual Psyches," *Journal of Social History* 20 (1987); see also Peter Burke, *Popular Culture in Early Modern Europe* (New York, 1978).

23. David Sabean, *Power in the Blood: Popular Culture and Village Discourse in Early Modern Germany* (New York, 1984); see also Burke, *Popular Culture;* Alan MacFarlane, *Marriage and Love in England: Modes of Reproduction, 1300–1840* (New York, 1986); Robert Muchembled, *Popular Culture and Elite Culture in France, 1400–1750* (Baton Rouge, 1985).

24. For fuller detail, Peter N. Stearns with Carol Z. Stearns, "Emotionology: Clarifying the History of Emotions and Emotional Standards," *American Historical Review* 90 (1985): 813–36.

25. This approach basically characterizes Peter Gay, *The Bourgeois Experience: Victoria to Freud* (New York, 1984), and Steven Ozment, *When Fathers Ruled: Family Life in Reformation Europe* (Cambridge, Mass., 1983).

26. Gay, *Bourgeois Experience;* Carl Degler, *At Odds: Women and the Family in America from the Revolution to the Present* (New York, 1980); Carol Z. Stearns and Peter N. Stearns, "Victorian Sexuality: Can Historians Do It Better?" *Journal of Social History* 18 (1985): 625–34.

27. Carol Z. Malatesta and Carroll E. Izard, eds., *Emotion in Adult Development* (New York, 1982).

28. Edward P. Thompson, review of Lawrence Stone, *The Family, Sex and Marriage in England,* in *New Society* 8 (1977): 499–501; Mitzman, "Civilizing Offensive."

29. Trumbach, *Egalitarian Family*.

30. See, for example, Michael Barton, *Goodmen: The Character of Civil War Soldiers* (University Park, Pa., 1981).

31. James R. Averill, "A Constructivist View of Emotion," in Robert A. Plutchik and Henry Kellerman, eds., *Emotion: Theory, Research, and Experience* (New York, 1980), pp. 305–39; Richard Shweder, "Anthropology's Romantic Rebellion against the Enlightenment, or There's More to Thinking than Reason and Evidence," in Shweder and LeVine, eds., *Culture Theory,* pp. 27–66.

32. John Demos, *Entertaining Satan. Witchcraft and the Culture of Early New England* (Oxford, 1982), pp. 184ff.; Gay, *Bourgeois Experience;* Greven, *Protestant Temperament*.

33. An example, heavily influenced by the work of Clifford Geertz, is Michelle Z.

Rosaldo, "Toward an Anthropology of Self and Feeling," in Shweder and LeVine, *Culture Theory*, pp. 137–57.

34. Michael MacDonald, *Mystical Bedlam: Anxiety and Healing in Seventeenth-Century England* (Cambridge, Eng., 1981); Charles Lloyd Cohen, *God's Caress. The Psychology of Puritan Religious Experience* (New York, 1986), pp. 20ff.

35. Stuart Clark, "French Historians and Early Modern Culture," *Past and Present* 100 (August 1983): 62–99.

36. Melford E. Spiro, "Some Reflections on Cultural Determinism and Relativism with Special Reference to Emotion and Reason," in Shweder and LeVine, *Culture Theory*, pp. 323–46.

37. Gertrude Himmelfarb, "Denigrating the Rule of Reason: The 'New History' Goes Bottoms Up," *Harper's Magazine* (April 1984).

38. George Rudé, *The Crowd in History: Popular Disturbances in France and England*, rev. ed. (New York, 1981); Charles Tilly and Edward Shorter, *Strikes in France, 1830–1974* (Cambridge, Mass., 1974); Charles Tilly, *From Mobilization to Revolution* (Reading, Mass., 1978).

39. Maris Vinovskis, "Recent Trends in American Historical Demography," *American Review of Sociology* 47 (1978); Edward Shorter, "Illegitimacy, Sexual Revolution and Social Change in Modern Europe," *Journal of Interdisciplinary History* 2 (1971): 237–72; Viviana Zelizer, *Pricing the Priceless Child: The Changing Social Value of Children* (New York, 1985).

40. Benjamin Nelson, *The Idea of Usury* (Chicago, 1969).

41. Abram de Swaan, "The Politics of Agoraphobia: On Changes in Emotional and Relational Management," *Theory and Society* 10 (1981): 359–85.

42. Alain Corbin, *The Foul and the Fragrant: Odor and the French Imagination* (Cambridge, Mass., 1986).

43. MacDonald, *Mystical Bedlam*; Sabean, *Power in the Blood*.

44. Theodore Zeldin, "Personal History and the History of the Emotions," *Journal of Social History* 15 (1982): 339–48.

45. Averill, "Constructivist View"; James R. Averill, *Anger and Aggression: An Essay on Emotion* (New York, 1982).

46. Jean L. Briggs, *Never in Anger: Portrait of an Eskimo Family* (Cambridge, Mass., 1970); but see also Robert I. Levy, *Tahitians: Mind and Experience in the Society Islands* (Chicago, 1973).

47. Arlie Russell Hochschild, *The Managed Heart: Commercialization of Human Feeling* (Berkeley and Los Angeles, 1983).

48. Helen B. Lewis, *Shame and Guilt in Neurosis* (New York, 1971); M. S. Clark, "Compatibility in the Context of Exchange versus Communal Relationships," in E. Ickes, ed., *Compatible and Incompatible Relationships* (New York, 1985), pp. 119–40.

49. Peter N. Stearns, "Historical Analysis in the Study of Emotion," *Motivation and Emotion* 10 (1986): 185–93, and "The Problem of Change in Emotions Research: New Standards for Anger in 20th-Century American Childrearing," *Symbolic Interaction* 11 (1987).

50. Paul R. Kleinginna and Anne M. Kleinginna, "A Categorized List of Emotion

Definitions, with Suggestions for a Consensual Definition," *Motivation and Emotion* 5 (1981): 354–59.

51. Levy, *Tahitians*.

52. Hochschild, *Managed Heart;* Sara Kiesler, T. McGuire, and J. Siegel, "Social Psychological Aspects of the Computer-Mediated Communication," *American Psychologist* 39 (1984): 1123–34.

1

Understanding Emotions: Some Interdisciplinary Considerations

Shula Sommers

Analyses of emotion have long concerned themselves with questions regarding the scope and range of processes that emotions involve. What is typically involved in the experience of emotions? Are emotions reflexive responses to situations or do they involve significant cognitive activity? Are emotions essentially a psychological and physiological phenomenon, or are they broader in scope? Do emotions mainly represent what the individual feels "inside," or do they also carry implications for the social context? Questions such as these that deal with highly complex issues have been difficult to tackle and are still the subject of much debate.[1] It is, therefore, not surprising that there is not yet general agreement as to what should constitute the focus of theoretical concern in the analysis of emotions. Theorists of emotion differ greatly on the type of questions they treat as central to the understanding of emotions. While some have argued that emotions need to be analyzed at the biological and psychological levels, others have suggested that there is a need to go beyond the individual and to take into account the social context of emotions.[2] In this paper I will elaborate on the latter position and I will suggest that emotions need to be studied in a much broader context than has heretofore been assumed. I will also suggest that an adequate study of the emotions requires us to go far beyond the disciplinary boundaries demarcated by traditional theories of emotion.

Toward an Interdisciplinary Approach to the Emotions

It seems instructive to begin with a brief review of recent developments in the field of psychology—a field where emotion was traditionally placed as a subject of inquiry. Amid persistent controversies regarding the basic determinants of emotions, there has been in recent years a growing consensus with respect to some key issues. First, there is a growing agreement among contemporary theorists on the general significance of emotions. In contrast to the trend that dominated psychological theorizing in the 1930s and 1940s to view emotion primarily as a disorganized or disorganizing response, most theorists today acknowledge that emotions involve constructive processes.[3] A number of theorists have insisted that emotions cannot be viewed as biological givens or as natural and passive states composed of sensations and feelings of arousal. Rather, it has been suggested that there is something active to the experience of emotion, since it involves cognition.[4] Likewise, during the past two decades theories have emerged that characterize the emotions as complex responses involving multiple factors. Schachter and Singer, as well as Mandler have presented a two-factor theory that accounts for emotions in terms of both physiological and cognitive processes.[5] Lazarus, Averill, and Opton characterize emotions as "coping responses" involving physiological, behavioral, and cognitive components.[6] And Leeper, who has strongly emphasized the "richness" of emotional processes, argued against viewing emotions in terms of the "frightened look" or the "angry reaction" which occurs when the organism is confronted with some problem in the environment. Instead, emotions are to be treated as the processes underlying the frightened look or the angry reaction.[7] In Leeper's account, the emotions become highly complex as they are imbued with a full cognitive character and are elevated to the status of a high-level human function. Leeper has also challenged the conception that emotions tend to make people engage in relatively primitive reactions that are at odds with their social responsibilities.[8] More recently there has been an elaboration on the theme that emotions are partly a social affair and that they serve an important social function.[9] Thus, Averill has insisted that an important task in the analysis of emotions is to understand the meaning of emotion within the sociocultural system.

The growing interest in what might be called the social aspects of emotions has spread in the past decade to the fields of sociology and anthropology, where emotions had previously received little attention. Sociological analyses such as those of Hochschild and Kemper suggest that emotions are subject to penetrating social influences.[10] Kemper views emotions largely as a product of social interactions and he maintains that social organizations and structures promote or inhibit different emotions. Implicit in the recent sociological analyses is the idea that societal influences on emotions cannot be understood as merely restrictive. Social agencies and institutions are not only involved in imposing constraints on the expression of emotions judged as inappropriate, but they play an important role in promoting emotions that are consistent with societal aims and interests.[11] Anthropologists have also argued against viewing emotions as matters of instinct, insisting that emotions are mediated by cultural rules and expectations. For Levy, Rosaldo, and

Lutz the experience of emotion is largely a cultural matter, since individuals define emotional realities in accordance with local cultural schemata.[12] Lutz's interesting study of what might be called emotional education among the Ifaluk reveals how parents try to ensure that their children acquire certain values that might have consequences for their emotional style.[13]

There is still another kind of analysis of emotion that has recently been offered. Stearns and Stearns have proposed a socio-historical framework for the study of emotion suggesting that emotions need to be understood not only in relation to the personal histories of individuals, but also in relation to the larger social history.[14] Thus, it is suggested that historical investigations should focus on the study of "emotionology"—"the collective emotional standards of societies across time"—and seek to identify links between change over time in emotional standards and changing social and ideological conditions.[15] The arguments of Stearns and Stearns deserve further consideration, and I will devote more attention to their proposals in a subsequent section.

The most general issue that emerges from the above discussion is the strong suggestion that the subject of emotion is no longer accounted for in strictly psychological terms. In view of the diversity of the new approaches to the emotions, one is led to consider the need for an interdisciplinary approach. Does a proper understanding of emotions require that we view this phenomenon from multiple viewpoints (e.g., the biological, cross-cultural, and historical)? What might be the contributions of the different approaches? Can the sociocultural approaches to emotion form meaningful links with the psychological perspective? In addressing these issues I will focus on work in the social sciences and other disciplines that aim at elucidating those aspects of the emotions that are more than physiological. Psychologists long tended to place a strong emphasis on the biological aspects of emotions and they have become convinced that they can benefit from research efforts in the discipline of biology.[16] But what has not yet been fully considered are the potential contributions of various socially oriented approaches to the emotions, such as the newly proposed socio-historical approach. It seems, therefore, appropriate to concentrate on this perspective on emotion, while considering the broader theme of the usefulness of an interdisciplinary effort in this area.

The justification for the need of a broad perspective on emotion—a perspective that extends beyond the individual psychological level of analysis—will be aided by a consideration of Bedford's interpretation of emotion concepts and their meaning.[17] Bedford has said:

> Emotion concepts . . . are not purely psychological: they presuppose concepts of social relationships and institutions, and concepts belonging to systems of judge-

ments, moral, aesthetic and legal. In using emotion words we are able, therefore, to relate behavior to the complex background in which it is enacted and so to make human action intelligible.[18]

Bedford argues that emotions cannot simply be treated as radically personal responses, the expression of feelings or other processes that are private, individual, and socially irrelevant. On this account emotions do not lie outside the social framework, but they have important social connotations. Emotions reflect, among other things, knowledge of the valuations of a community, concepts of social relationships as well as attitudes and beliefs held in common by members of a community. It follows that an individual's emotions are embedded in the social framework in which an individual functions and that analyses of emotions cannot ignore social phenomena. Emotions, then, cannot be "reduced" to a strictly psychological analysis.

Bedford's analysis could be understood as inviting explorations of new, emotion-related topics—topics whose understanding might be advanced by research efforts in various fields. Sociologists, anthropologists, and historians might well aid the psychologist to understand how the emotional life of the individual relates to broader modes of thought within a community. With this in mind, let us now turn to consider some methodological issues.

The Problem of Methodology

In evaluating the usefulness of multidisciplinary research efforts in the area of emotion, we must also address some methodological issues. Which research strategies should be accepted as useful methods? Which research strategies can tap important aspects of emotions? So far, recognition has been given to various methods used by psychologists (e.g., behavioral, self-reports, laboratory experiments), which follows from the general acknowledgment that emotion is accessible to the psychologist. What is less certain is the degree to which emotion is accessible to investigators within the boundaries of other disciplines. In this context it seems particularly necessary to pose some questions about the aptness of research strategies used by historians, since historians cannot study emotion directly. What, then, might be the nature of their contribution? Can historians contribute significantly to efforts directed toward the understanding of emotion? Stearns and Stearns have proposed that historians should concentrate on the study of "emotionology," that is, how emotions are appraised at different historical periods.[19] This focus on emotionology (as distinct from the study of emotional experience) is considered by Stearns and Stearns to be a legitimate research strategy, one that could add substantially to the traditional methods of studying emotions.

TABLE 1

Responses distribution (percentages) for questions about
the evaluation and experience of emotions.

N	Americans 60	Greeks 21	West Indians 20	Chinese 20
Which emotions are most useful and constructive to experience?*				
Which emotions do you experience regularly and often?**				
Enthusiasm	52 (55)	28 (14)	20 (10)	10 (10)
Happiness	61 (40)	47 (33)	60 (45)	50 (50)
Hope	47 (20)	61 (43)	30 (30)	40 (25)
Joy	45 (20)	42 (28)	35 (20)	55 (15)
Love	92 (47)	80 (38)	85 (65)	45 (25)
Pride	48 (25)	33 (33)	65 (60)	25 (15)
Respect	53 (23)	80 (52)	60 (30)	60 (25)

* Responses to this question, which pertain to the evaluation of emotions, are out of
parentheses.

** Responses to this question, which pertain to the experience of emotions, are in
parentheses.

Several questions emerge: Can the study of emotionology contribute to the understanding of emotional experience itself? What kinds of links exist between ways of evaluating emotions and the experience of emotions? Does the study of the former have a bearing on the latter? On the basis of recent research findings I will argue that there may be a close correspondence between the evaluation and experience of emotions. I will also suggest that it is important to study how emotions are perceived and evaluated, since the evaluation of emotions communicates valuable information about emotion itself.

Proposed Links between the Evaluation and Experience of Emotions

The first set of findings relevant to our discussion is presented in table 1. The data are part of a larger research project in which young adults of four cultural groups were interviewed on the way they view, evaluate, and experience emotions.[20] There were sixty Americans, twenty-one Greeks, twenty West Indians, and twenty Chinese. Table 1 presents one set of data pertaining to the evaluation and experience of emotions. The table summarizes subjects' responses to a question that deals with the way emotions are evaluated ("In your view which emotions are most useful and constructive to experience?"). A summary of subjects' responses to a question about their experience of emotions ("Which emotions do you experience regularly and often?") is also presented. An inspection of this table reveals a close association between the evaluation of emotions and the reported emotional experiences. The emotions that tended to be evaluated most positively within a group also emerged as the most frequently experienced emotions. Consider, for example, the findings with respect to enthusiasm. Americans tended more than the other cultural groups to value enthusiasm; more than 50 percent of the subjects in the American sample considered enthusiasm to be a useful and constructive emotion. Interestingly, Americans were also found to report more often the experience of enthusiasm than did other cultural groups.

Another emotion, pride, was prominent in the accounts of the West Indians. As can be seen, the majority of the West Indian subjects evaluated pride positively and they reported that pride was frequently felt. Once again, we see that cultural variations in the perceived value of an emotion parallel variations in its experience. Compared to other cultural groups there were more West Indians that referred to pride in their evaluation and reports of emotional experiences. The emotion of love was also the source of cultural differences. The findings reveal that in comparison to other cultural groups there were fewer subjects in the Chinese sample that considered love as one of the most useful and constructive emotions. At the same time there were comparatively fewer subjects in the Chinese sample reporting that love was frequently experienced.

The findings reported in table 2 reinforce the suggestion that there is close correlation between ways of thinking about emotions and the experience of emotion itself. Subjects' responses regarding the negativity of various emotions (i.e., "In your view, which emotions should be avoided as most dangerous and destructive?") reveal that the emotions of hate, terror, and rage were evaluated most negatively by a large number of subjects in the four cultural groups. Note, too, that these emotions tended to be reported as rare experiences. (See table 2, which also summarizes subjects' responses to the question "Which emotions do you experience very rarely or hardly ever?") Other interesting results involve the Chinese reactions to the so-called negative emotions. An inspection of table 2 also reveals that there were comparatively fewer Chinese who evaluated negatively emotions such as terror, rage, and hate—a finding that could be taken to indicate that the Chinese

TABLE 2
Responses distribution (percentages) for questions about
the evaluation and experience of emotions.

N	Americans 60	Greeks 21	West Indians 20	Chinese 20
Which emotions should be avoided as most dangerous and destructive?*				
Which emotions do you experience very rarely or hardly ever?**				
Envy	31 (13)	77 (48)	40 (35)	15 (30)
Guilt	30 (7)	38 (24)	40 (25)	50 (15)
Hate	77 (60)	77 (33)	65 (35)	50 (25)
Jealousy	61 (12)	55 (43)	50 (40)	20 (45)
Rage	60 (35)	66 (24)	50 (40)	35 (45)
Terror	43 (41)	66 (52)	50 (35)	35 (30)

* Responses to this question, which pertain to the evaluation of emotions, are out of parentheses.

** Responses to this question, which pertain to the experience of emotions, are in parentheses.

may be more accepting of the so-called negative emotions. Consistent with their evaluation of these emotions were the reports of emotional experiences. As can be seen, there were relatively fewer subjects in the Chinese sample reporting that the experience of negative emotions such as hate or terror was a rare experience.

How can we explain the suggestion put forward by the findings that there are links between the evaluation and experience of emotions? What kind of conceptions and ideas about emotions can be drawn upon to elaborate the proposed relationship? Cognitively oriented formulations that assume a tight connection between emotion and cognition seem to shed some light on this matter. Especially useful is Solomon's theory that views emotions not in isolation from the rest of our cognitive experiences, but in close association with them.[21] According to Solomon, emotions involve judgments (about the world, about other people, and about ourselves and our place in the world) that have conceptual connections with other attitudes and beliefs that the person holds. As he said: "Emotions are part of an elaborate web of experiences and beliefs tied to other judgements . . . by various logical connections. To understand another person's emotional life requires nothing less than an understanding of their view(s) of the world."[22] On this account emotions are "conceptual constructions" tied to ways of viewing life; they are presumed to be composed of values and beliefs that are structured within a "world view." The proposed relationship between the evaluation and experience of emotion can, then, be understood with reference to a system of values and beliefs or a world view that might influence both the evaluation and experience of emotions.

At this point, it might be useful to engage ourselves in a less abstract discussion of the relationship between emotional experiences, world views and the evaluations of emotions. I will, therefore, move on to discuss a set of anthropological observations that could offer more specific information about this matter.

Emotions and Ways of Thinking about Emotions in Diverse Cultures

We may begin our exploration of this topic by focusing on the ideology surrounding anger among the Utku Eskimos, described by Briggs as a people who rarely if ever experience anger.[23] The "never in anger thesis" put forward by Briggs suggests that Utku adults differ from other cultural groups not in that they do not express anger, but in that they do not experience anger.[24] To the extent that this is correct, how are we to understand the Utku emotional style? How is anger perceived in this cultural environment? Can we gain an understanding of the Utku emotional responsiveness via an exploration of their views of life? Such a suggestion was made by Solomon, who has argued that the Utku emotional style could be better understood if viewed in relation to the content of their world view.[25] From a cognitive perspective, anger is understood as involving an evaluation that leads one to make an accusation. It is presumed to involve concepts such as "wrong," "unfairness," "offense," and other notions that lead one to impute blame and responsibility on another.[26] But such concepts, according to Solomon, are not built into the Utku world view. Central to their world view is instead an attitude of fatalism or "resignation to the inevitable." Their philosophy is that hardships are unavoidable and must be tolerated. Anger does no good and the appropriate attitude, in their view, is calm acceptance (e.g., "it can't be helped").[27] It might be said, therefore, that the Utku do not view the world in terms that invite anger.

In sharp contrast to the Utku cultural orientation, consider the Kaluli culture that seems to value vigor, individual initiative, and personal assertiveness. What appears to coincide with this cultural orientation is an emotional style and an ideology of anger that stands in sharp contrast to the Utku's "never in anger" orientation. As Schiefflin's ethnographic study reveals, anger has high "visibility" within the Kaluli culture.[28] And there are other differences. Whereas the Utku ridicule anger, viewing it as a childish and immature response, the Kaluli view anger with admiration.[29]

The above discussion of cultural difference in the evaluation and experience of emotions in relation to world views reinforces the suggestion made earlier that emotions cannot be explained only in terms of individual psychological mechanisms. There seems to be a close association between cultural values and the emotional responses of individuals which, in turn, suggests that emotions need to be understood in terms of the rest of the culture and its ideology. An adequate understanding of emotions thus requires that we concern ourselves with much more than is assumed by traditional theories. For example, we need information about the way of life of a community, its distinctive value-emphasis, and the kind of attitudes toward emotions that are prevalent within this community.

Observations of Tahiti at different historical periods shed more light on the kind of issues we need to attend to in a comprehensive account of the emotions. Contemporary Tahiti has been described by Levy as a "gentle" environment where anger has "low visibility."[30] Interestingly, there seems to be a good deal of similarity between modern and pre-Christian Tahiti in responsiveness to anger. The accounts of travelers of the late eighteenth century and early nineteenth century contain very few reports of angry behavior.[31] The Tahitians impressed these observers as people that are "slow to anger and easily appeased."[32] As concerns the ideology of anger we learn from Levy's study of modern Tahiti that anger, although much discussed by the Tahitians, is viewed negatively. Anger tends to be perceived mainly in terms of its destructive effects.[33]

What aspects of the Tahitian culture may be of relevance for understanding the status of anger in Tahiti? Levy's continual references to Tahitians' concepts and expectations of the self, and of relationships between self and others, offer some useful information about this complex matter.[34] As suggested earlier, anger is a judgmental emotion and it is presumed to involve an evaluation that leads one to cast a judgment and impute blame and responsibility to another. Among other things, anger requires a conception of oneself that enables one to judge another.[35] But the Tahitians, as they emerge from Levy's descriptions, do not seem to define themselves in such terms. Their philosophy defines the self in terms of limitations and powerlessness and essentially as accepting and not as protesting.[36] Levy tells us that the Tahitians cultivate an attitude of calm acceptance—an attitude which is likely to minimize the seriousness of an offense and thus act as a deterrent to anger. Consistent with the way the self is defined is the Tahitian view of the world, a view that would seem to limit individual strivings and willfulness. Thus, the world or forces outside the individual are conceived to be powerful and not easily changed. And there are other aspects of the culture that may be considered in relation to the Tahitian's reaction to anger. We learn from Levy's study that in modern Tahiti timidity and docility are highly valued and considered the desirable qualities, whereas individual striving and ambition, qualities that might be associated with the disposition toward anger, are devalued.[37] To understand emotions within a social framework thus requires that we concern ourselves with concepts and definitions of the self that are context bound and culture specific. In addition, there is a need to inquire into the historical origins of cultural practices that are tied to various concepts. Future research might attempt to examine, for example, socialization techniques and child-rearing procedures in Tahiti in terms of the influences they might have on the shaping of one's sense of self and one's responsiveness to anger. It might be interesting to examine certain institutional patterns and, in particular, the highly prevalent custom of adoption as practiced in Tahiti in terms of its effects on the emotional life of individuals.[38] In this context we must note that Levy's informants have referred to felt emotional constraints due to adoption. Levy quotes an informant talking about her adoptive mother: "I never got angry at her, even if she whipped me, because I was aware that she had taken me. She took me so I thought I was the one who was at fault, that is why she hit me. . . . I did not get upset. I did not get angry because she took me from infancy and kept me. So I thought . . . it wasn't right to be angry with her."[39]

Historians can contribute to research efforts toward understanding the communal context of emotions, and they can point to the kind of factors we need to consider in attempting to understand societal attitudes toward various emotions. With respect to anger in Tahiti we need to learn more about the role of past trends in the shaping of Tahitians' attitudes toward anger. Is it indeed true that the transition from pre-Christian to modern Tahiti has not affected the way anger is understood? Does the evaluation of anger in contemporary Tahiti represent a continuity of traditional attitudes? Questions such as these await exploration.

I would like to pursue the question of the usefulness of an interdisciplinary approach in this area and, in particular, the potential contribution of historians by considering a case of emotional change within a group over time, and the ramification it has for the general study of emotion. Specifically, my discussion will consider accounts of grief and mourning behavior in pre-Christian and modern Tahiti. From Levy's study we learn that grief and mourning behavior in the present is emotionally restrained.[40] Even the nearest relatives are expected to make an effort to control the expression of grief. The following description is offered by Levy in his account of the ceremony related to the death of Tavana Vahine (the wife of Tavana, the chief of a community in Tahiti):

> The first villages that entered the room were mostly members of Teiva's congregation. . . . when everybody was seated, Teiva read from the Bible and then spoke, praising Tavana Vahine. As he began this, Tavana's eyes were brimming with tears, and he sobbed silently. After a few minutes of this he stopped sobbing and sat quietly with his eyes closed. The eyes of all the adult villagers in the room were full of tears, and all the women and some of the men held handkerchiefs with which they would wipe their eyes. During all this nobody looked at anyone else, looking either off into space or down at the floor. Once during the service Teiva's voice broke, and he started to sob quietly. Several of the other people in the room seemed to me at this time to be making a strong effort to restrain themselves from breaking down. When Teiva had finished, Tavana stood up and gave a quiet, formal speech of thanks.[41]

It is also noted by Levy that a short period of mourning is expected in modern Tahiti as the public emphasis is on getting over the loss quickly.

How different this seems from the way grief was expressed in Tahiti in earlier periods. From the reports of early observers we learn that in pre-Christian Tahiti the expression of grief was intense, even violent.[42] Typical of bereavement at that time was the loud wailing and the self-wounding of women, as some of the mourners cut their head with a shark tooth instrument. Consider, for example, the comments made by Ellis in his journal of 1829.

> Almost every native custom connected with the death of relations or friends, was singular, and none perhaps more so than the *otohaa*, which, though not confined to instances of death, was then most violent. It consisted in the most frantic expressions of grief, under which individuals acted as if bereft of reason. It commenced when the sick person appeared to be dying; the wailing then was often most distressing, but as soon as the spirit had departed, the individuals became quite ungovernable.
>
> They not only wailed in the loudest and most affecting tone, but tore their hair, rent their garments, and cut themselves with shark's teeth or knives in a most shocking manner . . .
>
> . . . they cut themselves unmercifully, striking the head, temples, cheek, and breast, till the blood flowed profusely from the wounds. At the same time they uttered the most deafening and agonizing cries; and the distortion of their countenances, their torn and dishevelled hair, the mingled tears and blood that covered their bodies, their wild gestures and unruly conduct, often gave them a frightful and almost inhuman appearance. This cruelty was principally performed by the females, but not by them only; the men committed on these occasions the same

enormities, and not only cut themselves, but came armed with clubs and other deadly weapons.[43]

One might begin the exploration of the causes for the change in mourning practices in Tahiti by posing some questions about the depth of this change. What does the change in mourning practices represent? Does the change in mourning behavior reflect a change in the intensity of experiencing grief? Does it suggest that there has been a change in reactions to loss and that such reactions now involve less distress and less sorrow? The more general question here is, of course, the question of the relationship between the experience of grief and its conventionalized public display. In this connection it is interesting to note that early observers expressed doubts about the sincerity of mourning behavior in ancient Tahiti and some have suggested that the violent expression of grief was not spontaneous but simulated.[44] Especially suspect was the strong emphasis on formality in what appeared to be violent and out-of-control emotional behavior. Joseph Banks in his journal of 1769 points to some peculiarities in the ceremonies related to death.

No sooner is the corpse fixed up within the House . . . than the ceremony of mourning begins again. The women . . . assemble led on by the nearest relation, who walking up to the door of the house swimming almost in tears, strikes a shark's tooth several times into the crown of her head, on which a large effusion of blood flows, which is *carefully* caught in their linen, and thrown under the bier. Her example is imitated by the rest of the women, and this ceremony is repeated at the interval of 2 or 3 days, as long as the women choose or can keep it up. Beside the blood which they believe to be an acceptable present to the deceased . . . they throw in cloths wet with tears, of which all that are shed are *carefully* preserved for that purpose.[45] (Italics mine)

Others noted that the intense display of grief was of an extremely short duration and that the mourners quickly resumed their activities and assumed a degree of cheerfulness.[46]

Historians could perhaps aid us in assessing the depth of the emotional change that occurred in Tahiti and they might help us understand whether the change was confined to the expression of grief or whether it extended to the experience of grief. Historians can also offer information about trends in Tahitian society that led to such a major change in the standards for expressing grief. Anthropological reports indicate that female self-wounding and other violent mourning practices disappeared after Christianity was introduced.[47] But we need to learn more about the kind of influences that the contact with the Europeans and Christianity had on the mode of expressing grief in Tahiti. Could the change be mainly attributed to the influence of the contact with European manners? Or, to the extent that the change was deeper (a change that entailed not only the expression but also the experience of grief), is it to be attributed to the influence of Christian doctrines? More particularly, does the change represent a shift in Tahitians' beliefs about death? Historians can offer information relevant for understanding the impetus for this change, and they can contribute significantly to the analysis of emotion by further addressing the important topic of change in various aspects of emotional functioning across time.

Concluding Comments

I began this paper with a set of questions concerning the kind and range of processes that emotions involve, and I have argued that in order to give emotions their due we need to study emotion not only at the physiological and psychological level of analysis, but also at the social level. The major thrust of this discussion was to suggest that it is incomplete to treat emotions as radically personal responses that are to be explained only with reference to the particular history of the individual. Rather, emotions are to be understood in terms of their communal context and in relation to the larger social history. Until fairly recently, investigators in this area have ignored the social connotations of emotions, thereby obscuring the complexities and richness of emotional responses. The development of an interdisciplinary approach is thus an important task in the study of emotions, since it might enable us to comprehend the more subtle qualities of emotions that have not received sufficient attention. It was pointed out in the above discussion that recent developments in theory and research on emotions seem to allow for a closer contact among psychologists, sociologists, and anthropologists, and I have also suggested that historians need to participate in research efforts directed toward understanding emotions in a broad social context.

The view of emotions that I have sketched in this paper also suggests that there are many ways to get hold of information pertaining to the emotions. Examinations of cultural world views and arrangements that may invite or preclude certain emotions, and examinations of the ways emotions themselves are evaluated, constitute appropriate and useful research strategies. Emotion, then, is also accessible to historians and it can be expected that our understanding of the social and cognitive aspects of emotions will be enhanced by historical investigations.

Notes

1. See Klaus R. Scherer and Paul Ekman, eds., *Approaches to Emotion* (Hillsdale, N.J., 1984); Robert Plutchik, *Emotion: A Psychoevolutionary Synthesis* (New York, 1980). See, e.g., Carroll E. Izard, *Human Emotions* (New York, 1977).

2. James R. Averill, "A Constructivist View of Emotion," in R. Plutchik and H. Kellerman, eds., *Emotion: Theory, Research and Experience* (New York, 1980), pp. 305–39.

3. R. W. Leeper, "A Motivational Theory of Emotion to Replace Emotion as Disorganized Response," *Psychological Review* 55 (1948): 5–21; Joseph de Rivera, *A Structural Theory of Emotions* (New York, 1977); Robert C. Solomon, *The Passions* (New York, 1976); William Lyons, *Emotion* (Cambridge, Eng., 1980); Richard S. Lazarus, "Cognitive and Coping Processes in Emotion," in R. S. Lazarus and A. Monat, eds., *Stress and Coping* (New York: 1977), pp. 145–51; Shula Sommers, "Emotionality Reconsidered: The Role of Cognition in Emotional Responsiveness," *Journal of Personality and Social Psychology* 41 (1981): 553–61.

4. See James R. Averill, "An Analysis of Psycho-physiological Symbolism and Its Influence on Theories of Emotion," *Journal for the Theory of Social Behavior* 4 (1974): 147–90. See also Shula Sommers and Anthony Scioli, "Emotional Range and Value Orientation: Toward a Cognitive View of Emotionality," *Journal of Personality and Social Psychology* 51 (1986): 417–22.

5. Stanley Schachter and Jerome Singer, "Cognitive, Social, and Physiological Determinants of Emotional State," *Psychological Review* 69 (1962): 379–99; George Mandler, *Mind and Emotion* (New York, 1975).

6. Richard S. Lazarus, James R. Averill and M. Opton, "Towards a Cognitive Theory of Emotion," in Magda B. Arnold, ed., *Feelings and Emotions* (New York, 1970), pp. 151–68.

7. R. W. Leeper, "The Motivational and Perceptual Properties of Emotions as Indicating their Fundamental Character and Role," in Magda B. Arnold, ed., *Feelings and Emotions* (New York, 1970), pp. 169–83.

8. R. W. Leeper, "Some Needed Developments in the Motivational Theory of Emotions," in D. Levine, ed., *Nebraska Symposium on Motivation* (Lincoln, 1965).

9. James R. Averill, "The Functions of Grief," in Carroll E. Izard, ed., *Emotions in Personality and Psychopathology* (New York, 1979).

10. Arlie R. Hochschild, *The Managed Heart: The Commercialization of Human Feelings* (Berkeley and Los Angeles, 1983); Theodore D. Kemper, *A Social Interactional Theory of Emotions* (New York, 1978).

11. Hochschild, *The Managed Heart*. See also Peggy A. Thoits, "Coping, Social Support and Psychological Outcomes: The General Role of Emotion," in Philip Shaver, ed., *Review of Personality and Social Psychology* (Beverly Hills, 1984).

12. Robert I. Levy, "Emotion, Knowing and Culture," in Richard A. Shweder and Robert A. LeVine, eds., *Culture Theory* (Cambridge, Eng., 1984), pp. 214–38; Michelle Z. Rosaldo, *Knowledge and Passion* (Cambridge, Eng., 1980); Catherine Lutz, "The Domain of Emotion Words on the Ifaluk," *American Ethnologist* 9 (1982): 113–29.

13. Catherine Lutz, "Parental Goals, Ethnopsychology and the Development of Emotional Meaning," *Ethnos* 11 (1983): 246–62.

14. Peter N. Stearns, with Carol Z. Stearns, "Emotionology: Clarifying the History of Emotions and Emotional Standards," *American Historical Review* 90 (1985): 813–36.

15. Stearns and Stearns, "Emotionology."

16. See, for example, Klaus R. Scherer and Paul Ekman, *Approaches to Emotion.*

17. Errol Bedford, "Emotions," *Aristotelian Society Proceedings* 57 (1957): 281–304.

18. Bedford, "Emotions," p. 304.

19. Stearns and Stearns, "Emotionology."

20. See Shula Sommers, "Adults Evaluating their Emotions: A Cross-Cultural Perspective," in Carol Z. Malatesta and Carroll E. Izard, eds., *Emotion in Adult Development* (Beverly Hills, 1984), pp. 314–38.

21. Robert C. Solomon, "Emotion and Anthropology: The Logic of Emotional Word Views," *Inquiry* 21 (1978): 181–99.

22. Ibid., p. 186.

23. Jean L. Briggs, *Never in Anger: Portrait of an Eskimo Family* (Cambridge, Mass., 1970). It should be emphasized that Briggs's descriptions suggest that the low visibility of anger among the Utku Eskimos is not due to a conscious or unconscious attempt to control anger. Rather, it is suggested that anger is not visible because it is rarely if ever experienced among Utku adults.

24. There have been some objections to Briggs's research and her conclusions. See, for example, Michelle Z. Rosaldo, "Toward an Anthropology of Self and Feeling," in Richard A. Shweder and Robert A. LeVine, eds., *Culture Theory* (Cambridge, Eng., 1984), pp. 137–52; See also Stearns and Stearns, "Emotionology," pp. 813–36.

25. Solomon, "Emotion and Anthropology."

26. From a cognitive perspective anger cannot be understood as a mere reaction to frustration. Rather, it is assumed that central to anger is a cognitive evaluation. See James R. Averill, *Anger and Aggression: An Essay on Emotion* (New York, 1982); John Sabini and Maury Silver, *The Moralities of Everyday Life* (New York, 1982).

27. Solomon, "Emotion and Anthropology." Solomon's paper offers an interesting discussion of the methodological problems surrounding anthropological research on emotions.

28. E. L. Schiefflin, "Anger and Shame in the Tropical Forest," *Ethos* 11 (1983): 181–91.

29. It should be noted that Schiefflin's account suggests that anger is both feared and admired by the Kaluli.

30. Robert I. Levy, *Tahitians: Mind and Experience in the Society Islands* (Chicago, 1973).

31. See James Morrison, *The Journal of James Morrison* (London, 1935); William Ellis, *A Voyage around the World in the Years 1772, 1773, 1774, 1775,* 2 vols. (London, 1977). See also Levy, *Tahitians,* pp. 288–91.

32. In Levy, *Tahitians,* p. 275.

33. Levy characterizes anger as a "hypercognized" emotion, since it is discussed extensively by the Tahitians. However, this is not to be taken as implying that anger is

evaluated positively in modern Tahiti. From Levy's informants one learns that only the *release* of anger is considered to be beneficial, as opposed to keeping anger inside. At the same time, it is believed that it is altogether preferable to avoid the experience of anger.

34. Levy, *Tahitians*.

35. See Robert C. Solomon, "Getting Angry: The Jamesian Theory of Emotion in Anthropology," in Richard R. Shweder and Robert A. Levine, eds., *Culture Theory* (Cambridge, Eng., 1984).

36. Levy, *Tahitians*, pp. 214–23.

37. Levy, *Tahitians*.

38. Adoption is a prevalent custom in Tahiti. According to some studies (see Levy, p. 474), 25 percent of the children in some rural communities are adopted. For various data and speculations on adoption in Tahiti and the possible effects of adoption on the personality dynamics of the people involved, see Levy, pp. 473–86. See also J. G. Weckler, "Adoption on Mokil," *American Anthropologist* 55 (1953): 555–69.

39. Levy, *Tahitians*, p. 482. It should be noted that the gist behind these remarks does not seem to characterize only adopted children's relationships with their parents, but also those of natural children themselves. Levy's study indicates that biological parentage in Tahiti does not imply unconditional obligation of parents toward their children. As some of Levy's informants remark, children must be perpetually grateful to their natural parents for having kept them.

40. Ibid., pp. 294–301.

41. Ibid., p. 294.

42. See Douglas L. Oliver, *Ancient Tahitian Society*, vol. 1 (Hawaii, 1974).

43. Quoted in Oliver, *Ancient Tahitian Society*, 1:492.

44. Ibid., 1:492–93.

45. Levy, *Tahitians*, pp. 289–90.

46. It is recognized, of course, that the impressions recorded by earlier observers cannot be treated as precise anthropological descriptions.

47. Levy, *Tahitians*, p. 291.

2

"Lord Help Me Walk Humbly": Anger and Sadness in England and America, 1570–1750

Carol Z. Stearns

Recent historical work on emotion, initially derived from an expanded exploration of family life, has raised questions about changes in personality associated with modernization. The focus, of course, has been on an eighteenth-century watershed. Yet it is love and sexuality, rather than a wider emotional spectrum, that have commanded attention. Recent revisionist work, furthermore, in arguing for continuity rather than change, makes it clear that the watershed itself is far from definitively established. The present essay addresses both the question of change and the problem of the range of emotions involved. It explores the ways in which people handled some negative emotions in the early modern period in England and America. It follows from the clear need to attend to emotions beyond love and sex, and it tries to address the eighteenth-century transformation with a subtlety missing in both the pioneer and the revisionist efforts in this area.

Since the historiography of emotion has thus far concentrated on making temporal rather than national distinctions, this article will take a transatlantic approach. This is not to suggest that there may not have been significant differences between the emotional climates of early modern England and America, but simply that until more basic work is done on delineating early modern emotionality in general, making national distinctions within a Western context is premature. I have limited my attention to English-language sources as a matter of convenience, but again not because I postulate that Anglo-American emotionality in this period was significantly different from say French or Dutch.[1]

This article is based on diaries and autobiographies because these are some of the best sources historians possess for exploring the personal goals and struggles of earlier generations. Although diaries as we know them did not exist before the sixteenth century, by the period we are considering they were becoming voluminous. Certainly, there are problems with these sources.

For one thing, diarists probably are never typical of their era, and so one must be careful not to draw conclusions about the larger population based on their products, except with caution. A second problem is that even when typical, diarists, like all of us, have a self-image to preserve, and like all of us cannot be totally honest with themselves even if they wish to be.[2] Thus, even if diarists are conscious of their emotions they may choose not to commit what they know to paper. This distortion, in the service of preservation of self-image, is an advantage as well as a problem, however, because it allows us to glimpse something of the diarist's emotionology as well as his emotions, and to learn a great deal about the struggle to keep the two in harmony.[3]

Finally, and obviously, there is a great deal about emotional life which does not appear in the pages of diaries. To get the full flavor of a culture's emotional life without being there to observe is certainly a formidable, and ultimately impossible, task, but many different sorts of sources, literary sources as well as records of interactions such as those at festivals, law courts, and riots, need to be used. The diaries are some help here, since most writers recorded a great deal of their observations of the behavior of others as well as chronicling their own feelings and thoughts, but certainly it would be good to use records which make such observations in a more systematic fashion, and certainly studying the diaries alone tends to exaggerate the importance of the cognitive aspect of emotions and to underrate the importance of behavior. Thus, the diaries are a good source with which to begin to study early modern emotions, but there is no claim here that from the diaries alone definitive statements can be made.[4]

This article uses, further, only a selection of diaries, and not all those available in print, or certainly in manuscript.[5] It is meant then to be a pilot study which will erect some hypotheses that can be tested in more extensive work on the history of early modern emotions. The writer admits first to historical prejudice. She believes that people's feelings and their experience change over time—that there are modal forms, within a culture, for emotional experience, and that these differ between cultures and chronological periods. These differences, which we all intuit with no difficulty when we experience the "differentness" of, say, Donne's poetry, a Puritan sermon, or a Jacobean tragedy, are often difficult to formulate precisely. This difficulty has in turn plagued historians of everyday life, and so although the first generation of historians to talk about love and family experience stressed the great gap between the premodern and modern experience, the more recent revisionist wave has essentially argued that there is no historical change in some of the fundamentals of life such as family interaction and emotional experience.[6] It is one purpose of this study, through using the diaries, to see if some testable formulations about change in emotional experience can be generated.[7]

This essay will concentrate on two emotions, anger and sadness, which are of interest to the author since she has worked on one of them, anger, before, and since it is widely believed that the two emotions are very much connected.[8]

Before the end of the seventeenth century, most diarists had difficulty thinking of themselves as angry. To be sure, many diarists had difficulty thinking of themselves as having emotions which could be named at all, and their records are useful to us only in making us aware of the lack of interest many had in their inner lives. But for the first introspective diarists, conscious anger was a rarity. Interactions or situations which were noxious often stimulated arousal, but the arousal would be labeled as sadness rather than as anger.

Roger Lowe, an apprentice during the years he kept his diary, had his most difficult interactions with his master, but experienced their conflicts as arousing grief rather than anger. For instance, "I thought it sad for me to be ingaged 9 yeares . . . to sell my Master's ware . . . and get no knowledge." When his master insists on commandeering money he has earned as a scribe, apart from his duties as apprentice, Lowe relates what happened "to my great greefe." Later, his Master promises and then refuses to give him a new set of clothes, "soe I would have none and parted with greefe."

Lest one argue that it was only toward social superiors that Lowe had difficulty conceptualizing anger, examples of a similar pattern in other situations will be offered. Lowe is out for the day and someone steals his horse so there is no easy way to go home: "I was highly perplexed, yet bore it very patiently." A woman starts some malicious gossip about him, and he is "in some greefe" about it. A friend steals his love letters and passes them around, which "was matter of much griefe to me and I was very sad upon it."[9]

Ralph Josselin, a Puritan clergyman, had similar disinclination to find himself angry. Conflictual situations would often be noted, a sign they were troubling him, yet he did not label his reaction. When his stepmother cheats him out of inheritance from his father he says only that "wee could not agree . . . I departed from her," and that "frends were not so kinde as I expected." When he is not paid as well as he has been promised in a new ministry, "I confesse I was stumbled at their dealings and some abuses offered mee." He sometimes seems to have a glimmer that something like anger may be bothering him, but he does not label the feeling and instead asks immediately that the feeling turn into something else. Thus, in a dispute about a living, "lord learne me patience and wisdome." In a dispute about doctrine where someone speaks to him "very unkind words, Lord . . . helpe me to walk humbly," and he later asks for help in "patienting my heart under some trialls, the Lord give mee an humble, condescending spirit, weaken my soule. . . ." In a dispute with his wife, he is aware of arousal and discomfort, but wants to skip over labeling his feeling, and get back to equanimity. "I find my heart apt to unquietnes . . . and it troubles mee . . . I thinke I have cause, but I am sure I should bee more patient and counsellable." It is interesting that what is repressed in the daytime emerges in dream material: "They say dreames declare a man's Temperament, this night I dreamd I was wondrous passion with a man that wrongd mee and my child insomuch as I was ashamed of my selfe, god in mercy keepe mee from that evill, in the day, I did that and that in passion for which I was sorry."[10]

Non-Puritans too, in this early period, are not eager to see themselves as angry, and are more likely to present themselves as sad. For instance, John Dee, involved in various disputes, wrote that his economic problems, "do not so much grieve my hart as the rash, lewde, fond and most untrue fables and reports of me."[11] Or Anne Clifford, whose diary covered a long dispute with her husband about his use of her money: "Sometimes I had fair words from him and sometimes foul, but I took all patiently, and did strive to give him . . . assurance of my love," and when he canceled her jointure said, "I am resolved to take all patiently, casting all my care upon GOD." Instead of becoming angry at her husband she became sad so that at Church, "my eyes were so blubbered with weeping that I could scarcely look up."[12] Mrs. Freke, of a less exalted social class, but involved in similar disputes with her spouse, resorted to a standard posture of tears, grief, and drug abuse, but not to anger.[13]

The anger of others made early modern people uncomfortable. Anger in other people was often observed and even labeled, and yet one could not respond in kind. Various solutions to this problem emerged. When a friend is angry, Roger Lowe is sad. One coping mechanism was to avoid angry situations. For instance, Lowe arranged to get someone else to broach his problems to his master. Another solution was to turn to God for support. When another woman is in a "rage" at his girl friend in his presence, "this was matter of great greife of harte unto me . . . my trust is in God who will helpe in trouble. Though the storme be now, yet I have hopes I shall see a calme." When he wrongly blames someone for forging his name and that man is offended with him this is "Great griefe. But God will help." It is intriguing to see that other people when angry are experienced as extremely threatening, perhaps a result of the repression of one's own anger leading to exaggerated projections of the anger of others. In a religious dispute, Lowe is worried that the "contention had like to have beene hott," and that the other man "should doe me some hurt."[14]

Others also found it uncomfortable to be confronted with anger. When Samuel Sewall, of New England, is involved in religious and governance disputes, a man speaks to him with "fierceness" and "I was stricken with this furious expression." When he asks to have a bill paid, and the response is anger, Sewall writes, "I know no reason for this Anger; the Lord sanctify it to me, and help me to seek more his Grace and favor."[15] Anger needs almost to be explained away, and certainly help is needed to bear it. When Ebenezer Parkman catechizes a dying woman, and her brother angrily objects to his questions, Parkman spends paragraphs in his diary defending himself, talks of this as a trial for days, and has difficulty sleeping. Years later he notes with pleasure that the man apologized.[16]

It would be mistaken, though, to conclude, because early modern people had difficulty recognizing their own anger, or feeling comfortable with anger in others, that angry behavior was not a commonplace in their culture. Other historians have commented upon the rough-and-tumble tone of early modern society, the readiness to start physical fights, the institutionalization of duels, the easy cursings and swearing, and violent games, sports, and punishments.[17] Obviously, the very discomfort with anger which has been described by the diarists is evidence that frequent anger did exist.

Fighting was common among people whom we would be surprised to find fighting today. For instance, Anthony Wood made no comment on seeing students pelting a man in the pillory with eggs or a priest fighting in the street. Richard Oglander was unsurprised to see gentlemen beating each other with sticks, and Oliver Heywood was not startled to see an adult severely beat rowdy boys. Dueling was not remarkable, even in Puritan New England.[18]

Abuse of servants was taken for granted, so that when another minister struck his maid causing her to "bleed much," Ralph Josselin's only comment was that "it might have been my condicion if mercy had not prevented it." Sewall also was unsurprised at a man who fell into an "angry passion with his servant."[19]

Quarrels between neighbors were probably frequent, and resulted in behavior that we might find surprising, but which elicited no particular comment from the diarists, such as an incident in which Elias Ashmole recorded that his neighbor piled garbage against his garden wall. Romantic difficulties might frequently lead to quarrels and even to violence. Ashmole reported one such in which the aggressor was blamed but no one seemed to take any steps regarding his attempt to kill a rival.[20]

Verbiage was often very angry, and on the part of people from whom today we might expect more restraint. For instance, Anthony Wood registered no surprise when the Master of Balliol said one of his books was "not fit to wipe one's arse with." Sewall related that in a dispute over a servant, a General Nicholson spoke with a "roaring voice" and was so "furiously Loud, that the Noise was plainly heard in the Council Chambers." Sewall frequently reported "vehement" fights and "fiery" words in council meetings.[21]

How can it be that so much anger existed in a culture in which people denied anger among themselves? Can it be that diarists were unusually restrained people? It may be that, tending to be more introspective than others, they might also have been less expressive, but it seems doubtful that they were totally different in their emotional styles from all they interacted with. It is notable that Sewall, who has difficulty admitting his own anger, observed high levels of anger in the other Puritan magistrates with whom he worked, men who, we can be certain, were loath to recognize anger in themselves. Oliver Heywood made similar observations of nonconformist ministers in England. The explanation seems to be that men who did not recognize in themselves the feeling of anger could yet act as though they were angry. For instance, Richard Norwood, who never called himself angry, described starting a fight with a quarterstaff when someone spoke to him scornfully. He said nothing about his feelings here.[22] Roger Lowe, always loath to say he was angry, when called a bastard, vowed to be the death of the offender and "buffeted hime very mery."[23] This was not the only time he got into a physical fight and yet recorded no emotion preceding it.[24] Sewall admitted that he and Cotton Mather had substantial public disputes, and refers to Mather's anger, though never admitting to the emotion in himself. Similarly, he admits to a dispute with a neighbor over digging a cellar, and that they "storm" and speak "opprobrious words" but he does not say he is angry.[25] It is as though there were a dissociation between feeling and action. These seventeenth-century people are acting as though they are in a Skinnerian paradigm where there is a stimulus and a response, but no recognized mediating ego or self. In other words, there is little cognition that emotions exist, and therefore little sense that behavior flows from conscious feelings and can be controlled.

It was this lack of cognition and of a sense that through cognition one could control behavior that was soon to change. Emotional styles do not change overnight and it is not being suggested here that a sharp break is discernible, but it is notable that by the late seventeenth century, more diarists began to write as though they had an awareness of feelings, and that from this awareness a sense came that behaviors could be controlled. Certainly, many diarists still maintained the older style, and many who used a newer style at times reverted. What is notable, though, is that a new style, which had hardly existed before, was being developed, and it was a style which was to become predominant by the nineteenth century. This new style suggested that behaviors could be controlled even if feelings were intense. For instance, Sewall, in dispute with another magistrate, noted that the man spoke "vehemently" and he told him he "was in a passion." The man denied this, and Sewall said that therefore "it was so much the worse."[26] In other words, if one is in control of one's feelings one should control one's behavior. A similar belief is seen in John Oglander's discussion of a gentleman who was "by nature very passionate, yet in his wisdome he conquered that passion so much that you would think him to be of a mild disposition."[27]

Henry Newcome was a Puritan minister who at the end of the seventeenth century wrote a book about the necessity for controlling the expression of anger. He said that men should not let themselves be ruled by passion but should protect the soul by erecting walls against passion, much like the walls around a city. He agreed with the old idea that men are born with temperaments, and some more easily angered than others, but his emphasis was on the fact that all could exert self-control.[28] This view was expressed clearly in his autobiography, in which the angry behavior of others was condemned as a failure, and rather than being simply assumed to result from temperament or passion, required explanation. For instance, "I was exceedingly perplexed about my wife. God knows what I should do. These four years have I now lived with her and do not know how to humor her. When she is angry, I do aggravate her passion by saying anything." He concludes that this must be because women were naturally weak. Dudley Ryder similarly judged angry behavior harshly and thought it could be controlled. He used the word *childish* to describe his sister's angry outbursts, and wrote of his parents:

> At supper father and mother had some little dispute, as they generally have every time they meet at table. I have been thinking which is in fault . . . but indeed they are both very much in fault, my mother for saying everything in a cross way . . . and my father for continuing the matter that gave offense and pushing it on.[29]

At the same time that anger is being condemned as controllable in others, diarists are beginning to be able to label it in themselves. For Roger Lowe, in the early seventeenth century, this was a rarity, though he did at one point admit to a quarrel that made him "very angry" and then to feeling upset about it. Writing in the early eighteenth century, Ebenezer Parkman had similarly allowed the possibility he might be angry in noting a falling-out between other ministers and hoping therefore that he would not "forget myself."[30] Oliver Heywood in 1673 censured himself for a "sharp dispute" in which "I was in some passion . . . my spirit was too warm." By the late seventeenth century Henry Newcome, more often than not, labeled his response to noxious experiences as anger. He mentioned, for example, expressing anger at a messenger who brought him bad news, and then condemned himself for doing it. He noted "peevish folly in my heart, envy and anger" when he was not invited to a fair. On a difficult journey, "I could not but observe the folly of my spirit, that I should be angry at the length and hardness of the way as if the inhabitants were in fault. . . . Should the earth be removed for thee?" In an argument over the repair of his house, "I urged it

too far and too hotly . . . passion never does good. I was troubled hereupon."
This is not to say that Newcome did not occasionally describe difficult
situations as making him "weary" rather than angry, or project his own anger
onto others, but for the most part, it is notable that he was able to label his
responses as anger, and that this gave him a sense that he could control his
behavior that seemed to be lacking in some of the earlier diarists.[31]

Dudley Ryder, writing in the early eighteenth century, had an even more
explicit notion of when he was angry. For instance, he commented that when
his maid sent his wig to London by mistake, "it put me into a great deal of
concern and I never spoke so angrily to a servant before." Spotting and
labeling his feelings gave him a sense that he could master them. Continuing
with the maid, "I was vexed to find the passion had so much power over me. I
began to suspect my own temper more than ever and afraid lest it should
betray me hereafter into some unlucky hit." He was developing, in sum, a
sense that he was not merely the agent of uncontrolled passions, but that he
had a character, a self, and that this afforded him some control: "Was in a
very ill humour all this evening, everything . . . disposed me to be angry . . . I
cannot but be concerned that I have such a disposition which may grow up in
time if not checked to be very ill humour and make me extremely troublesome." And commenting on his mother's bad temper, "I am too apt to be
guilty of the same kind of peevishness myself. I have too much of her temper
but I am resolved to endevor to quell at its first rise every secret resentment
and uneasiness that comes upon me. I know how to do it already pretty well
with respect to others by preventing its being discovered to others but this is
not enough."[32] Diarists like Newcome and Ryder, then, are developing a
new sense that there is a self, what we might call an ego, appearing in the
Skinnerian black box, and that the human self is not simply a stimulus-
response machine, but an agent of control. Thus, the dissociation between
self-perception and behavior, which was characteristic of the earlier diarists,
was no longer a prime mechanism for confronting noxious stimuli. The new
sense of the self, which was just beginning to emerge in late seventeenth-
century diarists' perception of their own anger, was to become the modal
form for dealing with the emotion by the nineteenth century. A change was
taking place, albeit slowly. Angry emotions, once denied, projected, or acted
out without acknowledgment, were now being identified and labeled, and in
the process, giving some men a sense that they had more control over their
behaviors. Some corollaries of this changing style in anger control will now
be explored.

There is a seeming paradox in the fact that although the earlier diarists
had difficulty seeing themselves as angry, they were more comfortable than
the later ones with the notion of an angry God. Exploring this apparent
puzzle leads to deeper understanding of both points of view and to the

reasons for change. Certainly, up to the last third of the seventeenth century, God's anger for minor trespasses was held to be a constant fact of life, and many diarists explained the slightest pieces of bad fortune as resulting from punishment by the wrathful Almighty. Lowe, worried about career plans, wrote that "I was in a troubled condition in my mind considering my unsettlednes, and that God was highly offended with me." Josselin frequently noted God's anger at him and at his town. Norwood had similar fears. Charles Lloyd Cohen finds it a commonplace of Puritan psychology that the individual felt subject to God's ire for all infractions, "lying under the wrath," perceiving "nothing but death and wrath . . . terrible expressions of wrath."[33]

Since God could be angry, and the individual could not, it was not surprising to find individuals indirectly expressing rage by counting on the Lord for revenge. For instance, when Lowe's love letters are purloined, he calls the thief a "stinking Raskell . . . a develish, malicious, dissembling, knavish rascall"; admitting to no anger on his own part, he says he feels only grief, but "God will not faile those that trust in him." A more clear-cut example comes when his girl friend's sister spreads malicious gossip about him. He writes this poem:

> Well, I'me content, though fortune on me frowne,
> God will me raise, though the world would cast me downe,
> And I with patience will their Mallice bear. . . .
> But vengeance will att last light on their head, . . .
> In time my quarrelle will revenged be,
> Till then I'll waite and only seeke to God . . .
> And they that are the acters of my greefe
> May they cry out and yet find no releife.[34]

In other words, the anger that Lowe could not feel himself could be projected onto God, and he could count on God to avenge him, for God, and only God, was allowed anger.

But by the late seventeenth century, some people were beginning to question God's wrath, and to postulate a more merciful Lord. Henry Newcome made this argument explicitly in his book against anger, asking men to stop fighting over religious matters, and to imitate God, who as incarnated in Christ, was meek and loving. In his own life, Newcome attempted to act on this. When a minister seized a pulpit cushion Newcome thought belonged to him, he wrote, "I could have taken these passages ill, but I thought it best to take no notice of it . . . for so I think Jesus Christ in such a case, would have done." Dudley Ryder found it common sense that God was forgiving, and wrote "we don't conceive . . . of God to suppose that He would be this inexorable malicious being."[35]

The change in the perception of God paralleled a changing view of the propriety of anger in hierarchy. Earlier, anger was clearly viewed as the prerogative of those on top, and led to no surprise. Anthony Wood displayed no shock in relating how RB, a chaplain, thrust his servant down the stairs and kicked her. Elizabeth Freke had no comment when her daughter-in-law told her maid she had a "good mind to kick her downe staires." Richard Norwood has no comment on the fact that when he tried to abandon his ship, his Captain "fell upon me with his truncheon, giving me three or four blows, and would have me ask him forgiveness." Roger Lowe was constantly expecting his Master to be angry with him, and was surprised whenever he was not.[36]

During the later seventeenth century, however, a new view was being developed that those on top in hierarchies, whether husbands, parents, or masters, should moderate their anger and rule by gentleness. The diarists who thought of God as gentle also had this view of hierarchies. Newcome wrote that inferiors should be spared anger. He was proud that as a minister he did better than in those congregations where "men [were] usually flying off," while he, writing mildly, masters opposition. Anger against children, or servants, when not controlled, was viewed as lower-class: "There is not a more disgusting sight," wrote John Witherspoon in 1797, "than the impotent rage of a parent who has no authority. Among the lower ranks of people, who are under no restraint from decency, you may sometimes see [a parent] . . . running out in the street after a child . . . with looks of fury . . . it fills every beholder with horror."[37]

The earlier view assuming that anger is justifiable when one is on the right side, and that God, always on the right side, may be angry, allowed conversion of anger to zeal. It is best, if one is clearly in the right, to be tough. As John Oglander put it, "Let thy sword, rather than thy tongue, give thy enemy the advantage." Early Puritan religious writers condemned lukewarmness, and argued that zeal for God was good. "Anger in strength and starkness intends the driving away, and despelling of the evill . . . against which it riseth." Zeal combines "love and anger" and "proceeds from love of the Lord."[38]

The new view has been discussed at length in other contexts. In England at least, disgust with the excesses of the Civil War and then the general context of early Enlightenment thought condemned zeal as unwarranted. It was not always clear which was the right and which was the wrong side. Translated into emotional direction, then, anger must be very modulated. The whole point of Newcome's book against anger was that religious differences were almost never so important as to justify ire, or "uncivil expression." He explicitly argued against the older view that those who moderated their anger were "pusillanimous." Dudley Ryder knew he had strong feelings about politics, but said that, just because those feelings worked him "up into a kind of heat . . . [which] . . . makes me speak with too much warmth and eagerness," he must restrain himself. Even if the opponent was a papist, it was distasteful to argue in a "noisy loud voice." Ryder observed explicitly that in his day there was a change in what was considered good manners even in a political argument. In arguing politics with him, his aunt "is extremely violent and cannot tell how to keep her temper. . . . She still keeps to the old way of saying the most absurd and shocking things that silence one at once. . . ."[39]

Another contrast between old and new emerged. While in the old view anger was the prerogative of those on the top of hierarchies, anger on the part of those at the bottom of hierarchies was so unacceptable, even shocking, that it was viewed not as anger but madness in the sense of insanity.[40] Interestingly enough, though, as we have seen, the early diarists almost uniformly did not feel entitled to the emotion. It would seem as though even in earthly relationships, they had a sense of being one down, and of being uncomfortable with self-assertion. Since children, even upper-class children, were socialized to feel that they were on the bottom, they may never have grown up to feel comfortable with assertive postures, or at least with acknowledging them as such even when they did flail out. David Hunt has made this point in his study of the child rearing of Louis XIII of France. He has argued that the whippings the child constantly received were designed, in some way, to suppress his sense of autonomy, and to prepare him for a role of submissiveness.[41] Thus, even those on the top of hierarchies were not to feel comfortable with experiencing themselves as on top, or with emotions that were clearly assertive. An example of such unease appears in the musings of Adam Eyre in 1647:

> This night I whipped Jane [a servant] for her foolishness, as yesterday I had done for her sloathfulness; and hence am induced to bewayle my sinfull life, for my failings in the presence of God Allmighty are questionless greater than hers are to me; wherefore, unless Thou, my most merciful God, be mercifull unto mee, what shall become of mee?[42]

This is old-fashioned in that the anxiety comes not so much from the view that one should be gentle, as God is gentle, but from the fear that no matter what one's position on earth, one is always in a servile position vis à vis the potentially angry Deity. Many writers have discussed, in Puritan thought, the emphasis placed on creating feelings of submission, and combatting pride. Discomfort with anger would seem to fit in here. Richard Norwood illustrates the connection between anxiety about pride and anger when relating his experience in a falling-out with another man:

wherein I gave place to passion even unto rage and fury, which . . . was stirred up
. . . chiefly by pride. . . . In the heat of which fury I had thoughts and inclinations
in my heart of cutting down his house, yea of killing him, and that if I should do so
God would yet be merciful and would be reconciled to me again.

Behold an example of the stupendous wickedness of the heart.[43]

We see here the notion that if one is certain one is in the right there is some
sense that anger is justifiable. But we see also that the idea of asserting
oneself so strongly makes people uncomfortable—it is in fact the sin of pride;
therefore anger must be repressed and left to God, the only being entitled to
that emotion. Thus there is a kind of wavering between the belief that
"zealous" anger is justifiable, and the inhibitory notion that to assume one
has a right to be zealous in this fashion is to be sinfully prideful. It may well
be, because this problem remained unresolved, that when anger did emerge,
it so often seemed unmodulated and accompanied by an inner sense of
conflict. There are cultures in which the legitimacy of anger is defined, as in
early modern Europe and America, by being in the right, but in which the
experience of anger is less conflicted. That is because in these cultures, which
value self-assertion, it is not necessarily sinful or dangerous to claim that one
is indeed in the right.[44]

The new view, beginning to emerge by the late seventeenth century, was
more democratic, made greater allowance for the possibility of the individual's reasonable assessment that he was in the right, and developed a new
view of God. In eighteenth-century religious thought, God was more like
man than he had been earlier. A sharp division between God who was
allowed anger and man who was allowed none no longer seemed reasonable.
In fact, God's likeness to a good man was the basis of Dudley Ryder's
discussion about whether God could be angry.[45] To admit anger now was
not so very terrible, because it no longer had the connotation of untoward
assertiveness. Contrast William Byrd's cheerful note that "I . . . was angry
with my man for not getting up and gave him warning," with the above-
mentioned Adam Eyre, who about a century earlier, had been so nervous
about berating his servant.[46] By the early eighteenth century, it was all right
to admit that one felt angry. Of course, angry behavior must be controlled,
but one could look at angry feelings and talk about them without abject
shame, as part of the effort to maintain behavior. This is one reason that in
the late eighteenth and early nineteenth centuries, spates of books attacking
anger became popular. Anger could be recognized, as it infrequently was
before, and this raised the whole new problem of what to do about it.[47]

No discussion of early modern anger can be complete without some
discussion of sadness in the same period. The word *aggrieved*, which once
meant saddened by an affront, before it took on its more modern con-

notation of "angered," is testimony to a past in which sadness and anger were less clearly differentiated than they are to us. In the early modern period, when anger in oneself could not be easily identified and labeled, sadness was much more acceptable than it was to become. One is struck, in reading the diaries, at how freely and unembarrassedly men burst into tears. Religious sympathies frequently drew tears from Samuel Sewall, but also from the Anglican Oglander.[48] Oglander "could do nothing but sigh and weep for two nights and a day," because of his worries about the fate of King Charles in 1647.[49] Ralph Josselin found himself in tears over money problems. Romantic problems also led grown men to cry. Sewall's son Sam "told me with Tears that these sorrows [arising from discord between him and his wife] would bring him to his Grave." Lowe cried to a woman friend over his failure to win a girl he had courted. Ryder, too, was frequently in tears, both privately and to confidantes, about girl problems. Heywood cried after a dispute with his wife. Norwood, both as a young adolescent and a youth, found it normal to cry over difficulties related to changes of residence.[50]

The early modern period showed a great fascination and sympathy with the idea of melancholy.[51] Newcome wrote of a young Michael Buxton who had fallen "into Melancholy. His condition much to be lamented; but it is far better than sin, which is the condition of too many." Many of the diarists felt it appropriate to portray themselves as doleful, and the sense they convey is that they felt that dolefulness was somehow opposed to sin. Norwood wrote that at one point his image of God was that "he allowed of no joy nor pleasure, but of a kind of melancholy demeanor and austerity." Parkman, after a pleasant visit with relatives, "grievously and sadly reflected upon my Levity this Evening," and had to justify himself by suggesting, "But there was nothing criminal in my conduct when one . . . considers what a time of Joy it was with us. However, I think I might have spent more time with the graver people." It was fashionable, in reflecting back on one's life, to admit to great sorrow and dolefulness.[52]

By the early eighteenth century, tears were still in fashion, but there was beginning to be some sense of the desirability of good cheer, as in Ryder's diary, or John Byrom's statement, in 1728: "it was the best thing one could do to be always cheerful . . . and not suffer any sullenness . . . a cheerful disposition and frame of mind being the best way of showing our thankfulness to God." In several diaries, the hint begins to emerge that it is in fact an obligation to be cheerful.[53] By the mid-nineteenth century, furthermore, male tears were quite out of fashion, and there was a generally felt responsibility even among evangelicals to be optimistic.[54]

The discomfort with identifying anger connected with the readiness to be sad. To be sad was to be passive, submissive, and helpless. Often the remedy was prayer. The sad person did not assert himself but begged for help from the Almighty. One is struck by a certain narcissism in some of these early reactions to other peoples' problems. When misfortune befalls others, the almost universal response is to think that such a thing could happen to oneself and pray God that it does not.[55] These people, presented with difficult situations, had little sense that they could assert themselves to control the situation, and therefore resorted to a supplicant, whiny posture, asking for help from above.[56] They were the exact opposite of the Kaluli of Papua New Guinea, as discussed by Edward L. Schieffelin, who modally value assertiveness, encourage anger rather than sadness, try to transform sadness into anger, and are rarely depressed. In Schieffelin's New Guinea, the connection here discussed between sadness and anger holds, but is simply turned on its head.[57]

Lack of ease with conscious anger and readiness to embrace the position of tearful supplicant seem to have something to do with the early modern sense that emotions assail rather than belong to one. Feelings were experienced often as overwhelming assaults, as when Lowe wrote of his fiancée that "att those times my effections ran out violently after her, so as that I was never contented . . . unles I had seene her." Josselin wrote constantly of the sense that he might be assailed by evil feelings, and that only God protected him. When an acquaintance seduced a widow, he felt that only "god's goodness [kept] . . . I and mine . . . not in the same condicion." Observing a drunkard, "lord thy name be blessed in keeping mee from that sin." Norwood, writing of his lusts, felt he had no self-control, and that only the fact that God would punish him with affliction could raise fear in him and prevent vice. Oliver Heywood, upset with worry about his children, mused, "Oh Lord, How weak and slippery is the soul of man! how easily is the mind put out of order! how hard to be settled and composed! . . . how little power have I over my own thoughts."[58] This sort of experience did not disappear all at once, so that even in the eighteenth century we find William Stout writing similarly of his attraction to a woman, his "affection and passion" as dangerous forces to be resisted.[59]

Richard Norwood, during the years of his spiritual conversion, suffered tremendous guilt over his lusts, and felt that he was being punished by a siege of dreadful nightmares. His nightmares, including visions of his father "greviously angry with me," in his understanding had nothing to do with his own conflicts and were totally out of his control. He explained his dreams of "strange-passions, affections, lusts, and blasphemies" as coming from the outside, the affliction of Satan, who also was "deforming my countenance," and he later attributed the problem to staying in a haunted house. Satan was also felt to be the source of angry dissension among neighbors by

Heywood.[60] The unquestioned assumption behind all this, however, is that one does not have control over one's feelings.

While Puritan thought, even in the late seventeenth century, had emphasized submission, and instructed people to rely on God's grace for help with troublesome emotions, in some diarists there emerged now an increasing sense of self-control. Ebenezer Parkman, writing in the early eighteenth century, for example, felt that he could develop systematic self-inspection to the point of self-regulation: "to look into Myself and view the state of my Heart . . . my Thoughts run more free from those confusions and interruptions than in the day," and he resolved to introspect regularly that "I may learn the most suitable regular method of forming my own Thoughts and Action."[61] Emory Elliott has noted the same emphasis on possibilities for assertion of the self and de-emphasis on submission in the preaching of Cotton Mather in the late seventeenth century.[62] That Mather and Parkman were Puritans, like the earlier Josselin, is certainly true; but the earlier Puritan had no such systematic sense of how to go about self-control, and evinced a much more pervasive sense that he was constantly being assailed by waves of inexplicable and uncontrollable emotion than emerges in the diary of the later Parkman. Parkman, in fact, shares more in this sense with the non-Puritan Ryder, his contemporary chronologically, than with Josselin. His passage is not unlike Ryder's, who in starting his diary said he intended "particularly to observe my own temper and state of mind" in order to seek out causes of disturbance and to enable him to "mend" himself. Ryder's stance was to be surprised when assailed by feeling and to endeavor immediately to "check myself" rather than to pray to God. Ryder, in commenting on others, clearly felt that people who fluctuated in their emotions lacked a certain self-control and were curiosities, requiring explanation.[63]

Both the old and new views shared the characteristic Western distinction between emotion, considered dangerous, and reason, considered superior.[64] For both, the picture of a man controlled by passion, and particularly angry passion, was quite stereotyped, deriving from classical descriptions, and was akin to the picture of a madman—thus the double meaning of the word *mad*, connoting both anger and insanity, and Walter Calverley's disdain for an acquaintance who "fell into a great fury, as is usually his way when contradicted. . . . By his behaviour one would have taken him to be a madman."[65]

What was new, then, was not a revision of the standard dichotomy— reason, superior; emotion, inferior—but rather, an increasing sense of the possibility that man did have some ability to control emotion. In fact, in the new view, if anger were under control, it was in some cases legitimate to display it, for anger could be useful, or instrumental. The early writer, Roger Lowe, could conceive of this sort of instrumental anger only in relation to non-humans. In a tussle with a ram, "I looked att [him] . . . with an angry countenance," in order to frighten him. Later writers, though, could picture instrumental anger as legitimate with people. For instance, Newcome wrote "A servant of mine . . . would not be ruled, but oft was overseen in drink, and I found at this time, that anger for this did quicken to duties and bring in comfort, whereas other anger works quite contrary." It feels all right to Newcome to choose to be angry, for he believes that God, in assessing man, will judge "without Passion." William Byrd similarly notes that he beat his servant Joe "for being very saucy, after which he was very sullen and very good." Anger has its purposes. And part of using it wisely came from staying in control. As Byrd wrote of an encounter with another troublesome employee: "found my man late, which made me very angry with him. However, I kept my temper pretty well, thank God."[66] Great emphasis was placed in the latter half of the seventeenth century and after, on the importance of keeping temper, of punishing children "calmly" and without "passion."[67] Thus, the new view, though clearer on the possibility of controlling behavior than of controlling feeling, did allow for the latter as well, and was more optimistic about its possibility than the old view had been. Anger in the earlier view had been legitimized only by being in the service of the right side, that is, God's side, and such anger needed its own word, *zeal*. The new view implied that man, through the use of reason, could judge when anger was justified; since reason must be paramount in such judgment, then anger could be acceptable only if it was anger without passion. "Zeal," was no longer virtuous.

All these changes added up, in fact, to a twofold shift in emotionology. The larger change was from the view that man had little control over his own feelings and behavior to the view that good men did have control. Secondly, while there was no change in the belief that unrighteous anger was reprehensible, there was a subtle alteration in understanding of what legitimized anger; the earlier view allowing it only to those on the upper level of hierarchical relationships, the new view legitimizing it solely by its reasonableness, which was identified in part by its dissociation from passion and its accompaniment by self-control.

The diaries offer striking evidence that the change in emotionology drastically affected emotional experience. The old emotionology almost never allowed people to acknowledge anger comfortably. In situations, which for modern people might arouse a consciousness that one was angry, the earlier diarists expressed instead a sense of unease or sadness. They evinced angry behavior, but did not conceptualize themselves as angry. When the emotionology began to change, anger was recognized and labeled in the self, and a connectedness between feeling and behavior was experienced, which reinforced a sense of self-control.

Earlier personalities frequently expressed a sense of lack of control, and not surprisingly, their feelings were often experienced as vague somatic complaints afflicting the self rather than as cognized emotions identified as part of the self. Although careful quantification has not been done here, one is certainly struck in reading the earlier diarists at the frequency of their complaints about minor physical difficulties.[68] It is also interesting that similar words were used for feelings and for fevers or diseases and pains, such as "violent," "senseless and raging" and "angry." "Distemper" was used without distinction for an emotion or a somatic condition. Words for good feelings were like words for sensuous experiences such as eating, as when Norwood, feeling happy, called life "savory."[69]

It was more characteristic of later personalities to display an interest in emotion as distinct from soma. To modern eyes, it is striking how many of the earlier diaries are simply recordings of events with no statement of the writer's emotions at all. Although certainly some later diarists did the same, it was more characteristic by the eighteenth century to display an introspective, self-conscious style.[70] It is also characteristic of the later diaries to display an interest in the subject of personality or character that was lacking in the earlier writers, for whom behavior was almost always seen as a vector resulting from the various forces of temper and humor, rather than as resulting from clearly defined personalities differing from man to man.[71] The novel, as a newly developing literary form, may thus be seen in the context of the history of emotions as resulting from a new interest in the personality of the individual. By the eighteenth century, a literary genre that viewed characters as often helpless creatures of fate and passion, assailed by emotion in much the same way they might be assailed by illness, would have been anachronistic. Jacobean plays would have seemed foreign. The novel, with its interest in the individual's personality, and its view that plot was determined by character, gave literary expression to a new emotionology, which held that behavior was determined by self.[72]

Both anthropologists and psychiatrists have displayed a great deal of interest in the question of whether modern, westernized personalities, with their emphasis on the self as a controlling agent, their interest in individual personality, and their highly developed sense of cognized emotions as opposed to somatic experience, are less prone to depression than more traditional personalities. Some writers have argued that it is typical of less developed countries, or lower socioeconomic groups, to have a more limited vocabulary for emotions and to somaticize all complaints. Recently, however, a revisionist view has argued that depression exists in all cultures, merely manifesting itself differently from place to place, and that some cultures, while lacking verbal distinctions for emotional differences that may seem important to us, have vocabularies for variations in emotion important to them but lacking in us.[73]

This study addresses some of these questions. It is striking, in reading the earlier diaries, how often the writers feel sad, although they seem to have no reason.[74] An emotionology which, as we have seen, encouraged people to feel sad rather than angry, often resulted in sad people. Although a recent work on the psychology of Puritanism has argued that the Puritan, through submission, usually found strength and joy, we are struck by how often doubt and moroseness persisted even after conversion.[75] Norwood's musings after his conversion reveal that his sufferings were far from over. He complains that he feels feeble, slow, and timorous, doubting and despairing, and that he seems "in general to have lost much of that youthful heat and vigour in the way of God which before I enjoyed."[76] In fact, it is typical of the earlier diarists to embrace a kind of depressive demeanor, reminiscent of what Robert Levy has noted in his work on Tahitians: "If depression is defined . . . subtly as 'a decrease in self-esteem; a sense of helplessness; the inhibition of ego functions to varying degrees; and a subjective feeling of sadness or loss' . . . then there is a suggestion of 'depressive tone' for most of the informants."[77]

It is hardly surprising, in view of the fact that the earlier diarists viewed feelings, including sad feelings, as coming from outside the self, that cures for their depressions involved external panaceas, like pills to take away anger, or healing rituals controlled by others.[78] There was little sense here, as began to appear later with Newcome and Ryder, that one can cure oneself from emotional disturbance through use of the ego. Clifford Geertz has noted that our view of the self as an agent that controls behavior and emotion is relatively unusual in the world today. This essay suggests that even in the West it is a relatively recent view.[79]

Why did a change take place? In offering causal explanations for a change in personality, both direct causes and functional explanations have some merit. One way to think about changes in personality is to consider changes in child rearing. Early seventeenth-century children were certainly raised in a world that must have appeared capricious. The pervasive sense of uncertainty about attaining even the basic requirements for life characteristic of early modern society has been discussed at length by both Keith Thomas and Robert Muchembled. Unquestionably, some of this uncertainty with which adults lived was experienced by their children. And in the specific case of children, indeed, one is struck by how unprotected they were, with near-fatal accidents a commonplace in the diaries.[80] The recording of these in part simply restated the view that one has no control over the world, but it indicated that the parents involved took little care to structure the environments of children in order to systematically protect them from danger. This certainly was to change somewhere in the middle of the eighteenth century.[81]

But why did parents not provide more protection at an earlier period? Surely, with easy access to manpower this would have been possible. The answer must be that they simply did not see the world as a controllable place and think in terms of controlling it. As Keith Thomas has discussed at length, this sense of lack of control began during the Enlightenment period to be replaced by the notion that man could take charge, but there is no one simple explanation for this change. It is hardly surprising that children raised in a world where they felt there was no control even over the basics of preserving life grew up with less of a sense of control than those raised, as was more typical in the middle and upper classes from the eighteenth century on, in carefully regulated environments. Although some historians have derided this sort of approach to a culture, and rightly warned against characterizing whole cultures as neurotic, the diaries themselves offer ample empirical evidence that the writers did experience themselves as lacking control.[82]

But a sense of lack of control was not simply taught by parent to child apart from cultural context. If emotional styles were simply passed on fixedly, they could never change. It can be argued that the older personalities were well-adapted to the requirements of their culture, and that child-rearing styles are maintained or changed according to cultural need. Hierarchical societies benefit from submissive, if slightly depressed participants, and the fact that even those on the upper ends of the hierarchy tended to have conflicts over assertion and to fancy themselves submissive to the greater Authority probably helped to curb extreme abuses of power. The dissociation between feeling and behavior that existed in this sort of society was not a serious problem, for most interactions were between individuals who knew each other, and seldom involved huge numbers of people.[83] If people acted in a rough-and-tumble and physically aggressive manner, their actions would rarely get out of hand or lead to major problems because of community supervision. Enough easily enforceable outside regulators of behavior existed to make the development of strong internal controls unnecessary. Thus, shame rather than guilt was typically used to punish infractions, and major sins were seen to be sins of self-assertion against higher authority rather than, as later, infractions of behavior by man against man.[84]

In the more complicated society developing in the eighteenth century, the new sort of personality was more adaptive. Economically, the society relied on people to be assertive rather than submissive and passive. But people now frequently interacted in larger groups, often where they were not known to others. In such situations, uncontrolled rough-and-tumble anger could be a serious problem. It was important that people develop inner controls. Thus some sense of the self as possessing control and initiative was useful and adaptive, as might not have been the case before.[85]

Yet while a change from a sad-submissive mode to a more assertive mode can be noted in men, it is vital to recognize that this change did not take place as clearly in women. Even nineteenth-century women were characteristically tearful rather than angry, and used the stance of martyr when aggrieved.[86] Women, in other words, remained in the older mold. Grasping this new differentiation in emotionology for the sexes may prove useful in future explorations of the relationship between modernization and changing gender distinctions. Clearly, although in some sense nineteenth-century women benefited from being placed on pedestals that denied anger to them, in another sense, they were being left behind as men modernized. One wonders, in this context, if there was not a certain hypocrisy in the prevalent emotionology that men offered to nineteenth-century women. Was this, indeed, simply a dressed-up version of what was essentially an outdated stance of self-abnegation? Perhaps, indeed, the older historiography that viewed Victorian women as oppressed saw a certain truth which the feminist/revisionist view, that Victorian women benefited from the moral pedestal, has overlooked.[87]

Reading the diaries, one sees that sadness is associated with helplessness and a withdrawing, pulling in, or even denial of the self. When confronted with difficulties, the diarists' sad responses have a submissive and frightened quality. To acknowledge one's anger in the face of obstacles is to legitimate the self and to retain initiative.[88] Even if for the most part one decides to suppress one's anger, one keeps, in the face of conflict, a sense that one is in charge, if only because one can exercise self-control. If middle- and upper-class men could do this increasingly from the early eighteenth century, while women and the lower classes were still saddled with an emotionology demanding submissiveness and passivity, then the gap between privileged men and their wives or social inferiors could only increase. A new world view created differentiated emotional experiences that reinforced inequalities.

The point is not, of course, that the new personalities were psychologically healthier or superior. The author believes firmly that psychological health can be defined only within a culture. However, the relativist implication that one cannot in any way negatively characterize the emotional tone of another culture seems as mistaken as a tendency to judge prematurely or without awareness of the culture's own standards. An assumption that all cultures have equivalent cognitive solutions to their worries prematurely cuts off the effort to listen attentively to what the culture reveals affectively. The assertion that there is a sad or helpless tone in the early modern diaries discussed is based not on modern prejudice, but on careful reading of the diarist's own statements. Historians who, in their zeal to respect the past, deny even the theoretical possibility that another culture could be more anxious or otherwise affectively troubled than our own, would be the equivalent of the good-natured but mistaken psychotherapist, who rushes to assure the patient that "you're fine" before listening to what the patient wants to say. There were emotional differences between early modern people and ourselves, and it would be unrealistic to imply that their style had no disadvantages. This is different from saying that they were all neurotic.[89]

The fact that, like the Tahitians, early modern people typically displayed a more depressive stance than our own, does not mean that they were depressed in the sense of being mentally ill.[90] While one is struck by the depressive tone of some of the earlier personalities, it is clear that increasing the sense of self-control has also led to a great deal of struggle and guilt in modern personalities. Though the later diarists, when acknowledging anger, demonstrated a certain sense of self-reliance, this was often accompanied by anxiety about self-control. The decline of the obligation to be sad was accompanied by hints of a new, perhaps equally onerous duty to be cheerful. The sense of the self, or ego, was often overwhelmed by the sense of duty, or superego. To be self-conscious, in modern parlance, is, after all, to be slightly uncomfortable. The increasing belief that behavior could be controlled took away an outlet for feeling which had previously been widely used. Now that behavior was so strictly judged, it could hardly be as spontaneous. For the early modern person, who conceptualized problems and controls as coming from outside, there may have been no more anxiety about feeling than for the modern person with his internalized superego.[91] The purpose, again, is certainly not to judge, but rather to depict a change. And thus one must return to the contention of those who deny significant emotional changes over time.

Revisionist historians of emotions, such as Peter Gay, Carl Degler, and Linda Pollock, have emphasized the relative constancy of human nature and stressed the determining aspects of biology in shaping human love or sexuality. A more subtle version of this point of view emerged in Philip Greven's book *The Protestant Temperament,* which stressed continuities in three basic personality types or temperaments from the colonial period through the mid-nineteenth century. Both theoretically and factually, this approach presents problems for historians. Greven seems to suggest that personalities or temperaments are equally distributed historically. If this is so, then modal personalities do not change from time to time, and the study of personality is one for the biologist or psychologist but not for the historian. This certainly seems counterintuitive, since most of us recognize evidence from the past as being foreign in some sense. It also seems to contradict Greven's own belief in the importance of child-rearing practices in the formation of personality, since we know that child-rearing practices do change over time. This is not to say that there are not huge differences and varieties in personalities within any one historical period. It might even be true that the differences within any one period are more significant and far-ranging than the differences between modal personalities from period to period. However, if there is any change in modal personality over time, it would seem to be the job of historians to delineate rather than to obscure this.

In practice, Greven's eagerness to find his three types unchanged through the centuries causes him to make two sorts of errors. Error one is to refuse to see that evangelicals of the seventeenth century differed significantly from those of the nineteenth century. Error two is to exaggerate differences between groups in any one century. An example of the first type of error is the equation of eighteenth-century attempts to suppress conscious anger with the unconscious displacement and projection of anger through witchcraft accusations found in seventeenth-century Salem. A similar mistake is to minimize the significance of the fact that the evangelicals of the earlier period were troubled by a wrathful God, while their nineteenth-century descendants had replaced him with a God of love. In the same vein, it is mistaken to use nineteenth-century evidence of the care with which evangelicals governed their children to argue that child rearing in the seventeenth century was similarly careful, when the evidence indicates how very poorly controlled the early child-rearing efforts were.[92]

The second sort of error Greven makes is to exaggerate distinctions among eighteenth-century people. Although evangelicals and moderates are clearly separated in his treatment, they were not so clearly separated in real life. The efforts of the evangelicals to deal with anger through suppression that Greven cites sound very much like those of his moderates.[93]

My argument, then, is not that there are not profound personality differences within historical periods—this is a truism—but rather that when historians go looking for them, they may obscure changes that do take place over time. My formulation of these changes, which I hope will be tested by more extensive historical research, is as follows: During the course of the seventeenth century, a new emotionology of the relationship between feeling and behavior was evolving, and along with this came new views on the relative appropriateness of sadness and anger. The increasing ability to see the self as angry seems to be connected with a new sense of control and of personal assertiveness, at least on the part of middle- and upper-class men, and this in turn seems associated with the needs of a modernizing society. The new emotionology was far from an academic exercise; it profoundly altered the emotional experience of many ordinary people.

Appendix: Diaries Used in This Essay

1. Elias Ashmole. *The Diary and Will of Elias Ashmole.* Edited by R. T. Gunther. Oxford, 1927. Ashmole, a royalist scientist, was born in 1617. The diary goes from about 1633 to 1687. There is little recording of emotion.

2. Nicholas Assheton. *Journal.* Edited by Rev. F. R. Raines. Chetham Society, 1848. The journal covers 1617–18 and is remarkable for almost no discussion of emotions.

3. Richard Boyle. *The Lismore Papers. . . . Diaries of Sir Richard Boyle . . . Earl of Cork.* Edited by Alexander B. Grosart. London, 1886, 5 volumes. No significant recorded emotions. Years covered are 1611–37.

4. Robert Bulkeley. "The Diary of Bulkeley of Dronwy, Anglesey 1630–1636." Edited by Hugh Owen, in *Transactions Anglesey Antiquarian Society and Field Club.* Liverpool, 1936. A gentleman farmer and J.P., with little recording of emotions.

5. William Byrd. *William Byrd of Virginia. The London Diary (1717–1721).* Edited by Louis B. Wright and Marion Tinling. New York, 1958. Virginia planter educated as a lawyer.

6. John Byrom. *The Private Journal and Literary Remains of John Byrom.* Edited by Richard Parkinson. Vols. 32, 34, 44. Manchester, 1853–57. The writer was born in 1691. Letters start about 1707.

7. Walter Calverley. "Memorandum Book of Sir Walter Calverley, Bart." *In Yorkshire Diaries and Autobiographies in the Seventeenth and Eighteenth Centuries.* Edited by James Raine. Durham, 1883?. Very little introspection. Years covered are 1663–1748.

8. Anne Clifford. *The Diary of the Lady Anne Clifford.* Edited by Vita Sackville-West. London, 1923. She was born in 1590, the daughter of an earl. The diary goes only to 1619.

9. John Dee. *Autobiographical Tracts.* Edited by James Crosley. Chetham Society, 1851. An astrologer. Dates from the 1570s to the 1590s.

10. Adam Eyre. "A Dyurnall. . . ." In *Yorkshire Diaries and Autobiographies in the Seventeenth and Eighteenth Centuries.* Edited by James Raine. Durham, 1877. Eyre was a yeoman who fought for Parliament in the Civil War. The diary covers 1647–49.

11. Elizabeth Freke. *Mrs. Elizabeth Freke Her Diary 1671 to 1714.* Edited by Mary Carbery. Cork, 1913. Diary of a wealthy English lady.

12. James Fretwell. "A Family History." In *Yorkshire Diaries* (see item 10). Years from end of seventeenth to mid-eighteenth centuries. Few emotions.

13. Oliver Heywood. *The Reverend Oliver Heywood, Autobiography, Diaries.* Edited by J. Horsfall Turner. Brighouse, Eng., 1882–85. Diary of a nonconformist born in 1629. Diary covers 1660s through 1702, but mostly 1660s and 1670s.

14. John Hobson. "The Journal of Mr. J. H." In *Yorkshire Diaries* (see item 10). Years from 1725 to 1726. Writer was a tanner. Doesn't record much on feelings.

15. William Jefferay. *The Journal of William Jefferay, Gentleman.* Edited by John Osborne Austin. Providence, R.I., 1899. Diary of an English gentleman farmer who

emigrated to New England but was not a Puritan. Covers years from 1591 to 1623, though not written until about 1650.

16. Ralph Josselin. *The Diary of Ralph Josselin 1616–1683.* Edited by Alan MacFarlane. Cambridge, Eng., 1976. Introspective Puritan.

17. Roger Lowe. *The Diary of Roger Lowe.* Edited by William Sachse. London, 1938. Puritan apprentice. Covers 1663–74.

18. Henry Machyn. *The Diary of Henry Machyn 1550–1553.* Edited by John Gough Nichols. London, 1848. Not much introspection but plenty of observation of the behavior of others.

19. Adam Martindale. *The Life of Adam Martindale.* Edited by Rev. Richard Parkinson. Chetham Society, 1844. Covers through 1684. Written retrospectively. Author, a Puritan minister, born 1623.

20. Henry Newcome. *The Autobiography of Henry Newcome, MA.* Edited by Richard Parkinson. Manchester, 1852. Puritan minister, born 1627, who was nonetheless a loyalist in Civil War. Covers through 1690s. Mostly written retrospectively.

21. Richard Norwood. *The Journal of Richard Norwood.* Edited by Wesley Frank Craven and Walter B. Hayward. New York, 1945. English Puritan who later traveled to Bermuda. Written in 1639 but covers his early life. He was born in 1590.

22. John Oglander. *Sir John Oglander. A Royalist's Notebook.* Edited by Francis Bamford. New York, 1971. Covers 1585–1655.

23. Ebenezer Parkman. *The Diary of Ebenezer Parkman, first part 1719–55.* Edited by Francis G. Walett. Worcester, 1974. New England Puritan minister.

24. John Penry. *The Notebook of John Penry, 1593.* Edited by Albert Peel. London, 1944. A Welsh Congregationalist, born in 1563 and involved with the Marprelate tracts. Not really a diary and little on emotion.

25. Walter Powell. *The Diary of Walter Powell 1603–1654.* Edited by Joseph Alfred Bradney. Bristol, 1907. Steward to the Earl of Worcester. Little on emotions.

26. Dudley Ryder. *The Diary of Dudley Ryder 1715–1716.* Edited by William Mathews. London, 1939. Nonconformist who later became parliamentarian. Diary starts at age twenty-four.

27. Samuel Sewall. *Samuel Sewall's Diary.* Edited by Mark Van Doren. New York, 1963. This is an abridgment of the original diary of the New England Puritan magistrate and official. Covers 1675–1729.

28. William Stout. *The Autobiography of William Stout of Lancaster 1665–1752.* Edited by J. D. Marshall. Manchester, 1967. A Quaker merchant.

29. Anthony à Wood. *The Life and Times of Anthony à Wood.* Edited by Llewelyn Powys. London, 1961. Abridgment not entirely satisfactory. Covers 1632–95. Oxford antiquarian and anti-Puritan.

Notes

1. The author disagrees with approaches such as Emory Elliott's, which postulate the uniqueness of the American experience and explain changes in American emotionology as resulting solely from changes in local conditions (*Power and the Pulpit in Puritan New England* [Princeton, 1975], p. 65).

2. For a discussion of how much ideas about emotion color what people actually

claim to feel, see Carol Zisowitz Stearns and Peter N. Stearns, *Anger: The Struggle for Emotional Control in America's History* (Chicago, 1986), passim.

3. For a discussion of the meaning of emotionology, see Peter N. Stearns with Carol Z. Stearns, "Emotionology: Clarifying the History of Emotions and Emotional Standards," *American Historical Review* 90, no. 4 (1985): 813–36.

4. For a good statement on the uses and limitations of diaries, see Linda A. Pollock, *Forgotten Children, Parent-Child Relations from 1500 to 1900* (Cambridge, 1983), pp. 69ff. On the particular genre of Puritan diaries, see Owen C. Watkins, *The Puritan Experience. Studies in Spiritual Autobiography* (New York, 1972).

5. For an annotated list of the diaries used, see appendix to this chapter.

6. For a discussion of the controversy, see Stearns with Stearns, "Emotionology."

7. The author does not have much sympathy with the notion of trying to quantify the diaries, which are different enough from one another to make such rigorous comparison almost impossible. An example of such a quantitative approach is Michael Barton, *Goodmen: The Character of Civil War Soldiers* (University Park, Pa., 1981).

8. Arthur Kleinman and Byron Good, "Introduction," Kleinman and Good, *Culture and Depression. Studies in the Anthropology and Cross-Cultural Psychiatry of Affect and Disorder* (Berkeley and Los Angeles, 1985), pp. 4, 30.

9. Roger Lowe, *The Diary of Roger Lowe*, ed. William Sachse (London, 1938), pp. 74–5, 19, 50, 70, 55, 46–47.

10. Ralph Josselin, *The Diary of Ralph Josselin 1616–1683*, ed. Alan MacFarlane (London, 1976), pp. 5, 10, 43, 56, 289, 20. For a similar reaction, see Oliver Heywood, *The Reverend Oliver Heywood, Autobiography, Diaries. . . .*, ed. J. Horsfall Turner (Brighouse, Eng., 1882–85), 1:266.

11. John Dee, *Autobiographical Tracts*, ed. James Crosley (Chetham Society, 1851), pp. 78–79.

12. Anne Clifford, *The Diary of The Lady Anne Clifford*, ed. Vita Sackville-West (London, 1923), pp. 62, 69, 70, 73.

13. Elizabeth Freke, *Mrs. Elizabeth Freke Her Diary 1671 to 1714*, ed. Mary Carbery (Cork, 1913), pp. 35, 41–42, 118.

14. Lowe, *Diary*, pp. 114, 91, 56, 52. For discussion of Puritan "projection" in dealing with anger, see John Putnam Demos, *Entertaining Satan; Witchcraft and the Culture of Early New England* (Oxford, 1982), pp. 187–88, 195–97.

15. Samuel Sewall, *Samuel Sewall's Diary*, ed. Mark Van Doren (New York, 1963), pp. 199, 191.

16. Ebenezer Parkman, *The Diary of Ebenezer Parkman 1719–55*, ed. Francis G. Walett (Worcester, 1974), pp. 24–25, 45.

17. Rhys Isaac, *The Transformation of Virginia 1740–1790* (Chapel Hill, 1982), p. 119. See also Stearns and Stearns, *Anger*, chap. 2; Michael MacDonald, *Mystical Bedlam: Madness, Anxiety and Healing in Seventeenth-Century England* (Cambridge, 1981), pp. 109ff.; Robert Muchembled, *Popular Culture and Elite Culture in France 1400–1750*, trans. Lydia Cochrane (Baton Rouge, 1985), pp. 31–33, 119ff.

Walter Ong sees this as typical of preliterate cultures (Walter J. Ong, *Orality and Literacy* [London, 1982], pp. 43–45).

18. Anthony à Wood, *The Life and Times of Anthony à Wood*, ed. Llewelyn Powys (London, 1961), pp. 287, 298; John Oglander, *Sir John Oglander. A Royalist's Notebook*, ed. Francis Bamford (New York, 1971), p. 87; Sewall, *Diary*, p. 207; Heywood, *Autobiography*, 1:345.

19. Josselin, *Diary*, p. 40; Sewall, *Diary*, pp. 115–16.

20. Elias Ashmole, *The Diary and Will of Elias Ashmole*, ed. R. T. Gunther (Oxford, 1927), pp. 165–68, 30–31.

21. Wood, *Life*, p. 331; Sewall, *Diary*, pp. 220–21.

22. Heywood, *Autobiography* 2:240ff., 294. Richard Norwood, *The Journal of Richard Norwood*, ed. Wesley Frank Craven and Walter B. Hayward (New York, 1945), p. 32.

23. Lowe, *Diary*, p. 105.

24. Lowe, *Diary*, p. 70.

25. Sewall, *Diary*, pp. 164–65, 185, 195.

26. Sewall, *Diary*, pp. 200–202, 210. Also, Heywood, *Autobiography*, 1:333, 338; 2:278.

27. Oglander, *Notebook*, p. 166.

28. Henry Newcome, *A Plain Discourse about Rash and Sinful Anger . . .* (Manchester, 1693).

29. Henry Newcome, *The Autobiography of Henry Newcome, MA*, ed. Richard Parkinson (Manchester, 1852), p. 296; Dudley Ryder, *The Diary of Dudley Ryder 1715–1716*, ed. William Mathews (London, 1939), pp. 53–54 and 311.

30. Lowe, *Diary*, p. 62; Parkman, *Diary*, p. 21.

31. Heywood, *Autobiography*, 1:333. Newcome, *Autobiography*, pp. 99, 197–98, 58.

32. Ryder, *Diary*, pp. 281, 132, 38; and similarly pp. 119, 371, 38–39.

33. Lowe, *Diary*, p. 70; John Wesley, in Philip J. C. Greven, Jr., *Child-Rearing Concepts, 1628–1861* (Itasca, Ill., 1973), p. 65; Muchembled, *Popular Culture*, pp. 26ff.; Alan MacFarlane, *The Family Life of Ralph Josselin* (Cambridge, Eng., 1970), pp. 172ff.; Charles Lloyd Cohen, *God's Caress. The Psychology of Puritan Religious Experience* (New York and Oxford, 1986), pp. 204–5.

34. Lowe, *Diary*, pp. 46–47, 80.

35. Newcome, "To the reader" in *Anger; Autobiography*, pp. 144–45; Ryder, *Diary*, pp. 303–4.

36. Wood, *Life*, pp. 141–42; Freke, *Diary*, p. 57; Norwood, *Journal*, p. 47; Lowe, *Diary*, pp. 16, 28, 50. See also Stearns and Stearns, *Anger*, pp. 21ff.

37. Newcome, *Anger*, p. 42; *Autobiography*, p. 16. Witherspoon in Greven, *Child-Rearing*, pp. 90, 85; Jean-Louis Flandrin, *Families in Former Times: Kinship, Household and Sexuality*, trans. Richard Southern (Cambridge, 1979), pp. 127ff. For identification of both God and father as angry, see Paul S. Seaver, *Wallington's World. A Puritan Artisan in Seventeenth-Century London* (Stanford, 1985), p. 75.

38. Oglander, *Notebook*, p. 239; John Robinson, *Essayes . . .* (London, 1638), pp. 446–47, 494; Cohen, *God's Caress*, p. 131.

39. Newcome, *Anger,* pp. 6, 10–11, 65ff.; *Autobiography,* pp. 296–97; Ryder, *Diary,* pp. 125, 155, 60.

40. MacDonald, *Mystical Bedlam,* 126–28.

41. David Hunt, *Parents and Children in History* (New York, 1970), chap. 7.

42. Adam Eyre, "A Dyurnall," in *Yorkshire Diaries and Autobiographies in the Seventeenth and Eighteenth Centuries,* ed. James Raine (Durham, 1877), p. 67. See also Seaver, *Wallington,* p. 8.

43. Norwood, *Journal,* p. 77. For similar stress on submission and fear of pride, see Josselin, *Diary,* pp. 43, 56–57; also Seaver, *Wallington,* p. 10. For a discussion of fear as the appropriate and pervasive emotional stance of early modern people, see Muchembled, *Popular Culture,* chap. 1.

44. On legitimation of anger in other cultures, see Edward L. Schieffelin, "The Cultural Analysis of Depressive Affect: An Example from New Guinea," pp. 101–3, and Catherine Lutz, "Depression and the Translation of Emotional Worlds," pp. 63–100, in Kleinman and Good, *Culture and Depression.* For an argument that anger always implies a judgment about being in the right, see Robert C. Solomon, "The Jamesian Theory of Emotion in Anthropology," in Richard Shweder and Robert A. LeVine, *Culture Theory, Essays on Mind, Self, and Emotion* (Cambridge, Eng., 1984), p. 250.

45. Ryder, *Diary,* pp. 303–4. This is not to argue, of course, that the old view disappeared entirely. The writings of Jonathan Edwards clearly were "old-fashioned" on God's anger. The point is that an alternative view was emerging.

46. William Byrd, *William Byrd of Virignia. The London Diary (1717–1721),* ed. Louis B. Wright and Marion Tinling (New York, 1958), pp. 209. Also 213, 254, 269, 276, 282, 315, 435, 437, 440.

47. Clearly, I take issue with Emory Elliott's view that this change was unique to the local situation in New England (*Power,* pp. 13–14).

48. Sewall, *Diary,* pp. 89–90, 125; Oglander, *Notebook,* p. 245; *Oxford English Dictionary.* Also, Heywood, *Autobiography,* 1:261, 300.

49. Oglander, *Notebook,* p. 113.

50. Josselin, *Diary,* p. 5; Sewall, *Diary,* p. 216. Lowe; *Diary,* p. 68; Ryder, *Diary,* pp. 282, 294–96; Norwood, *Journal,* p. 12.

51. MacDonald, *Mystical Bedlam,* pp. 150ff. For a discussion of some other cultures which dignify sadness, see Kleinman and Good, "Introduction," p. 3.

52. Newcome, *Autobiography,* pp. 207–8; also 197, 216–17. Parkman, *Diary,* p. 23; Norwood, *Journal,* p. 64.

53. Ryder, *Diary,* pp. 141, 91, 63. John Byrom, *The Private Journal and Literary Remains of John Byrom,* ed. Richard Parkinson (Manchester, 1853–57), p. 295.

54. Joe L. Dubbert, *A Man's Place: Masculinity in Transition* (Englewood Cliffs, N.J., 1979), pp. 32–34.

55. Josselin, *Diary,* pp. 50, 54–56, 17, 32; Sewall, *Diary,* p. 124.

56. Clifford, *Diary,* p. 32; Lowe, *Diary,* p. 15; Sewall, *Diary,* pp. 155, 78, 215; Josselin, *Diary.*

57. "Cultural Analysis of Depressive Affect: An Example from New Guinea," in Kleinman and Good, *Culture and Depression,* pp. 101–33.

58. Josselin, *Diary*, pp. 51, 17; Lowe, *Diary*, p. 24; Norwood, *Journal*, p. 17; Heywood, *Autobiography*, 1:319.

59. William Stout, *The Autobiography of William Stout of Lancaster 1665–1752*, ed. J. D. Marshall (Manchester, 1967), pp. 103–4, 141–42.

60. Norwood, *Journal*, pp. 26–27, 93–99, 104. Heywood, *Autobiography*, 2:238.

61. Parkman, *Diary*, pp. 7–8.

62. Elliott, *Power*, pp. 197–98.

63. Ryder, *Diary*, pp. 29, 334, 229.

64. MacDonald, *Mystical Bedlam*, pp. 180ff.; Watkins, *Experience*, p. 6.

65. MacDonald, *Mystical Bedlam*, p. 140; Newcome, *Anger*, pp. 26–28. Walter Calverley, "Memorandum Book of Sir Walter Calverley, Bart.," in *Yorkshire Diaries*, pp. 139–40.

66. Lowe, *Diary*, p. 38; Newcome, *Autobiography*, p. 48; Byrd, *Diary*, pp. 375, 276.

67. Newcome, *Anger*, 46; Adam Martindale, *The Life of Adam Martindale*, ed. Richard Parkinson (Chetham Society, 1844), pp. 22, 25; Sereno E. Dwight "The Works of President Edwards . . ." (1829), and John Locke "Some Thoughts Concerning Education" (1690), in Greven, *Childrearing*, 77, 41.

68. Alan MacFarlane, *Ralph Josselin*, p. 170. For another example, see Ashmole, *Diary*, pp. 103, 106, 121, 129, 138–39, and passim; Eyre, "Dyurnall," p. 68.

69. Ashmole, *Diary*, pp. 31, 49; Norwood, *Journal*, p. 41.

70. For an example, see Walter Powell, who records no emotion on the death of a wife, a new marriage, or the birth of a child (*The Diary of Walter Powell 1603–1654*, ed. Joseph Alfred Bradney [Bristol, 1907], p. 4). Ashmole, *Diary*, pp. 12–13, records no emotion on his father's death or his own marriage.

71. Ryder, *Diary*, pp. 32, 46.

72. Though Ong, in *Orality and Literacy*, would argue that degrees of literacy and literary expression cause changes in emotionality rather than the reverse.

73. For the older view, see J. Leff, "Culture and the Differentiation of Emotional States," *British Journal of Psychiatry* 123 (1973): 299–306. For a revisionist view, see Kleinman and Good, "Introduction" and "Epilogue," in *Culture and Depression*.

74. Lowe, *Diary*, pp. 532, 55; Josselin, *Diary*, passim.

75. Cohen, *God's Caress*, p. 239, chap. 8. Cohen himself admits that the experience of grace after conversion is not well documented (pp. 212–13). His discussion of John Winthrop's diary ignores the very evidence it presents of the diarist's conflict and suffering even after conversion. See also Seaver, *Wallington*, pp. 19–20.

76. Norwood, *Journal*, p. 106.

77. Robert I. Levy, *Tahitians; Mind and Experience in the Society Islands* (Chicago, 1973), p. 405.

78. Oglander, *Notebook*, pp. 215–16; Norwood, *Journal*, pp. 101–3. MacDonald, *Mystical Bedlam*, 173ff.

79. Clifford Geertz, *Local Knowledge* (New York, 1983), p. 59. See also Arthur Mitzman, "The Civilizing Offensive: Mentalities, High Culture and Individual Psyches," *Journal of Social History* 20:4 (1987), pp. 663–87.

80. Keith Thomas, *Religion and the Decline of Magic* (New York, 1971); Muchembled, *Popular Culture;* Josselin, *Diary,* pp. 53, 56, 57, passim; Sewall, *Diary,* p. 124; Newcome, *Autobiography,* pp. 104, 108; Norwood, *Journal,* p. 4; Ashmole, *Diary,* pp. 8–9; Seaver, *Wallington,* p. 90.

81. This certainly is not to argue that the early diarists did not love their children deeply. The evidence strongly supports Linda Pollock's revisionist view on that question. But Pollock has ignored the question of how differently love may have expressed itself over changing centuries, and has therefore been seemingly unaware of the relative neglect that early modern parents had for the safety of their offspring. She has nowhere dealt with the frequency of accidents that happened to early modern children. *(Forgotten Children.)*

82. Thomas, *Religion and the Decline of Magic.* Stuart Clark has argued that it is theoretically impossible for early modern people to have experienced themselves as lacking control since they could not have been aware of something they never had. He also has suggested that cognitive structures and behaviors such as rituals should not be explained in terms of emotional needs unless one can offer evidence that the emotional states can be identified independently of the cognitions or behaviors ("French Historians and Early Modern Popular Culture," *Past and Present* 100 [1983]: 62–99, especially pp.88–90). Study of these diaries proves that Clark is wrong in suggesting that early modern people experienced no discomfort from lack of control. This essay also shows that it is indeed possible to discuss the emotionality of a culture by examining what members state about their own emotions. Clark is also wrong, then, in suggesting that "emotionalist" explanations must be ex post facto, prejudiced, "reductionist" approaches to behavior and cognition.

83. Muchembled, *Popular Culture,* pp. 39ff.

84. John Demos, "Shame and Guilt in Early New England," in this volume. Elliott, *Power,* pp. 68–69; Cohen, *God's Caress,* pp. 218–20.

85. The author takes issue with Elliott's analysis of similar changes as resulting solely from generational changes in New England (*Power,* pp. 174ff.). Clearly the changes were more widespread than he realized.

86. Stearns and Stearns, *Anger,* chap. 3.

87. A traditional view of the damage caused by nineteenth-century views of emotionality is Bernard I. Murstein, *Love, Sex, and Marriage through the Ages* (New York, 1974), pp. 260–64. Also John Haller and Robin Haller, *The Physician and Sexuality in Victorian America* (New York, 1977), pp. 24–42. Toward a partial revision, stressing moral elevation through control of emotions such as anger, see Nancy Cott, *The Bonds of Womanhood: Women's Sphere in New England 1780–1833* (New Haven, 1977), pp. 64–69; Patricia Branca, *Silent Sisterhood* (Pittsburgh, 1975).

88. For an analysis of the relationships between anger and assertion, see Joseph De Rivera, *A Structural Theory of the Emotions* (New York, 1977), pp. 83ff. de Rivera further argues, as do I, that depression is an alternative to anger "when values are being challenged but anger seems unprofitable and there are reasons (such as dependency) against exercising alternatives that create distance." Depression as a contracting of the self or experience of being "pressed down" is also described by de

Rivera (pp. 121–22). The distinction brings to mind a patient of mine, a young woman formerly depressed and now often angry, who told me, "when I'm angry, it's like I know I have a self."

89. Again, I take issue with Stuart Clark, "French Historians and Early Modern Culture." The assumption here, that one must always take cultures entirely at face value, seems to rest on several conceptual errors. Error one is to argue that there are no mental structures which affect a culture but of which the culture may be unaware (p. 99). This is, in effect, a statement that the unconscious does not exist, a statement with which few sensitive social scientists can be entirely comfortable. Error two is the assumption that it is somehow dignified for people to develop cognitive structures to explain their world, but undignified for them to develop structures to allay anxiety. This assumption, which runs throughout Clark's article, leads to his accusing historians such as Muchembled with a lack of respect for the past. One must point out, then, that it is Clark, not Muchembled, who is unable to accept the reality that one of man's universal activities is to try to allay anxiety. A discussion of early modern anxiety is not equivalent to a statement that early modern people are inferior or that modern people have less anxiety. Clark needs to reassess his motives in suggesting that it is proper for historians to look only at the cognitive, and not at the emotional, difficulties of our forefathers. Finally, Clark is misguided in positing a rigid distinction between historians who look at the past in terms of its own meanings and those who come as "sociologically privileged observers" (p. 95). An either/or approach can hardly aid our collective endeavor to understand human experience. We must respect other cultures on their own terms, but also, in delineating them, make them comprehensible to ourselves. There is a kind of romanticism in an approach which overstresses the "differentness" of other cultures. It is not a sign of disrespect, but rather of respect, to employ the wisdom of modern social science in an effort to understand the past. To do otherwise is to make our ancestors noble savages. Empathic and objective understanding are both useful and should not be mutually exclusive. For an argument that historians need in some sense to see beyond the past's own meanings in order to understand change, see Keith Thomas, "An Anthropology of Religion and Magic, II," *Journal of Interdisciplinary History* 6, no. 1 (Summer 1975): 102–3. For a general argument in favor of objective as well as empathic understanding, see Melford E. Spiro, "Some Reflections on Cultural Determinism and Relativism with Special Reference to Emotion and Reason," in Shweder and LeVine, *Culture Theory*, pp. 323–46.

90. For a discussion of the necessity of making a distinction between feelings and mental illness, see Kleinman and Good, "Epilogue," in *Culture and Depression*.

91. I dispute Muchembled's view that early modern people because of external anxieties were more pervasively anxious or neurotic than modern ones (*Popular Culture*, 30–31).

92. Greven, *The Protestant Temperament. Patterns of Child-Rearing, Religious Experience and the Self in Early America* (New York, 1977), pp. 74, 11, 113, 123, 28ff., 43ff.).

93. Greven, *Protestant Temperament*, pp. 113, 253.

3

Shame and Guilt
in Early New England

John Demos

*F*orty years ago Ruth Benedict made this comparison of American life, past and present:

> The early Puritans who settled in the United States tried to base their entire morality on guilt, and all psychiatrists know what trouble contemporary Americans have with their consciences. But shame is an increasingly heavy burden . . . and guilt is less extremely felt than in earlier generations. In the United States this is interpreted as a relaxation of morals, because we do not expect shame to do the heavy work of morality. We do not harness the acute personal chagrin which accompanies shame to our fundamental system of morality.[1]

Benedict was, of course, a distinguished anthropologist, not a historian. And the foregoing statement seems mistaken—as history. But it does contain a pithy piece of phrase-making, which serves to pose a question. What aspects of American character have traditionally been made to "do the heavy work of morality"?

The question could be asked about any part of our history, early, late, or in between; but the discussion that follows will be limited to a single geographical region and two segments of historical time. It begins by arguing—in opposition to Benedict—that the "early Puritans" were notably shame-prone, and that shame performed the largest part of their moral "heavy work." It further suggests how, in the era of the Early Republic, the burden began to shift—away from shame, toward guilt and "conscience." Its focus is New England life and culture,* its framework is straightforward comparison. The result is argument, not finished exposition; evidence is introduced more to illustrate than to "prove" a given point. To these disclaimers

---

* "New England culture" is rather loosely construed here. For the first ("Puritan") period the boundaries are conventional enough; for the second they expand to include the hinterland (New York, the Upper Midwest) peopled largely by New Englanders.

must be added two more. Little is said here about the process of change. The period 1650–1750 seems to be one sort of moral/psychological world, and the period 1800–1850 another; but the interim remains (for now) largely obscure. Finally, readers may note an avoidance of certain knotty methodological problems. The psychological disposition of large populations— "national character," in its most familiar phrasing—is itself a *conundrum,* if not a bottomless pit of academic controversy. And it is necessary to invoke a temporary suspension of disbelief on that score as well.

I

   Shame and *guilt:* small words for large and complex forms of experience. Most of us can distinguish them, intuitively, in our personal lives; but it is well, nonetheless, to make some effort at formal definition. Fortunately, there is an abundant scientific literature to bring to bear on that task.[2]

   Close to the level of visible behavior, the distinction seems to turn on the presence—and salience—of other persons. *Shame* has an "external" reference; the pain it inflicts comes by way of an "audience." To be sure, the audience is sometimes imagined, not real; but the sense of being watched, of being exposed and unfavorably scrutinized, is central either way. A morality based on shame makes much of *appearances;* one does the right thing because one is concerned to preserve a good reputation. *Guilt,* by contrast, is based on a process that is largely "internalized." There is a "code" of values that individuals carry around inside them—and that serves to regulate their actual deeds. A guilt-prone person feels distressed whenever s/he acts contrary to the inner code—regardless of whether or not anyone else is watching.

   The distinction has other, "deeper" aspects as well, some of which are captured in the following comparative statements. (1) Shame occurs when a standard (a goal; a hope; a fantasy) is not reached; in this almost literal sense it involves "shortcoming." Guilt occurs when a norm (a rule; a precept; a principle) is violated—or, one might say, when a boundary is crossed; it amounts, therefore, to "transgression." (2) In experiential terms, shame means, "I am weak, inadequate, inferior"; whereas guilt means, "I do bad things." The point implied here is that guilt always has moral connotations, while shame may or may not have them—and also that shame is about the whole self, while guilt is more closely tied to specific acts. (3) The pain experienced, in each case, derives from different unconscious sources. In shame one feels that one is on the receiving end of an attitude of scorn, of contempt; and behind this lies a dread of abandonment. In guilt one seems to be the object, rather, of hatred; and the punishment one fears, at the deepest intrapsychic level, is some form of mutilation. (In psychoanalytic terms, the developmental line leads back to what is called "castration anxiety.") These three propositions, in turn, underlie one more: namely, that shame and guilt may both be operant at once, yet usually one of them is in some sense preferred to the other. In practice, shame may cover (or mask, or defend against) guilt—and vice versa.

II

With these theoretical props roughly in place, attention turns to the first part of our comparison—early New England, and, above all, "Puritanism." This patch of the historical landscape has, of course, been endlessly picked over by scholars; yet some features remain more or less neglected. Consider the legal system—especially, the punishment system. Here indeed is something wonderfully quaint and curious—and, by most scholarly accounts, inessential, even trivial.[3] It deserves to be taken quite seriously.

Fines were the most common sanction imposed on wrongdoers in early New England. Fines were also, evidently, considered least painful; whenever a choice was offered—pay so much cash, or accept another form of punishment—New Englanders elected to pay. And what were the other punishments? Sitting in the stocks; standing on a pillory; wearing a so-called "badge of infamy" (in the manner of Hawthorne's scarlet letter) or a simple "paper" describing the offense in question; branding (in effect, a way of making the "badge" permanent); being dragged through the streets, tied to a "cart's tail"; standing in the gallows with a rope tied around one's neck: these were the favorites, with occasional added refinements as circumstances might warrant. What they all had in common was the element of invidious public exposure. And often, in individual cases, the "public" part was given explicit emphasis. Thus the time and place of punishment would be specified as follows: "upon some public meeting day," "on a public training day," "in the open market place," "in the open street," "in the public congregation," "in some open place in the meeting house." The purpose of such directions was clear enough: "that he may be seen of the people," "so as they may be visibly seen," "to the open view of spectators," and so on. There was one more kind of punishment—at least as common as the others, and somewhat different in its effects—namely, whipping. The difference, of course, was the physical pain. But scattered evidence from the case files suggests that the pain was not *only* physical. It was an assumed and important part of all whippings that they were public; indeed the term "public correction" often served, in court records, as a shorthand reference to this procedure.[4]

At least occasionally, shame—that is, the psychological experience itself—was directly mentioned in the records. A man convicted of sexual misconduct was sentenced to be whipped; the woman involved was spared the same punishment, "considering the weakness of her body," but was ordered to "be present at the whipping post . . . that she may in some measure bear the shame of her sin." Another convict boasted, after his punishment, "that he did not value his whipping the skip of a flea, only for a little shame." (In one remarkable instance such considerations obtained even with a capital sentence: a murderer "desired to have been beheaded [rather than hanged], giving this reason, that it was less painful and less shameful.")[5]

Church congregations, no less than the courts, sought to discipline errant members by way of shaming. "Admonition" was the means most often employed. "Temperance Baldwin . . . was called forth in the open congregation . . . and solemnly admonished of her great sin, which was spread before her in diverse particulars": thus one instance among many. Sinners like Temperance Baldwin were urged to "confess"—or, as it was put in another case, to "take shame unto her face." Typically, the result was a long recital of wickedness, given in a tone of abject self-abasement. (For example: "With all submissive respect, prostrating himself at the feet of your clemency, . . . your poor petitioner . . . humbly desires to acknowledge the justice of God, who . . . hath made his sin obvious to his shame . . . ,"etc.)[6] If the tone seemed insufficiently abject—if shame was not willingly and visibly expressed—confession was considered meaningless, and the original offense stood compounded. And if admonition failed of results altogether, a church might decide to invoke its most terrible sanction of all, outright excommunication. The gravity of this procedure was underscored in the language used as the minister pronounced sentence:

> For these and many more foul and sinful transgressions, I do here in the name of the whole church . . . pronounce you to be a leprous and unclean person, and I do cast you out and cut you off from the enjoyment of all those blessed privileges and ordinances which God hath entrusted his church withal. . . . And so, as an unclean beast and unfit for the society of God's people, I do from this time forward pronounce you an excommunicated person from God and His people.[7]

If the Puritans were indeed shame-prone, and if the inward experience of shame is rooted in a fearful expectation of abandonment, then surely these words were calculated for maximum effect.

In fact, however, the record of the law and of ecclesiastical discipline does not by itself evince the *experience* of shame in the population at large. It shows that the leaders—those who made the laws and ran the churches—credited shame with great power, and perhaps it reflects their own psychological tendency. But it is obviously dangerous, when analyzing penal systems, to assume a symmetry of intended and actual effects. How well a given form of punishment "works" in the offender, or whether indeed it works at all—this is another sort of question.

Unfortunately, we cannot look inside the experience of actual offenders subjected to one or another punishment three centuries ago. We must look, instead, for different—but congruent—evidence. Consider, then, the extraordinary prominence in early New England court records of lawsuits for slander and defamation. In sheer quantitative terms this category of cases makes one of the very largest. And it shows us (as the punishment system does not) many individual persons choosing to act in a particular way. Furthermore, it shows us (at least occasionally) some of the feeling that prompted such action. Here is an illustrative example:

> William Edwards hath entered an action of defamation against Benjamin Price and his wife, his wife saying that the wife of William Edwards was a base, lying woman, and that she would prove her a liar in many particulars.

That is the summary notice on the Court docket; then the depositional evidence begins, with a statement from Edwards himself:

> William Edwards, plaintiff, declares it is a deep wound that is laid upon his wife in that which is expressed against her by Goody Price, for *her life lieth at stake* in this defamation in that it is laid against her that she is a base, lying woman, and that she will prove her a liar in many particulars. Which I also take to be a great defamation to me and my posterity, in that hereafter it may be spoken, "here go the brats of a base liar. . . ." I declare that the defamation is such as I would not have made out against my wife for a hundred pounds.[8]

The plaintiff in this case estimated the damage to his wife's reputation as equivalent in monetary terms to more than £100, and other New Englanders made similar calculations. A Rhode Island man, who considered himself "most ignominiously slandered" by an accusation of theft, pleaded in court as follows: "Seeing that a man's good name is worth more than wealth, I cannot but charge him [the defendant] with one hundred pounds damage, though it be not a sufficient recompense." A Massachusetts man challenged a slanderer to fight, saying "I had rather thou should cut my flesh than give me such words." A Connecticut town, in establishing its own code of local justice, set the penalty for assault at ten shillings, and that for slander at five pounds—a tenfold difference. And the poet Anne Bradstreet offered this comparison: "We read in Scriptures of three sorts of arrows: the arrow of an enemy, the arrow of pestilence, and the arrow of a slanderer's tongue. The two first kill the body, the last the good name; the two former leave a man when he is once dead, but the last mangles him in his grave."[9]

Lawsuits for slander often resulted from larger episodes of personal conflict, and conflict itself bears consideration here. The sources of conflict, the manner, the tone, the results: there is much to be learned from cross-cultural comparison of the ways people *fight*. In early New England the characteristic tone was (what might be called) "narcissistic insult." It is heard again and again, whenever the parties to conflict are directly quoted. Here is a modest sampling taken from a variety of depositional records.

He said . . . that Swan was a weak man, and he could drive a dozen such as he before him through the town.[10]

She said that she would make him bare as a bird's tail.[11]

He said he did not care a fart for the Court.[12]

He said, "We met old Mr. Bradstreet; and my brother . . . crouched and conjured to him, but I knew him well enough, and for my part I never stoved my hat to him, nor reverenced him more than I would an Indian."[13]

He answered that he would not suffer such an affront from a man—no, not from King Charles himself if he was here, but would trample him under his foot.[14]

He said, . . . "I shall make a fool of you before I have done with you."[15]

He put one hand in the waistband of his breeches and said . . . he would deal with him with one hand.[16]

She said . . . that the teacher [i.e., minister] was fitter to be a lady's chambermaid than to be in the pulpit.[17]

He said . . . "You are too high, you must be brought down."[18]

She said . . . "we'll kill them, and flea them, and carry them home in the cart."[19]

He said that he had as leave to hear a dog bark as to hear Mr. Cobbet preach.[20]

He said . . . that they were but a company of fools for meddling and making themselves ridiculous amongst men.[21]

He said he would humble him, for he had always been a pimping knave to him.[22]

He challenged us [to get] off our horses to try our manhood, and said that he would take me by the eyelids and make my heels strike fire against the element.[23]

He said that his dog's tail would make as good a [church-] member as she.[24]

High versus low, strong versus weak; reverencing versus humbling, trampling versus crouching; smart men versus fools, good men versus knaves, Englishmen versus Indians; kings versus chambermaids, preachers versus dogs; deeds that command respect versus farts and fleas and bare birds' tails. The issues are "narcissistic" ones* in that they involve the management of and, more especially, of self-*esteem*. When these folk faced off in situations of conflict (with its attendant excitements and dangers), they instinctively sought to inflate themselves, and to denigrate their opponents. Or—to make the same point in other words—efforts of shaming, and of defense against shame, virtually *defined* conflict for many of them.

The causes of conflict are no less revealing than the tonal qualities; and often, in early New England, the cause was some form of "narcissistic injury." One man began to fight after declaring that "his spirit could not bear to be made such a fool of." Another sued his neighbor in order to "vindicate my blasted reputation. . . . The world might think that I did cast off the care of my own credit, if I did suffer such reproaches to be laid on me." And still another—an eminent New England clergyman—lamented man's "vengeful" nature thus: "Nothing is more natural . . . than to say so and do so: 'I'll be even with him; I'll give him as good as he brings.' They think it a disgrace for them to put up [with] an affront, or pass by an injury, without revenge or satisfaction, notwithstanding the Lord chargeth them to forgive those that have done them wrong."[26]

This last comment leads into the subject of religion; and religion, no less than the law, furnishes important material for the present discussion. Indeed "Puritan" belief may be viewed as a kind of screen on which the believers could (and did) project a vivid cluster of fantasies, anxieties, and other forms of psychological preoccupation. Consider: A "good" man is characterized, above all, by "humility," "meekness," and the "forbearance" of pride. (Thus Anne Bradstreet wrote, in praise of her "honored father": "High thoughts he gave no harbor in his heart; nor honours puffed him up when he had part.")[27] To become good—or rather to obtain some prospect of "saving grace"—is to recognize one's profound spiritual weaknesses. (Recall the subjective experience of shame, as defined earlier: "I am weak, inadequate, inferior.") Self-importance is the sin of sins, self-abasement the way to improvement. ("And so the Lord did help me," wrote Thomas Shepard in his *Autobiography*, "to loathe myself in some measure, and to say often, 'Why should I seek the glory and good of myself . . . which self ruins me and blinds me.' ")[28]

---

*The term is used advisedly, and with some intentional reference to the psychodynamic pattern associated (by clinical theorists) with narcissism. This is not the place to open such a large subject—what psychoanalysts now understand as the "psychology of the self"[25]— but it does seem to *fit* the Puritans in interesting ways. That fit is explored at some length in John Putnam Demos, *Entertaining Satan: Witchcraft and the Culture of Early New England* (New York, 1982), chaps. 4, 6.

Shepard's autobiography and other personal documents from the period reflect at every point the importance of self-scrutiny in New England religious experience. "Watchfulness" was perhaps the single most common, and resonant, term for this attitude. Puritans were endlessly watching themselves, and God, of course, was watching them too. Nothing should be—or ultimately *could* be—concealed, not even one's innermost preoccupations. In fact, the ability to see everything was a key attribute of the Deity. Thus, one clergyman referred repeatedly in his private correspondence to "the eye of God's providence." A second lamented the tendency of "foolish creatures . . . to think themselves safe if they can but hide their sins from the knowledge of men, not considering that the eye of God is upon them in all their ways." A third told his congregation that "it is no matter whether our neighbors do see our virtuous carriage or no; *God's angels,* they see it." And a fourth described the Judgment Day as final, humiliating exposure: "We shall every one of us stand naked before Christ's Judgment Seat . . . [and] all, even the most secret, sins shall be laid open before the whole world." (A local court, meanwhile, might admonish an offender "that she hath to do with an all-seeing God, who can write her sin in her forehead"—i.e., for other *people* to see as well.) Seeing and being seen, watching and hiding: thus a vital nexus of Puritan thought and feeling. Not surprisingly, Increase Mather believed that "the eye is the most excellent member of the body . . . for which way so ever the eye goeth the heart walks after it."[29]

Another recurrent element of Puritan religious discourse was the imagery of height. Shepard repeatedly described himself as "low sunk in my spirit." John Winthrop reported how prayer "brought me lower in mine own eyes." The Reverend Michael Wigglesworth wrote in his diary: "Lord, I lie down in my shame, worthy to be rejected." And the Reverend William Adams, writing in *his* diary, gave an interesting account of a mishap experienced while traveling from his home to explore an "invitation" (in the ministry) elsewhere: "As we were coming, . . . my horse stumbled and I had a fall, though I received no hurt; which causeth me to reflect upon myself whether I had not been something *lifted up,* that there were so many come to attend on me; and to adore the wisdom and grace of God in that he can and doth effectively *bring down high thoughts.*"[30]

Height, of course, is something to be measured; and shame, as noted earlier, has much to do with subjective measurement. ("I come short of, I stand below," one or another standard.) The Puritans were much inclined to measure things, and above all to measure themselves. (To "watch" the self was also to measure it.) The pattern could be explored at length in their various individual writings, and it runs through their collective preoccupations as well. Consider "declension"—that quintessential category of Puritan experience. And consider, too, some further points in the psychological interpretation of shame. According to psychoanalytic theory, shame occurs in relation to that part of personality structure termed the "ego ideal." Simply described, the ego ideal is a composite of the goals a person has for him/herself—of all that s/he would most like to be. From a developmental standpoint, it originates in the very early years, when a child identifies with—and, in a sense, takes into himself—the image he has of his parents. This image has both positive and negative elements. The negative side is the terrifyingly powerful and malevolent "castrating parent"; this forms the basis of the punishing "superego." The ego ideal, by contrast, represents the admired parent—the parent one yearns to emulate—and, in experiences of shame, it becomes the internal point of reference against which one's failings are measured.[31]

These constructs can be pointed directly toward the Puritans, for whom "declension" meant, first and last, a sense of failure to carry on with the high standards of the founding generation. Cotton Mather's essay *Things for a Distressed People to Think Upon* offers a characteristic statement: "New England once abounded with Heroes worthy to have their lives written, as copies for future ages. . . . But . . . there seems to be a shameful *shrink,* in all sorts of men among us from the greatness and goodness which adorned our ancestors: We grow little every way; little in our civil matters, little in our military matters, little in our ecclesiastical matters: we dwindle away to nothing." Recent scholarship has done much to unravel the intellectual history of all this;[32] but perhaps we can better grasp the *emotional* energies involved if we appreciate the pervasive orientation of the Puritans to shame. The failure to "measure up" to the standards of the founding fathers of New England would be experienced with special intensity by people whose psychic life was structured, in substantial part, around an anxious concern with another—very personal and internalized—father.

Just as "declension" has served to organize our understanding of Puritan history, so John Winthrop's "Lecture on Christian charity" is widely taken as an epitome of Puritan ideals. Listen to its most famous passage:

We must consider that we shall be as a city upon a hill; the eyes of all people are upon us. So that if we shall deal falsely with our God in this work, . . . and so cause Him to withdraw his present help from us, we shall be made a story and a byword through the world. We shall open the mouths of enemies to speak evil of the ways of God and all professors for God's sake. We shall shame the faces of many of God's worthy servants, and cause their prayers to be turned into curses upon us, till we are consumed out of the good land whither we are going.[33]

Here, in one densely compacted mass, are virtually all the elements discussed so far: a high hill; staring eyes, open mouths, red faces; curses, false dealing, scornful stories; shame and the threat of abandonment.

Governor Winthrop's private writings reflect on the risks and difficulties involved in embracing the cause of religious reform. And the terms of such reflection recall his famous "lecture." "Methought I heard all men telling me I was a fool, to set so light by honor, credit, wealth, jollity, etc.," he wrote; yet God assured him that he was "in a right course." Moreover, God "and all experience tells me . . . that those which do walk openly in this way shall be despised, pointed at, hated of the world, made a byword, reviled, slandered, rebuked, made a gazing stock, called Puritans, nice fools, hypocrites, hairbrained fellows, rash, indiscreet, vainglorious, and all that nought is." The city on the hill and the gazing stock are opposite faces of the same psychological coin.[34]

Indeed, Puritans maintained an expectation of *attack* as part of their cultural repertoire. For this, of course, their experience furnished considerable ground; but their psychology contributed as well. The aforementioned Winthrop passages convey a positive reveling in the details of derision. And the same overstated tone appears elsewhere: for example, in the preface of Cotton Mather's important work *Bonifacius, or Essays to Do Good.* These essays, Mather predicted, "shall be derided, with all the art and wit that [the Devil] can inspire. . . . Exquisite profaneness and buffoonery shall try their skill to laugh people out of them. The men who abound in them shall be exposed on the stage; libels, lampoons, and satires, the most poignant that ever were invented, shall be darted at them; and pamphlets full of lying stories be scattered with a design to make them ridiculous. . . ."[35]

One can summarize all this, and hint at its broader significance, by attempting a sketch of the New England Puritan as a character type. He displayed, as perhaps his most striking personal trait, an extreme sensitivity to the opinions and attitudes of others. Time and again one feels, in the records he has left us, his propensity to search for cues to behavior outside rather than within the self. Has he achieved an important goal, gained some new position or mark of honor?—he will describe in detail the admiration of his friends and neighbors. Has he been disappointed in one or another personal quest?—he will present the view of supposedly neutral parties that he should by all rights have succeeded. Has he been criticized or slighted by other members of his community?—he will immediately call them to account. Does such criticism have some reasonable foundation in fact?—he will jump to his own defense, and will probably try to shift the blame elsewhere. Is he uncertain as to his particular worth and character?—he will ponder how others have defined him.

There is in all this a concern for reputation, an instinct of face saving, a deep dread of appearing deficient in any way, that reaches right to the center of personality. The New England Puritan—considered once again as a social type—was not a weak person; he could act effectively when the occasion required. But often he was reluctant to claim the motives of action as his own. He preferred to picture himself as responding to external influences, especially when his conduct might be open to reproach. He was, in short, not fully self-determining, and he was unable or unwilling to cultivate that existential awareness which modern man has prized so highly. His world was characterized less by stark confrontation with self and more by intense, face-to-face contacts with a variety of significant others.

III

The argument so far has scarcely touched on childhood experience—which must, in any culture, reflect and reinforce the prevalent pattern of moral "heavy work." Puritan childhood has, in fact, been widely canvassed in recent historical writing, and there is little need to go over the same ground here. Suffice it to say that "shaming" does seem to have been key to child-rearing practice in early New England—and that psychological development, beginning from infancy, laid strong foundations for such practice.[36]

However: child-rearing can serve as an entry-point for the second part of the story. Picture a living room (in a home we would now describe as "middle-class") where husband, wife, and several children are grouped together, yet are occupied with various individual pursuits. Suddenly, one of the children—a boy named Wallace—spies the family cat despoiling a favorite plaything. Infuriated, he dashes the unfortunate creature into a pot of boiling water. Shrieks of horror come from his siblings—followed by a tension-filled silence. Then father speaks in a measured tone: "Wallace, go to your room." Without a murmur, the boy complies. And, hour after hour, day after day, Wallace remains sequestered upstairs, emerging only to go to school. His meals are taken to him, and his other needs remembered; but he has no regular contact with family-members. Finally, after two full weeks of this, he comes solemnly downstairs. He declares to his father his sorrow over his violent misconduct and his determination to prevent any reoccurrence. (He has just withstood—that is, without yielding to anger—some extreme "provocations" at the hands of schoolmates.) Forgiveness is asked, and received.

This little vignette was, in fact, the centerpiece of a much-read and broadly representative novel by a New England author of the mid-nineteenth century.[37] It may appear, at first glance, to be a tale of "excommunication"—and thus a domestic replica of "Puritan" morality from two centuries before. But a second look suggests otherwise. For one thing, the quiet command of the father to "go to your room" is no equivalent to the minister's sentence of excommunication, as quoted above. For another, the attitude of *all* parties seems significantly different. Initially, they are "horrified," to be sure; but this feeling is soon superseded by others—by prayerful concern, by "grief," and above all by deep personal sympathy. Wallace, it seems, is engaged upstairs in some vitally important work with himself; his family cannot help, but then can (and do) *hope*. They are not scorning or censorious; on the contrary, they are openly supportive. Wallace is isolated so that he can more effectively *punish himself*. The penalty for wrongdoing must, in short, be exacted internally (i.e., without reference to an "audience"). And—in terms of the present discussion—it is a penalty rooted in guilt rather than shame.

Viewed thus, Wallace's lonely struggle was paradigmatic of trends and tendencies in the society at large. His room became, for the space of those critical days, a virtual penitentiary. And surely it is no coincidence that the same era, roughly the first half of the nineteenth century, witnessed the founding of *actual* penitentiaries in New England, and all across the land. Indeed the entire system of judicially imposed punishment now became transformed. Gone were the old forms of "public correction" and their various accoutrements (the stocks, the pillory, the whipping post, the branding irons, the badges of infamy). In their place arose the prisons which are with us still—though "penitentiary" does seem the more accurate term for the first, germinal phase. The process of change was, of course, immensely variegated and complex, and one cannot reduce it all to a set of psychological vectors. But surely there were psychological *correlates*. A motive to isolate offenders was central to projects of prison building. And the idea behind such isolation was explicitly—even smugly—psychological. Thus one advocate of the "Pennsylvania system" of prison organization (which featured a regimen of solitary confinement) could write as follows: "Each individual [convict] will necessarily be made the instrument of his own punishment; his conscience will be the avenger of society." And a colleague would point up the inner-life details: "[Each convict] will be compelled to reflect on the error of his ways [and] to listen to the reproaches of his conscience."[38]

Penitentiaries, as several scholars have shown us, were infused with the whole spirit of nineteenth-century moral reform. And reform's other branches—peculiarly associated with New England, as they were—deserve our notice too. Consider, for a moment, the temperance movement, that long and ultimately successful effort to curtail the consumption of alcoholic beverages. The literature of temperance was, of course, voluminous: printed sermons and lectures, tracts and pamphlets, personal memoirs and autobiographies. Reduced to their thematic essentials, they told a single story: Hero takes to drink and experiences various forms of personal degradation (loss of job, loss of property, loss of social standing). Hero's family (faithful wife, innocent children, doting parents) are deeply hurt (impoverished, exploited, physically abused, or left "broken-hearted") in direct consequence. Hero belatedly sees the harm he is causing to those whom he loves most, becomes "conscience-stricken," and vows to change.[39] Again, it is the relationship between the sin, the sinner, and the others that bears our special consideration. Under the old moral regime, sin might bring shame to the family members (insofar as they shared in the disgrace of the sinner), but it did not injure them otherwise. Moreover, outside the family sin evoked disapproval, disgust, scorn. It was, indeed, to avoid such unpleasant "external" consequences that one behaved morally, in the first place. The new regime rearranged these elements to a very different end. The inducements away from sin were cast in terms of hurt given *to* others (not inflicted *by* others). And this was precisely the stuff and substance of *guilt*.

The most famous branch of nineteenth-century reform, and the one that left the biggest impression on American history, was, of course, antislavery. The moral and psychological dynamic of antislavery seems considerably more complex than is the case, for example, with temperance, and there is space here only to sample some particulars. One part of the complexity involves the artifacts of language itself; for abolitionists chose to employ the language of *both* shame and guilt. Thus, for instance, William Lloyd Garrison's antislavery newspaper *The Liberator* includes articles entitled, on the one hand, "O! SHAME! SHAME! SHAME!" and, on the other, "WE ARE ALL GUILTY . . . ." And it does appear that antislavery leaders sought to move their compatriots to action by any and every psychological means possible. Still, one feels that the largest share of their energies was devoted to arousing feelings of guilt. They defined slave holding, first and last, as a *sin*, as a pattern of behavior which crossed an absolutely fundamental moral boundary. And they drew that boundary—spotlighted it, and dug it deep—again and again and again. Moreover, the sin of slaveholding was for them expressed in the wrong it did, the *hurt* it *gave*, to other human beings. A favorite abolitionist tactic was to pile up accounts of specific sufferings inflicted on individual slaves; and the most famous, most efficacious, single document in all this literature—Harriet Beecher Stowe's novel *Uncle Tom's Cabin*—is an unrelenting portrayal of slave suffering. The idea was to "rend the conscience" (as one commentator put it) of "decent folk" everywhere.

There is another aspect of abolitionist rhetoric that may deserve mention here. Recall, for a start, the prevalent style of conflict in the colonial period (the first part of our comparison). The main thrust, we noted, was by way of narcissistic insult: a tone of disdain, an effort, in short, to belittle one's opponents as much as possible. This seemed consistent with the clinical definition of shame, centered as it is on the dread of becoming an object of scorn, of contempt, of ridicule. Guilt, according to those same definitional categories, involves the sense of being *hated* (something quite different). And hatred—far more than scorn—indeed describes the abolitionists' attitude toward their adversaries. Certainly, they did not belittle those adversaries; on the contrary, their attitude tended toward magnification. Slavery was, in their eyes and words, an "infernal monster" which "legalized on an enormous scale, licentiousness, fraud, cruelty, and murder." Individual slaveholders were "manstealers," "tyrants," "oppressors," and so on. The list could be made very long, but the point is immediately clear. The enemy was in all ways outsize; and the response expressed a fierceness, a hatred, of corresponding dimensions.

And now, one more time, the "screen" of Protestant religion. Immediately we can see how much the imagery has changed with the passage of two centuries. This is, of course, a well-known story; it bears mention here only to flag some psychological meanings. For example: In the early period the emphasis had fallen on the Lord's all-encompassing sovereignty—and, in explicit contrast, on man's inherent weakness; to be "saved" was to acknowledge this gap and at the same time to bridge it. Now (that is, in the nineteenth century) the spotlight moved to Christ's sacrifice and suffering; to "convert" was to accept his sacrifice, even (in a sense) to redeem it. Moreover, resistance to conversion now carried the implication of spurning Christ's sacrifice—and thus of "hurting" him further. There is an echo here of the reform literature (mentioned previously), in which the wages of sin are exacted from the sinner's family and closest friends. Indeed revival preachers would sometimes present them*selves* as liable to injury by unresponsive congregants. "I could mention some cases," wrote the famous evangelist Charles G. Finney, "where ministers have died in consequence of their labors to promote a revival where the church hung back from the work. . . . The state of the people, and of sinners, rests upon their mind, they travail in soul day and night, and they labor in season and out of season, beyond the power of the human constitution to bear, until they wear out and die."[40] Prayerful wives and children were also at risk; to remain unconverted was to dash *their* hopes and frustrate their labors as well. In short: *convert*, or you will add to Christ's sufferings; *convert*, or you will kill off the preacher; *convert*, or you will distress and demoralize your loved ones.[41] This particular brand of moral "heavy work" is easy enough to recognize—in the argot of our own time, a "guilt trip" all the way.

IV

This essay concludes, as it began, with a brace of qualifiers. Its "coverage" seems in some respects impossibly large, in others painfully thin and sketchy. At best it frames a hypothesis, and samples the evidence that might be used to develop a full-fledged scholarly project. It does not explore possible class differences around the main thematic line—nor, for that matter, differences of gender, age, and political orientation. The hypothesis stands as a simple (perhaps *over*simple) piece of comparative history in two parts, and treatment of the second part is especially brief. Were the parts to be developed further, they would have to be shaded more carefully. The change between them was not a matter of movement from *all* shame to *all* guilt, but rather a shift in the overall emotional balance. Every regime of moral heavy work taps both kinds of psychological energy (and maintains nonpsychological sanctions as well). Hence this presentation overstates the case—in order to make it more clearly.

But enough of Historian's Humble Pie. The issues here are important ones; the hypothesis itself supports yet another call to "further research." Fortunately, New England historians (of both the "Puritan" and the "early national" periods) are discovering troves of hitherto unused materials that should make suitable grist for this particular scholarly mill. Court records (especially for the seventeenth and early eighteenth centuries), personal documents (especially for the nineteenth), a huge host of evidence from and about local experience: here, if anywhere, is the basis for reconstructing past emotional life. With all deliberate speed—and with *neither* shame nor guilt—historians must rise to the task.

Notes

1. Ruth Benedict, *The Chrysanthemum and the Sword* (Boston, 1946), pp. 223–24.

2. The following studies have proved especially helpful on the psychology of shame and guilt: Gerhart Piers and Milton B. Singer, *Shame and Guilt* (Springfield, Ill., 1953); Helen Merrell Lynd, *On Shame and the Search for Identity* (New York, 1958); Helen B. Lewis, *Shame and Guilt in Neurosis* (New York, 1971); Erik Erikson, *Childhood and Society* (New York, 1950), chap. 7; Heinz Kohut, "Thoughts on Narcissism and Narcissistic Rage," *The Psychoanalytic Study of the Child* 27 (1972): 360–400.

3. Puritan punishments are examined at length in Edwin Powers, *Crime and Punishment in Early Massachusetts, 1620–1692* (Boston, 1966). However, this study is of a purely descriptive nature; its author makes little effort to set his material in the context of Puritan society—or of Puritan psychology.

4. The details of Puritan punishment can be examined in any set of early New England court records. See, for example, *Records and Files of the Quarterly Courts of Essex County, Massachusetts,* 8 vols. (Salem, Mass., 1911–21). This collection will be cited hereafter as *Essex Court Records*.

5. Charles J. Hoadly, ed., *Records of the Colony and Plantation of New Haven,* 2 vols. (Hartford, Conn., 1867–68), 2:136; *Essex Court Records,* VIII, 303; J. K. Hosmer, ed., *Winthrop's Journal,* 2 vols. (Boston, 1908), 1:283.

6. Massachusetts Historical Society, *Proceedings,* 2d series, VI, 481; *Essex Court Records,* IV, 38.

7. This was the sentence pronounced on Mrs. Anne Hibbins of Boston in February 1641, as noted in Robert Keayne's "Notes on John Cotton's Sermons" (manuscript document, Massachusetts Historical Society, Boston) and published in John Demos, *Remarkable Providences: The American Culture, 1600–1760* (New York, 1972), pp. 238–39.

8. *Records of the Town of Easthampton, Long Island, Suffolk County, N.Y.,* 5 vols. (Sag Harbor, N.Y., 1887–1904), 1:33–34.

9. *Records of the Court of Trials of the Town of Warwick, Rhode Island, 1659–1674* (Providence, 1922), 15; *Essex Court Records,* I, 31; *Records of the Town of Easthampton,* 1:104–5; Anne Bradstreet, "Meditations, Divine and Moral," in *The Works of Anne Bradstreet,* ed. Jeannine Hensley (Cambridge, Mass., 1967), p. 278.

10. *Essex Court Records,* II, 277.

11. Testimony of Thomas Bennett, at the examination of Mercy Disborough (Fairfield, Conn., 1692), MS document, the Willys Papers, Connecticut State Library, Hartford, W-33.

12. *Records of the Suffolk County Court, 1671–1680,* in Colonial Society of Massachusetts, *Publications,* 30:891.

13. *Essex Court Records,* IV, 105.

14. Ibid., IV, 105.

15. Ibid., II, 353.

16. Ibid., II, 241.

17. Ibid., I, 275.

18. Ibid., V, 310.

19. Ibid., IV, 162.

20. Ibid., I, 59.

21. Ibid., IV, 343.

22. Ibid., VIII, 272.

23. Ibid., VI, 257.

24. Manuscript deposition by Samuel Reynolds, in Files Papers of the Quarterly Courts of Middlesex County, Massachusetts (Middlesex County Courthouse, East Cambridge, Mass.), folder 42.

25. The preeminent theorist of "self-psychology" is the late Heinz Kohut. See especially his *The Psychology of the Self* (New York, 1971) and *The Restoration of the Self* (New York, 1977).

26. *Essex Court Records,* VI, 329; ibid., V, 63; Increase Mather, *Solemn Advice to Young Men* (Boston, 1695), p. 23.

27. *The Works of Anne Bradstreet,* p. 202.

28. *The Autobiography of Thomas Shepard,* ed. Nehemiah Davis (Boston, 1832), p. 26.

29. *The Letters of John Davenport,* ed. Isabel M. Calder (New Haven, Conn., 1937), p. 66 and passim; Mather, *Solemn Advice,* pp. 36–37; Commonplace Book of Joseph Green, as printed in Demos, *Remarkable Providences,* p. 356; Hoadly, *Records of the Colony of New Haven,* 2:268; Mather, *Solemn Advice,* pp. 9, 14.

30. *The Autobiography of Thomas Shepard,* p. 38; John Winthrop, "Experiencia," in *The Winthrop Papers,* 1:201; *The Diary of Michael Wigglesworth, 1653–1657,* ed. Edmund Morgan (New York, 1946), p. 20; William Adams, "His Book," in Massachusetts Historical Society, *Collections,* 4th series, 1:19.

31. See, for the formulation of all this, Piers and Singer, *Shame and Guilt.*

32. I refer here to the work of Perry Miller and his colleagues.

33. John Winthrop, "A Model of Christian Charity," as printed in George M. Waller, ed., *Puritanism in Early America,* 2d ed. (Lexington, Mass., 1973), p. 5.

34. Winthrop, "Experiencia," in *The Winthrop Papers,* 1:196.

35. Quoted in Kenneth Silverman, *The Life and Times of Cotton Mather* (New York, 1984), p. 226.

36. See John Demos, *A Little Commonwealth: Family Life in Plymouth Colony* (New York, 1970), chap. 9.

37. Catharine Maria Sedgwick, *Home* (Boston, 1854).

38. Quoted in David Rothman, *The Discovery of the Asylum: Social Order and Disorder in the New Republic* (Boston, 1971), p. 85.

39. A good example of this plot line can be found in the immensely popular story by T. S. Arthur, *Ten Nights in a Bar-Room,* first published in 1854, and recently reprinted, Donald A. Koch, ed. (Cambridge, Mass., 1964).

40. Charles G. Finney, *Lectures on Revivals of Religion* (repr., Cambridge, Mass., 1960), pp. 226–27. A sermon by Cotton Mather, more than a century earlier, stands in direct contrast. The minister, Mather declared to his congregation, "is above the reach of hurt from your malignity. . . . Do, go on still in your trespasses. You will wound yourselves, and none but yourselves, wretches. Silly children, the minister of God is above all your silly attempts. You can't hurt *him!*"

41. On the matter of shame and guilt in nineteenth-century revivalism, I wish to acknowledge a profound debt to the work of E. Anthony Rotundo. In particular, I am grateful for permission to consult Dr. Rotundo's two (as yet) unpublished essays, "The Conflict Between Active and Passive in Charles G. Finney's Revival Imagery," and "Charles G. Finney's Upstate Revivals: Some Emotional Themes and Social Implications."

4

From Ritual to Romance:
Toward an Alternative History of Love

J o h n   R .   G i l l i s

*U*ntil very recently few historians cared to dig deeply into the history of the emotions. It was assumed that too much was concealed; the investment of time and effort, especially in periods that have left us few personal accounts, was simply not worth it. The few energetic scholars who did mine private papers, diaries, and letters reported that they found little emotional depth. Philippe Ariès's explorations left the impression that prior to the nineteenth century personal affection was of secondary importance. Lawrence Stone and Edward Shorter agreed that love was rare before the eighteenth century, even though they differed on which social group ultimately released love from age-old restraints, thus ushering in the modern era of the emotions. Shorter was eager to designate the proletariat as the liberators of emotion; Stone was insistent that credit be given to the well-bred and literate classes. Both, however, were determined to link love with modernization, a judgment from which, until recently, there has been remarkably little dissent.[1]

Now, however, British historians are beginning to question the notion of an affectionless past. Alan Macfarlane has recently detected love as early as the fourteenth century; Keith Wrightson has confirmed the existence of affectionate relationships in the sixteenth and seventeenth centuries.[2] On sifting more carefully those diaries and personal accounts that were the tailings of Stone's original digs, Linda Pollock has found that Stone had overlooked much evidence that did not conform to his conception of pre-eighteenth-century family relations as essentially cold and aloof.[3] Another rich vein, the notebooks of the seventeenth-century healer Richard Napier, has yielded Michael MacDonald yet more convincing evidence of the passionate character of early modern people.[4] Meanwhile, American historians have also been hard at work in the archival depths, showing that a capacity for affection, defined as tenderness, empathy, and intimacy, was also present in the colonial period.[5]

However, rummaging the past for evidence of the feelings that we now associate with love may do more to distort than to illuminate the social history of emotions. As Francesca Cancian has recently argued, defining love exclusively in terms of capacity for sharing feeling and intimacy ignores equally valid definitions of love emphasizing cooperation and mutual assistance, definitions that were the norm in earlier periods. Our contemporary determination to define love in terms of feelings rather than actions is the end product of what Cancian calls the "feminization" of love, an ideological process, traceable to the beginnings of the nineteenth- century, by which love came to be identified with pure feeling, with the domestic sphere, and specifically with the women confined to that sphere. The tendency to view women as having greater capacity for feelings and intimacy, and therefore as more loving, is strongly pronounced in both nineteenth- and twentieth-century psychological literature. Because of their stronger association with the impersonal worlds of work and power, men are portrayed as lacking in the capacity for real affection.[6]

This feminized definition of love still dominates popular as well as scientific thinking, and it is not surprising that historians have also chosen it as their standard for judging the past. It is Stone's and Shorter's measure, but also that of their critics. Therefore, in moving the dawn of love back in time, historians like Macfarlane are not really so revisionist as they might seem. In reality, they share with Stone and Shorter a notion of true love that ignores many of the ways that men and women in the past created and signified their most enduring relationships.

But what Cancian calls the feminization of love can just as well be described in class terms, for there has been a powerful tendency to identify the capacity for affection with the middle class. It is possible to accept Stone's notion that, beginning in the eighteenth century, this class created and nurtured the idea of love as feeling and intimacy without accepting his assertion that in the process the bourgeoisie liberated true love from a long dark history of neglect and repression. Stone's view of the emotions is implicitly essentialist or naturalistic, and ignores the degree to which love is something culturally and socially constructed. Holding the view that love is a universal drive or instinct waiting to be discovered or liberated, both Stone and Shorter are led to regard alternative notions of love that do not emphasize feeling and intimacy as inherently repressive, mere survivals, bound to disappear with the spread of enlightenment and liberation.

However, if one rejects the naturalistic or essentialist perspective, and views love as historically constructed rather than repressed or liberated, a very different kind of history immediately emerges. In what follows, I will be attempting to place the history of love in the context of the cultures of class, gender, and generation, demonstrating its multiple, competing definitions, showing why the naturalistic evolutionary account preferred by Stone and Shorter cannot account for the complexity and contradictions of love over the past three centuries. Their teleology, which assumes a deficit of love prior to the late eighteenth and early nineteenth centuries, proves inadequate, for, when we begin to look at the seventeenth and eighteenth centuries through the eyes of the men and women who courted and married during the early modern period, the idea of a progressively more loving society is called into question.

If one looks to a full range of expression, to physical as well as verbal expression—to ritual as well as to romance—we find abundant evidence that early modern people, men as well as women, were fully capable of loving relationships, as they defined them. They expressed their love in a way that later generations would perceive as vulgar and uncaring, yet, understood on their own terms, the rituals symbolizing cooperation and mutual sharing favored by early modern people reveal a capacity for loving relationships in no way inferior to that of modern society.

I

Excavating the past for traces of emotion is bound to be a haphazard, frustrating enterprise. As everyone knows, ordinary people leave few of the kind of private, verbal expressions that historians have tended to rely on for evidence of emotions. So, it is little wonder that historians have concluded on the basis of the usual diary and memoir material that loving relationships are more prevalent now than in earlier periods. Most have refused to look elsewhere for evidence of love, partly because, by training, they trust only the usual written sources, but also because they hold the prevailing view that love is something that comes from within, a drive or instinct of a highly personal nature.

The conventions of nineteenth- and twentieth-century psychology tell us that love is most likely to be encountered only in those most private forms of expression, the intimate conversation, the diary, or the letter. However, new work in psychology, as well as by anthropologists and the symbolic interactionist school of sociology, suggests that the historian need not confine his or her investigation to these traditional sources. There is now an extensive literature on nonverbal expression.[7] Furthermore, post-Freudian and postbehaviorist psychology has questioned the idea that emotions are the product solely of individualized instincts or drives, and, instead, proposes a conception of emotions as socially and historically created, as something that can be "worked" and altered.[8] Reinforcing these findings are symbolic interactionists, who see gender, sex, and love not as naturalistic things but as a socially and historically constructed behavior. They prefer the metaphor of a script to that of a drive because it attributes greater agency not only to groups but to individuals. Love is conceived of as drama, whose script is constantly being rewritten, and therefore a part of history rather than of nature.

Symbolic interactionism has already transformed the field of sex research in ways described by one of its leading advocates, Ken Plummer:

> The focus turns to the way in which individuals throughout their life cycle come to be defined by themselves and others as sexual beings, how they come to hook themselves on to the wider cultural meanings, and how these are renegotiated or stabilized. Gone is the view that socialization is concerned with the management of some inner pre-existing sexual "condition" or "motive"; gone is the view of "latent" sexual conditions; gone is the view of people "essentially being" that of which they are unaware.[9]

Applying a symbolic interactionist approach to the history of love produces an equally dramatic change of perspective and method. Having dispensed with the idea of love as a latent condition, the task of the historian is no longer to tell the story of its progressive triumph. Instead, the challenge is to ask specific questions about the nature of love (or, better yet, loves) in any given period. The question of whether one period is more liberated or repressed is irrelevant. Instead, it is the meaning that the actors themselves bring to a particular situation, action, or "scene" which becomes the focus of historical investigation. This means we begin with an ethnographic account of the highly ritualized courtship of the seventeenth and eighteenth centuries, and then turn to the rise of romantic notions of love at the beginning of the nineteenth century.

II

It is little wonder that historians who view love as pure feeling have had such difficulty recognizing loving situations prior to the nineteenth century. Neither the educated elite nor illiterate folk of the early modern period viewed love as having a separate, disembodied existence. Because we do not have an adequate history of popular ideas of love for this period, I have been forced to impute much about people's perceptions from their behavior, always a somewhat risky enterprise. Nevertheless, it seems fair to conclude that early modern people did not perceive the heart as having a separate existence apart from the mind and body. Psychological and physical healing were closely related; feeling and action, emotion and speech, were regarded as inseparably joined. As we shall see, early modern people were less likely to make the distinction between action and feeling. It would not have occurred to them to dig deep to find emotions. "Feeling" still meant both physical and internal sensation; and, at a time when medical authorities made no sharp distinction between psyche and soma, anger and love were seen as having an actual physical presence in the "cold stare" or the "warm embrace." Love and hate could be transmitted through bodily orifices by emission or ingestion. They were identified with body fluids—blood, urine, saliva, excrement—but also communicated through visible and ritualized body movement.[10] In short, the early modern view of love comes much closer to contemporary symbolic interactionist notions than it does to classic nineteenth-century theories. Love was treated more like a script than a drive, something to be negotiated, acted out, worked on, with a public as well as a private dimension.

Failure to understand the popular emotionology of earlier periods has cut historians off from obvious sources. Because they persist in seeing love through an essentially nineteenth-century perspective as an inner thing, they burrow ever deeper into diaries and letters, hoping to "find" love, but invariably coming up empty because they are looking in all the wrong places.[11] Had they turned to that which is public and manifest, namely to speech acts and body language, they would have had access to the grammar of love common to both elites and common people.

The best way to comprehend early modern understandings of affection is not through conduct books, sermons, and love poetry, but by observing the way people actually courted, betrothed, and married. These visible behaviors tell us that early modern people viewed love as something tangible, felt in the same way as we feel a blow, savor a taste, or sense a stare. Just as much as they feared the harm that could be transmitted by the evil eye, women and men of the seventeenth and eighteenth centuries reveled in the effects of a potion, a charm, the power of a lover's gaze, kiss, embrace, even a blow.[12] Kissing was not yet a private, intimate activity. It was still more like the modern handshake, a public social act signifying a pledge, which, if properly witnessed, was considered legally binding.[13] Our notion of kissing as a private, purely pleasurable activity was unthinkable at a time when sexuality was not yet conceived of as a thing in and of itself. In reality, love kisses were probably not particularly pleasurable. They were more like bites, intended to be felt, to leave a mark, and even to draw blood. Any physical contact, and especially with blood, was believed to have a powerful binding effect. As late as 1906, an Irish boy who had drawn blood from a girl while roughhousing was told by his nurse: "Now you'll have to marry her."[14]

Like kissing, the exchange of body fluids by sharing a meal or drinking from a common cup was "thought to comingle their spirits, and to be made one human life."[15] Similarly, in this still largely oral culture, public speech-acts (as opposed to private or written words) were thought of as having a physical effect, powerful enough to wound or heal, as the case might be.[16] Gestures, body language, and especially the emissions of the body itself had similar powers. In Wales, a young man proved his love to a girl by urinating on her dress, a practice known locally as *rhythu*.[17] Emotions were so closely identified with the body fluids that blood and urine were also used to drive away rivals and punish evildoers.[18] In this case, the body was not simply expressing emotion; it was emotion itself.

Everything depended, of course, on the intention and social context. A vow had meaning according to the place in which it was made, in what company, and with what degree of publicity.[19] A kiss between friends was not expected to have the same effect as one between lovers. A blow struck in anger was not the same as a love slap. Courting by blows was common in the French countryside throughout the nineteenth century:

> First they exchange glances, then casual remarks, then heavy witticisms. The young man shoves at the girl, thumps her hard on the back, takes her hand and squeezes it in a bone-cracking grip. She responds to this tender gesture by punching him in the back.[20]

Love in the early modern period was not something particularly mysterious or spiritual.[21] As something associated with the body, it was subject to the same control as any other physical function. Love could be worked on, consciously managed in any number of ways, some medical, others magical, but all quite deliberate.[22] Educated elites and ordinary people shared a common corpus of beliefs based on analogical rather than scientific reasoning, and, as a result, many resorted to white magic when faced with physical and emotional problems. As S. J. Tambiah defines it, magic is "usually compounded of verbal utterance and object manipulation, [constituting] 'performative' acts by which a property is imperatively transferred to a recipient object or person on an analogical basis." In the case of love magic, the body itself often provided both the vehicle for performance and the medium by which love was communicated. Sharing the common set of assumptions about the power of particular gestures or objects, the person to whom the performance was directed was thereby impelled to feel the appropriate emotion.[23]

In the seventeenth century we find all elements of the population, literate and illiterate, indulging in love magic, consulting dream and recipe books, using the same ritual performances to ensure love and exorcise envy and jealousy. They shared a somatic understanding of the emotions that caused them to believe they could cure "lovesickness" just as they could treat the gout or toothache.[24] Even the Puritans, who were otherwise critical of magic, shared the belief that the emotions could be worked on. "Keep up your Conjugal Love in a constant heat and vigor," counseled Baxter.[25] Where the Puritans departed from popular belief was their insistence on the private, inner character of the emotions and the kind of effort necessary to activate and control personal feelings. Whereas they exhorted the lovesick to introspection, other, more orthodox practitioners, like Richard Napier, continued to offer herbal and magical remedies, usually in combination with some advice about the social relationships that were the cause of the emotional distress in the first place. Napier urged his clients to reconcile the conflicts that he perceived as the cause of their anguish. The social side of his practice was essentially conservative. Quarreling couples were told to settle their differences; defiant daughters and prodigal sons were urged to be reconciled to their parents, advice that was ideologically consistent with the current emphasis on family solidarity, even though it was not invariably followed by Napier's clients, many of whom were clearly expressing guilt about their own autonomy. [26]

Magical uses of the body proved such an effective persuasive device because people believed the operations of the body and those of society analogous. We need not accept Mary Douglas's functionalist assertion that in all close-knit communities we should expect to find "the human body actively expressing the solidarity of the social body" in order to acknowledge that at both the popular and elite levels this analogical premise was accepted and operative in the seventeenth century.[27] Society was perceived organically, and men as well as women were taught from childhood to think of themselves as connected interdependent parts of a larger whole, whether it be the family or community. Boundaries between persons were viewed as porous. The body itself was seen as vulnerable to invasion, but its emissions were also regarded as very powerful. If used correctly—i.e., ritually—body parts and fluids, such as blood, saliva, excrement, hair, urine, the lips, tongue, even the eye, could transmit love or ward off envy.

Wise women and cunning men were sought out in critical situations, but, for the most part, ritual was self-administered. Both men and women were involved in all manner of love magic, including potions, charms, and divination. One seventeenth-century text, which was still being used a century later, advised maidens wishing "to drawe a heart" to put the blood of a young lamb's heart on their left breast. They were then to wash it off, mixing the water with blood from their own fingers and a little wine, before serving it to their sweethearts.[28] Burning dragon's blood, a red resin, was commonly employed, accompanied by incantations:

> This is not dragon's blood to burn
> But [name of lover] heart I mean to turn
> Be he asleep or be he awake
> He shall come with me to speak.[29]

In the small town as well as in the countryside virtually everyone knew the arts of divining, had access to love potions and charms, and kept track of those days and months most propitious for lovemaking.[30] White magic was invariably a group activity. The Salem witchcraft panic began with a little innocent divining. Young women had gathered to peer at the white of an egg suspended in water to determine "what trade their sweethearts should be of," when one of them thought she saw a coffin and hysteria developed.[31]

In most cases, however, a conjuring or divining session had much happier results. It was a semipublic event, a time for young men as well as women to make explicit their preferences in a subtle nonverbal manner and, using the persuasive power of magic, to influence the result. Young Welsh women would set a table in hope of conjuring lovers: "The 4 women hideing themselves in ye corners of ye room. The sweethearts will come in & eat, though a Hundred miles off." Divining remained a very popular mode of communication at the village level, where a more direct verbal approach might cause embarrassment or even conflict. Knowing he or she had been conjured, the dream lover could choose to accept or reject without loss of face or hurt feelings to either party, a device which, in a village community where the roles of lover, friend, and coworker overlapped, was essential to preserving communal solidarity.[32]

It must also be remembered that this was a society where marriage was long delayed and premature pairing off strongly discouraged. Courtship in the seventeenth and eighteenth centuries was invariably a polygamous affair, with girls entertaining several suitors simultaneously and boys striving to keep the friendship of many women until such time as an inheritance or trade opened up and they could establish a household. When the time was right, lovemaking occurred with a rapidity that later generations were to find both baffling and repulsive. But, prior to betrothal, care was taken to prevent relationships from becoming too personal, thereby keeping open the options of both men and women. Here both male and female peer groups, with their rich associational and ritual life, also remained very significant in channeling the affections in a homosocial direction. In a period when individual autonomy was discouraged, the ego was permitted a much greater variety of attachments. The kinds of homoerotic and polygamous affections that the nineteenth century would label pathological were a normal part of both male and female youth cultures in the sixteenth and seventeenth centuries.[33]

Divining on St. Agnes Eve, casting lots on Valentine's Day, or any other of the social activities associated with the magical moments of the amatory calendar were also a clear reflection of the wide choice enjoyed by both women and men in early modern Britain and America.[34] Love magic of this kind would have made no sense in a society where choices were dictated by parents or guardians. We now know that it was only among the very rich and powerful that arranged marriage was at all common. Love magic therefore reflected both the freedom of choice and the anxieties that accompanied those liberties. The fact that it was used by men as well as women in Britain suggests that males may have felt some of the same uncertainty and vulnerability as females when it came to matters of the heart. It is significant that in fifteenth-century Venice love magic was used only by plebeian women to secure the attention of more powerful upper-class men, whereas in Britain, where there was greater equality between the sexes, men also felt the need of magical assistance.[35]

John Demos has demonstrated for New England that it was young men and adolescent women, precisely those groups poised on the brink of major life decisions, who were most likely to experience that porousness of self which made magic conceivable and effective. Both sexes resorted to divining and other magical rites as instruments of the ego at the point in their lives when they were trying to establish themselves as separate from families and peers. At this crucial juncture, they were particularly aware of the ambiguity of the world, feeling simultaneously more powerful and more vulnerable. Looking into the crystal ball caused no harm in most cases, and probably helped make up the minds of the undecided, but, where conflict was present, normal anxieties could be transformed into abnormal hysteria, leading to accusations of witchcraft, directed at middle-aged persons, especially women, who, as magically powerful figures in the eyes of the young, were perceived as causes of the lovers' problems.[36]

We know more about this dark side of magic because witchcraft accusations left the most visible historical record. However, white magic was much more pervasive, so integral to the courtship process as to go virtually unnoticed except by folklorists. North Yorkshire women, who went to St. Cedd's Well at Lestingham on magical St. Agnes Eve intending to enhance the power of their love garters by washing them in the waters, understood the social pressures that gossip would put on their young men. St. Cedd's was also the place where a man could test the faithfulness of his sweetheart. To prove herself a true lover, the woman would allow her breasts to be covered with wet linen. If no mark showed, the man was bound to her, but, if a stain should appear, she was proven false. George Calvert reported that "so great was the fear of this trial held that none but a true maid dast venture thereupon. . . ."[37] In North Yorkshire it was thought possible to discover the father of a bastard child by placing a number of basins filled with holy water, each representing a suspected man, around an anvil. A red-hot horseshoe was then struck and the basin in which the sparks landed indicated paternity. Such a procedure was not always necessary, however, because it was said that the very threat of such a test brought about a quick confession from the putative father.[38]

We can see from these examples that, throughout the seventeenth and eighteenth centuries, men experienced a sense of connectedness very similar to that of women. Their sense of self was no less porous; and they thought of themselves not as autonomous individuals but as part of an interdependent whole.[39] Young people were most likely to resort to ritual and magic, but adults also turned to healers like Napier when they found vital relationships—and thus their sense of self—threatened.[40] The body was simultaneously the symbol of their connectedness and the means through which men as well as women managed to secure and repair cooperative connections.

Gifts of clothing, hair, and food all served to bind sweethearts. Love knots were favored virtually everywhere.[41] In North Yorkshire, it was the woman's garter, worn above the knee, which was yielded to the suitor "after that she hath proved him true and it shall hold them both true unto each other." The young man would wear this around his neck during the course of their betrothal, but on the wedding day it was the bride's to give away to a lucky bachelor, thus transferring love's magic to those who would need it in the future.[42] Similarly, garters plaited from the number of straws equal to that of the desired numbers of children were said to guarantee fruitful motherhood.[43]

For those who did not wish to rely on their own magical powers, there were the local wise women and cunning men to turn to. Betty Strother, who died about 1775, had a reputation in the North Yorkshire Moors of being both a witch and a sorceress. It was said that "her power when she was fairly putten to it was oft past ought man or woman can do unaided by themselves . . . ," and she was particularly sought after for her power to divine future husbands. Local clergy also entered into the magic business, selling what were called "Holy Seals," which suitors pressed against their sweethearts' legs, thus closing these "against himself untill [sic] they be wed and against all other men," and thus guaranteeing chastity among the young people of the Yorkshire Dales.[44] For jilted lovers there was Nansy Glandwr of Cardiganshire, reputed to have special powers to cure the lovesick. A formula similar to hers, consisting of a mixture of gin, beer, and saffron, together with a ritual incantation, was still being sold in Wales in the 1850s.[45] Throughout the British Isles, but particularly in those places in Wales, Scotland, and the North of England where homogeneous farming or industrial communities existed, these and other magical practices remained a part of working-class courtship and marriage well into the Victorian era.[46]

III

In the twentieth century, our understanding of the body is so privatized and sexualized that we have great difficulty understanding the magical communicative meaning it holds for other peoples. We think of touching and feeling as sexual "foreplay," when in fact these had quite other, much more symbolic meanings for the early modern people. Our contemporary "feminized" conception of affection tells us that love must be expressed through soft words and tender caresses. Love must be an individualized experience, best kept quiet and private if it is to flourish. Nothing could be further from the early modern conception, which refused to separate body and feeling, provided little space for sexual intimacy, and insisted that love, defined as cooperation and sharing, express itself through those prime symbols of mutuality, the body social as well as the body biological. The same acute sense of the porosity of self that made magic so potent was reflected in the rituals that accompanied every step of the courtship and marriage process.

Courtship, betrothal, and wedding were all public ritualized events, using the body, the traditional symbol of interdependence, as their principal means of communication. Love was expressed loudly and visibly, not only in a series of formalized speech acts, but also through a grammar of individual and collective body movement. While we go out of our way to give lovers as much privacy as possible, early modern society thought publicity absolutely necessary to the success of any amorous arrangement. Only the very earliest stages of courtship were carried on in secrecy. Couples were very careful not to appear together in public until they were seriously considering marriage.[47] Courtship was normally confined to the hours of darkness until very near the couple's betrothal:

> Everyone who knows the ways of country people is aware that courting throughout the night was the custom and a young man going courting was terrified lest anyone should see him in "broad daylight."[48]

Today, betrothal licenses withdrawal from the peer group and the beginnings of the privacy that we associate with conjugal love, but in the seventeenth century the same step plunged the couple into a rite of passage that involved progressively greater publicity and communal involvement. Betrothal was anything but quiet or clandestine. It rivaled the wedding itself in ritual and festivity. Spousals, trothplights, and handfasting—the various regional terms for betrothal—remained until 1753 the legal equivalent of church marriage. Throughout the sixteenth and seventeenth centuries it was a major social event, the beginnings for many people of the real marriage.[49] Couples who had encountered parental or parish obstacles had to resort to "private spousals" or clandestine marriages, but, as a rule, the betrothal was a public event, involving not just family but the larger community.[50]

Betrothals were sometimes conducted by clergy, though in the seventeenth century it was just as likely to be a layman, like the Somerset blacksmith,

John Reed, who served as master of ceremonies. He had the couple, Robert and Marjorie, join right hands while they gave their mutual vows—"to have and to hold for better for worse, till death do us part"—and then, like the church service, had them kiss. Robert "in confirmation of the contract [did] break a piece of silver of sixpence and gave . . . Marjorie one part thereof and kept the other himself. And then they acknowledged that they were man and wife."[51] In the 1530s, when William Sampson had decided to make "a goode woman" of Joan Smith, who had provided him four children out of wedlock, he sent for a neighbor to witness the act.[52] Such ceremonies were invariably witnessed and followed by some kind of festivity, in Somerset by a "bankett [banquet] . . . commonlie called a trothing feaste."[53]

Publicity guaranteed that the betrothal would stand up if challenged in church court. Having a betrothal ritualized gave it legitimacy, but also added that element of magic regarded as essential to any successful conjugal relationship. Betrothals thus had all the elements of a persuasive act, including the verbal utterances and the manipulations of certain objects, bodily and otherwise. Exchanging kisses, toasts, coins, or gifts was as important, if not more so, as the verbal promises. The gifts took their value not from their monetary worth, but from their role in the magical performance. In the seventeenth century, when women as well as men carried knives useful to their work, these were a popular item of exchange. By the eighteenth century women were no longer carrying knives, and the practice was virtually forgotten. By then the gift of a knife was the cause of considerable apprehension, for it was said to "cut love." So great was the fear that the betrothed would refuse such a gift "unless the giver would receive a small coin as nominal payment," thus giving the knife a purely monetary value and depriving it of magic powers.[54]

Nevertheless, other personal artifacts retained their magic. When Edward Arden betrothed Bridget Rose in Nottinghamshire during the 1590s, he gave her "a paire of sweete gloves and after then an English crowne of golde," which, according to testimony, had moved her to proclaim "this golde hath warm [sic] mine harte for ever and nowe I will never forsake thee." In turn, she had sent him sixpence and a cluster of nettles, instructing her intermediary to tell him "that as close on those thee did stick together, so fast shoulde her harte stick to him."[55] Clearly, these tokens had a power far beyond their material value. Giving rings, hair, or dividing coins made magical claims on both men and women so powerful that the termination of a betrothal had to partake of the same public, ritual character, with both parties returning the love tokens (men were required to return all, but women only half of the items given). Only then was one person thought to be completely free of obligation.[56]

It is significant that Bridget was as active as Edward in this ritual process.

In later centuries, and especially among the propertied classes, women were said to be betrothed when they had received a ring. It is clear from the seventeenth-century accounts that she also did some giving, confirming her acceptance of his proposals by giving a gift in return. This is particularly evident in the exchange of rings, something originally associated with the betrothal and only later appropriated by the marriage ceremony. To the analogically minded, the ring suggested eternity, but its power to transmit love was physical as well as symbolic. The ring finger was thought to give direct access to the heart, and precious metals, especially gold, were guaranteed to stir the passions.[57] Once a ring was put on, it could not be removed except in a ritual manner. To lose a ring or break it was thought, even as late as the Victorian period, to be a bad omen, especially among the working classes. "I thought I should lose him, for I broke my wedding ring the other day, and my sister lost her husband after breaking her ring. It is a sure sign!" observed an Essex widow.[58] By that time, the educated regarded ring magic as a quaint custom, a "superstition," of interest only to folklorists. In the early modern period, however, rings played a central role not only in courtship, but also in making informal marriages. When people were too poor to afford a proper gold or silver band, a curtain ring, church key, or a twist of tobacco was substituted.[59]

The body played a very important role in betrothal ritual. In addition to kissing, drinking, and eating, there was also a highly publicized joining of bodies. William Gouge noted that "many make it a very marriage, and thereupon have a greater solemnity at their contract than at their marriage; yea many take liberty after a contract to know their spouse, as if they were married, an unwarrantable and dishonest practice."[60] In interpreting the bedding ceremony as carnal and therefore sinful, Puritans like Gouge mistook for hedonism that which had a meaning that transcended sexual pleasure. In sixteenth-century Leicestershire, it was "common use and custom" for the man to remain "in the house where the woman doth abide the night next following after such contracte otherwyse he doth departe without staying the night."[61] We, like the Puritans, would tend to give a sexual reading to this rite, though seeing it as liberating rather than sinful. However, both interpretations are misplaced, for it is not entirely clear that ritual bedding at betrothal always involved intercourse. In fact, there is no firm evidence that a tradition of trial marriage for the purpose of testing a woman's fertility ever existed in Britain. Some couples may have begun regular intercourse at this point, but most who were bedded probably did not.[62] For the majority, the initial bedding was probably more like the kiss, more magical than erotic, more public statement than private pleasure. If witnessed, as it often was, bedding was the ultimate proof of a couple's claim on one another.[63] Here the use of the fusion of two bodies was more symbolic than sensual, an expression of the physical sharing that defined love during the period.

IV

Each phase in the early modern marriage process required ever greater ritual publicity. After betrothal, the next step was the posting of banns, an event which made manifest the public social nature of marriage.[64] The banns were called "askings," and in seventeenth-century Yorkshire they were the occasion of noisy public demonstration of communal feelings. If the parish approved, there would be a shout of "God speed 'em well" after the third posting.[65] It was a time of teasing, ritual joking, which tested the couple's willingness to go through with the wedding but also worked to counteract tensions that were invariably present when any single persons were removed from the pool of eligible mates.[66]

All this led directly to the big wedding; and, here again, we are confronted by what is to us a strange, almost impersonal event, that offends the modern sense of love as pure feeling and intimacy. Because the couple's bond had already been settled at the time of betrothal, the early modern big wedding was concerned with a set of issues more practical than purely personal. With the terms of the conjugal contract already settled, it was a time for legislating the social contract between the heads of a new household and the rest of the community, ritually and magically defining the cooperative arrangements that society understood to be the basis of a successful household.

So public was the early modern big wedding that even the immediate family played an insignificant role. The day began with the fetching of the bride by the groom and his men. There was often a mock struggle as the woman departed her home for the last time, but this was the only point at which her family played a prominent role in the day's performance. Parents did not normally accompany their children to church, and it was neighbors and peers who were the principal actors in an extended communal drama that followed.[67] The actual religious ceremony was conducted in an atmosphere that few modern couples would tolerate. Fiddlers played, friends drank, joked, and jostled, as if the nave were a fairground. Puritans complained that this made "a Maie game of marriage, [rather] than a holy institution of God," but in many places the clergy were no more able to control what went on within the church than what happened in its yard and at its gates.[68] Well into the eighteenth century, many parsons, rural and urban, wisely chose to join in the fun, initiating the kissing, dancing, and joking that began as soon as the vows were said and did not end until the couple returned to church several days later to take up their rightful place among the ranks of the privileged householders.

It will not be possible to explore here all the richness and variety of the early modern big wedding.[69] I focus instead only on a few of the most prominent rituals aimed at establishing the proper relationship between husband and wife, and, what was of equal importance, the relationship between the newlyweds and the larger community. The first of these occurred as the couple attempted to leave the church. The door would be barred from the outside and the groom was forced to ransom himself and his new bride by shoving coins to the crowd outside, "the idea being, the twain should meet and overcome their first trouble or obstacle in life within the church."[70]

Setting the right precedent was no less important in the subsequent rite of jumping the petting stone, normally performed on the church's steps, but sometimes at its gates. A stone or bench was placed across the path; the groom jumped first, demonstrating the authority and initiative expected of this newly ordained master of a household. The bride was more often lifted across, but it was very important that she, as a new mistress, perform in the appropriate manner, for a woman who would not jump was thought to make an ill-tempered shrew. By jumping with good humor, she was said to have left her "pets" or bad humors behind, thus ensuring that she would be a good mistress to all those who might serve in her household.[71]

Weddings were a time for establishing relationships, not for expressing feelings. As Yorkshire newlyweds made their way to the wedding feast, the husband always crossed the bridges first, "for was it not right that he, as master, and still more as protector of his bride, his wife, should go first and overcome all danger." But both also took the opportunity to throw small objects into the water below in the belief that "it might carry with it every evil wish and ill spell wrought by wicked hearts that day."[72] In the same way, the community used ritual to deal with the tensions that were bound to occur when two persons were removed from the ranks of the unmarried. By barring the door, erecting the petting stone, or obstructing the couple's path, peers of the bride and groom were able to act out their envy in a socially approved manner. Very common was the practice of roping or chaining the path, demanding coins from the groom before the couple was allowed to pass. In Yorkshire, young men, "gaily dressed and with blackened faces," made explicit the emotional dynamics of this particular ritual.[73] The captain of this band cried a halt, declaring

that he and his merry men were in need of wives, and unless the bridegroom paid them instantly "bride guest money" his bride and every bonny bride's maid would be kidnapped.

A similar purpose was served by the Yorkshire practice of racing for the garter. In Bedale, Yorkshire, the winner of the dash from the church would kneel before the bride to make his claim:

> Good bride of thee I beg thou'lt lift
> Thy bridal goon an' stand,
> I ask fra thou a lover's gift,
> 'Tis this, thy garter band.

It was a major breach not to give the garter, which, having the proven love power, was much coveted as a charm by both bachelors and spinsters. As late as 1800, it was thought very unlucky, as well as unfriendly, for new brides, whatever their social status, to refuse this request.[74]

Propitiatory rites, aimed at warding off envy, are found at moments of marriage in many cultures. Newlyweds are considered very powerful, but also exceptionally vulnerable, a major reason why such care was taken to select a lucky day, the right clothing, together with the correct body language and social behavior. Witchcraft was an ever-present threat and every effort was made not to offend those thought to be instruments of malevolence.[75]

Today, a wedding is seen as a moment of emotional release. We expect mothers to sob, brides to blush, and fathers to show pride. However, direct expression of feeling was noticeably absent in the traditional big wedding. It was a time for emotional management rather than expression, when the participants were expected to play certain well-defined roles rather than show what we would regard as their sincere feelings. This is not to say that people in the past did not recognize personal feelings, but they did not think in terms of a "hydraulic" model of the emotions, assuming them to be an uncontrollable force, always latent, the built-up pressure tending toward eruption. On the contrary, their view was quite like that which has emerged recently in the psychological as well as the symbolic interactionist literature, seeing the emotions as scripts rather than drives, to be "worked" on through a variety of devices, which, in the case of the early modern period, meant magic and ritual.

For example, in Wales, it was customary to send a white hazel stick and a bit of ginger to jilted lovers, reminders of loss but also healing gestures.[76] To us the pranks played on losers—mocking notes, the wedding garland stuffed down the chimney, a bottle of urine hung on the door—seem cruel, but they can best be seen as what Victor Turner has called "social dramas," involving the wounded parties in the larger performance, thereby producing a kind of catharsis which would prevent the further simmering of malevolence.[77] The same theatricality was involved in the ritual treatment of siblings who had been passed over in marriage. The older brother or sister would be forced to dance shoeless or in green stockings, acting out his or her envy, and thereby reconciling the person to the new situation.[78]

A similar function was served by the rough music that was the accompaniment of every nuptial evening. Rude cries, the blowing of horns, and incessant tin-panning prevented repose until the new husband paid his "footing" in coin, or submitted to further ritual humiliation at the hands of the gathered crowd. In Cornwall the groom was likely to be ridden in a wheel barrow; in other places the couple might be pelted or assaulted in their bed, but always within a certain set of rules that allowed for the proper propitiatory response.[79] In effect, the carnival atmosphere reinforced rather than undermined the privileged status of the newlyweds. Like other such highly visible and audible rites of inversion, wedding's rough music tradition assumed superiority of those who were the objects of its peculiar attentions.[80] In doing so, the big wedding created much more than a new couple; its rituals defined an entire social order.

V

The big wedding, and the definition of love as mutual cooperation and physical sharing that it exemplified, persisted among smallholders and artisans well into the nineteenth century. Many magical and ritual elements would persist in working-class culture (particularly in youth culture) even into our own century. However, among the educated elites new definitions of love antithetical to the old practices were apparent from the mideighteenth century onward.[81] In 1753 the Hardwicke Marriage Act abrogated the parity previously enjoyed by both betrothals and clandestine marriages with church weddings. Henceforth, the only ritual capable of legitimating a marriage was that of the Church of England.[82]

Furthermore, the upper classes withdrew their approval from all those symbols which had expressed the old notion of love as mutual cooperation. Among the elites verbal expressions of affections replaced the exchange of tokens, the handclasp, and ritual bedding. Magic lost its place in the courtship process when the middle classes began to define love as an inner feeling, requiring a sincerity and transparency of expression that was incompatible with the theatrical traditions of the old courtship and marriage practices. The public rites of the old betrothal were replaced by the private engagement, witnessed only by immediate family. The ring lost its magical properties and became a mere symbol; the binding power was now invested in law of church and state, witnessed to by the contracts drawn up in lawyers' offices.

As early as the beginning of the eighteenth century, the upper classes were refusing to have their banns called and were marrying as privately and quietly as possible. Henri Misson noted that wealthy Londoners were purchasing special licenses so as to avoid publicity:

> To proclaim Banns is a Thing no Body now dares to have done; very few are willing to have their Affairs declar'd to all the World in a publick Place, when for a Guinea they may do it *snug* and without Noise. . . . [83]

It was the crush of the "mob," the stares, as well as the shouts and music, which Fanny Burney found most distressing when she witnessed a provincial wedding in 1770. "I don't suppose anything can be so dreadful as a public wedding—my stars! I should never be able to support it."[84] Until banns regained their popularity among the upper and middle classes late in the nineteenth century, genteel weddings were family affairs by invitation only. A license permitted the parties to arrive at a nearly empty church, perform a brief ceremony, and depart by the side door, thus avoiding all of the festivities traditionally associated with weddings. The reception became very exclusive; and honeymoon, another of the genteel innovations of the period, underlined the new association of love with intimacy.[85]

What began as fashion became a matter of conviction in the course of the century. Antiritualism, already evident among dissenters in the seventeenth century, became respectable in the course of the next century. By the 1790s there was growing sentiment, reinforced by class antagonism, for the repression of all those old rituals and symbols that many educated persons now despised as incompatible with sincere expressions of feelings, and therefore vulgar and demeaning. In the decades that followed, a direct attack was launched in the name of true love on all the old courtship and marriage customs.[86] In North Yorkshire, where the clergy had once sold love seals to promote chastity among their flocks, the church now took the lead in condemning all forms of love lore as irreligious and obscene.[87] The seals, which had once had a high market value, were said to have lost all practical value and were now given "unto bairns for to play with and so come to be lost. . . ."[88]

The conflict between elite and popular notions of love took on a particularly bitter edge in the North Yorkshire region around Bedale during the 1790s when a clergyman's wife, new to the area, tried to prevent local women from knitting love garters. She regarded these as evidence of sexual license, to which the defenders of the tradition replied that it was but an "old and loved custom, their fathers and mothers had indulged in the rite, they saw no harm, and truly there was none."[89] In this confrontation of cultures, no quarter was given. The clergy threatened to absent themselves from any wedding where the garter custom was kept. But "so ancient a custom about which was woven with so much superstition, so many rites, and honoured beliefs, was not to be set aside because the parson—all powerful as he was in those days—wagged his finger."[90] A certain part of the male community, including most of the smallholders and a part of the literate artisanate, took up custom's cause. Against them were ranged Bedale's gentry, clergy, and the wealthier farmers, who forbade their daughters to wear the garter.

The Bedale struggles ran pretty much along lines defined by class. The smallholders of both sexes defended the old ways; those of upper-class status, and those aspiring to it, tended to side with the clergy. Social tension was particularly evident in the ribald songs directed against the farmers' daughters. Probably because the smallholders feared to attack these powerful men directly, it was girls' boarding-school manners and low-cut Empire dresses that were subjected to rhymed assault in numerous ballads suggesting the hypocrisy of an elite culture that approved of décolletage but could not bear the sight of a bare leg at a wedding:

> Was learnt other tricks with their tutors from France
> But to blush she's forgotten, indeed she will dance
> As no modest maiden would dream of or dare
> With gown so lifted, with bosom so bare.[91]

In the end, it was the parsons and wealthy farmers who had their way. Their dutiful daughters set the fashion for other brides; and, by the 1820s, local lads were racing for a token ribbon rather than a real garter. Brides no longer lifted their gowns for all to see; and the people of Bedale resigned themselves to quieter, more decorous celebrations of weddings, rationalizing the giving up of the old love magic as a matter of "different days, a's different ways."[92]

VI

The events in Bedale were symptomatic of the tensions throughout Britain occasioned when the new romance of feeling and intimacy confronted the older rituals of cooperation and mutual assistance. The contest was most intense in regions, like Yorkshire, where economies sustained by family and communal cooperation persisted. Where there occurred a division between home and work, love was more likely to undergo what Cancian has described as "feminization." But nowhere did this take place suddenly or completely. It made its initial advances among the middle and upper classes, and was slowest to take hold in rural areas and among those elements of the urban working classes where cooperation between the couple, and between the couple and the community, continued to have real meaning.

And, within the bourgeoisie itself, the "feminization" of love produced paradoxes. On the one hand, middle-class males, now defined as the sole breadwinners, tended to combine the new notions of romantic passion with older concepts of love as practical support. As for middle-class women, they became identified as the more emotional sex, without necessarily accepting the idea of love as pure passion. We must not confuse the feminine with the female (or, for that matter, the masculine with the male). It is important to note that the love that was now identified with the feminine did not necessarily reflect the needs or values of women as such.

Nevertheless, the ideal of love as feeling came to dominate middle-class emotionology during the nineteenth century. Psyche and soma underwent a radical separation. Heterosexual love was redefined as pure feeling, whose expression was limited to spoken or written language. The old ways of symbolizing love, using the body, became taboo. The body itself underwent a radical sexualization, ceasing to be the vehicle for public performance and becoming a thing of private pleasure. We can trace this shift in the changing meaning of the term *emotion,* which in the mideighteenth century still meant physical movement. Locke could speak of the emotion of blood, but, by the early nineteenth century, the term was used only in connection with invisible feeling.[93] The evolution of the term *feeling* reflected the perceived separation of psyche and soma; and the period also coined the terms *psychological* and *unconscious.*[94]

Love, now defined as disembodied feeling, was radically disassociated from the physical act of loving, which was coming to be defined for the first time in the modern terminology of "sex." While men continued to view sex as an expression of love, it lost that meaning for women, particularly those middle-class women who were taught to view the physical as vulgar and demeaning.[95]

Changes in the meaning of love demanded new courtship and marriage conventions. The new emphasis on pure feeling and sincerity was initially reflected in an intense antiritualism, which rejected all stereotypical performances as antithetical to authentic expression of feeling, and thus to love itself. But, in a process not unlike that which has been traced by Karen Haltunen for nineteenth-century America, the British antiritualists eventually developed their own "sentimental rituals," creating forms more compatible with the new definitions of love.[96]

By and large, it was the women of the middle class who were instrumental in the creation of sentimental rituals. Men of the class held ambivalent attitudes toward love, defining it both in terms of helping and as pure feeling. As is the case today, men were simultaneously more practical and more romantic than women. They combined the older view of love as providing with a notion of love as something mysterious, beyond human or ritual control, an ambivalence which is reflected in their role in the courtship and marriage process. For men, and for young men in particular, love was a spontaneous inner force, something that only women were supposed to be able to channel and manage successfully.[97]

Male romanticism was implicitly antiritualistic. The idea of love as a powerful inner impulse, as private experience transcendent of all social and moral considerations, arose simultaneous with the emergence of middle-class male concepts of individualism that identified manliness with the autonomous, rational, and always firmly bounded self. Middle-class males were reared to distrust both their bodies and feelings. In contrast to earlier notions of the self as porous and vulnerable, their body image was that of the hard impervious shell, invulnerable to invasion but equally incapable of effective communication of feeling. Love of a woman—*the* woman—was the only relationship that licensed the autonomous male to lower his ego boundaries and experience that unity of body and feeling from which he had been weaned from a very early stage of childhood. No wonder that for many middle-class males falling in love was experienced as something akin to religious conversion.[98]

However, because respectable young men were raised to idealize women of their own class, even the permission that monogamous love provided did not automatically guarantee that the sought-after reunion of psyche and soma would be accomplished. Middle-class bachelors imagined marriage to be a state of grace, only to find their wives "passionless" and their sexual and emotional desires unfulfilled. Mistresses, prostitutes, and lower class women generally provided what wives could not. But these clandestine liaisons, reinforced the bourgeois separation of "true love" and sexuality, of feelings and body. For many bourgeois men love remained an amoral, asocial power, a mysterious and irrational force irreconcilable with their otherwise highly rational, respectable existence. Passion was also a convenient rationalization for behavior licensed by men's overwhelming power over material and human resources, including any woman who was not protected by another man.[99]

Because men were supposedly driven by stronger inner impulses, they were expected to take the initiative in love as well as in sex. The older forms of courtship, in which women had often acted forcefully both physically and symbolically, gave way to a new etiquette in which the male was invariably the suitor. However, once engagement was reached and the practical aspects of the marriage contract arranged, men, in their role as providers, were expected to take little or no interest in the marriage rites themselves, becoming virtual spectators of their own weddings. Secure in their position as principal breadwinners in the new bourgeois division of labor, men of that class were able to combine an intense romanticism with an older definition of love as providing and sharing. Once engagement was completed, they felt no need for ritual, since the definition of man as the sole breadwinner negated the need to establish publicly the structures of shared work and cooperation that had been given so much symbolic attention in the traditional big wedding.

VII

As Mary Douglass has pointed out, the kind of individualism that was characteristic of middle-class men is often associated with negative attitudes toward ritualistic behavior.[100] Women, however, remained embedded within a web of dependencies much more like those which had existed in early modern society generally. Their need to create and sustain relationships (particularly female relationships) through symbolic interaction remained undiminished, though the new rites were of a very different dimension and quality. Indeed, it fell to women to create the plethora of sentimental rituals that were characteristic of the Victorian era, rites that reflected the "feminized" ideal of love as shared feeling and intimacy, but also met the practical needs of the largely powerless and dependent female.

With respect to courtship and marriage, the new rituals differed from the old with respect to the use of the body. Physical contact during courtship was discouraged.[101] Kissing, dancing, touching—which earlier generations had seen as perfectly chaste expressions of love—were now forbidden to respectable women, who were told by Mrs. Trimmer that they must avoid at all costs "improper display of personal beauty or indecorous agility."[102] Writing in the 1770s, one authority had already warned that:

> One of the chief beauties in the female character is that modest reserve, that retiring delicacy, which avoids the public eye and is disconcerted at the gaze of admiration. When a girl ceases to blush, she has lost the most powerful charm of beauty.[103]

Here is a new meaning of charm, not as a magical device useful to men as well as women, but as something wholly feminine, identified with receptivity rather than initiative. Women were supposed to be objects of attention and, as such, passive rather than active in the courtship process. This supposedly natural division between men and women was also the source of the split in the image of woman into idealized lady and dangerous whore. While lower-class women continued to be thought of as active, even aggressive, sensual beings, the object of male fear as well as masculine desire, genteel women were conceived of as weak emotional creatures, whose destiny was to respond rather than to take initiative.[104]

Victorian conduct books, like the popular *How to Woo*, told young women that "matrimony should be considered an incident in life which, if it comes at all, must come without any contrivance of yours."[105] The woman could be kissed, but must never kiss; she could be loved and be the source of love's grace, but she must never express love physically. One conduct book even went so far as to advise: "If you do love your husband, do not ever say so."[106]

While everyone now assumed women were better at expressing feelings than were men, it was still the men who were expected to be the actors. A girl could become engaged, but she must have no part in the engaging. As Lady Bracknell says to Gwendolyn:

> Pardon me, you are not engaged to anyone. When you do become engaged to some one, I, or your father, should his health permit him, will inform you of the fact. An engagement should come on a young girl as a surprise, pleasant or unpleasant, as the case may be. It is hardly a matter that she could be allowed to arrange herself.[107]

Female love, regarded as passive, could be roused only by male activity. Men regarded feelings as a mysterious force, idealized, disembodied, beyond control, a license for male extramarital affairs and an excuse to keep respectable females carefully cloistered.[108] Seventeenth-century Puritans had believed love to be accessible by deep introspection, but according to nineteenth-century romantic formulations, feelings lay too deep for conscious management, swallowed up in what the Victorians came to call the "unconscious," accessible only to specialized practitioners, male doctors, and, later, psychologists.[109]

However, middle-class women never wholly shared men's conception of love as an uncontrollable force. They continued to act as if feelings were manageable and could be given appropriate formal expression without undermining the all important ingredient of sincerity. This was reflected in women's greater involvement with the development of a whole range of what Karen Haltunen has called sentimental rituals, which ranged from the minor etiquettes of calling and visiting to the elaborate rites of mourning, and, of course, the white wedding.

Consistent with the greater emphasis on personal feeling and intimacy, the white wedding was much more private and domesticated. While the families were more involved, the community was less so. The white wedding eliminated all reference to both the body biological and the body social. The newly invented honeymoon emphasized intimacy; the bride in white was a symbol of pure feeling. By the midnineteenth century the body was hidden and the face veiled. All movements were reduced to the minimum required for the father to lead his daughter to the altar (a wholly new patriarchal innovation of the period) and the groom to take her off to the honeymoon.

No jokes, songs, or other references to marriage's productive or reproductive functions were permitted. The petting stone, race for the garter, rough music were all unthinkably physical and undignified.[110] The material basis of marriage, now vested entirely in the male, was taken for granted, and required no symbolic representation in a ceremony that now emphasized only a feminized vision of affection.[111]

VIII

The white wedding, the embodiment of the Victorian separation of soma and psyche, reveals in a striking manner a notion of love, new in the nineteenth century, which is still dominant in our own time. Paradoxically, it represented the ritualization of something—feeling—that was supposedly not at all amenable to stereotypical expression. Clearly, the women who were involved in the creation of these and other sentimental rituals did not share the male view of love as a mysterious force, beyond their control. If bourgeois men liked to think of women as the more emotional sex, this was not necessarily the way women of that class regarded themselves. Early nine-teenth-century women's magazines by no means wallowed in feelings; and female writers were openly critical of romantic passion, insisting that feelings should not be given priority over moral and social considerations. Mary Wollstonecraft had warned that "love from its very nature is transitory . . ."; and another early feminist Anna Wheeler argued that the belief that women were naturally more loving "had been made a superstition," a reflection of men's felt needs rather than the real interests of women. Like others of her generation who suspected that romantic emotionology represented "silken fetters," Wheeler argued: "let . . . reason teach passion to submit to neces-sity."[112]

Middle-class men tended to define women as the objects of love, denying them the agency attributed to the male, reserving for themselves initiative and control in the courtship process by defining themselves as lovers and the women as the loved. But it is abundantly clear that many women, middle- as well as working-class, continued to act as lovers, and not just within the prescribed boundaries of the heterosexual. Not allowed by Victorian culture to aspire to autonomous individuality, bourgeois women were dependent on relationships of cooperation and sharing with other members of their fam-ilies, and especially with other females. In sustaining these relationships, they continued to use the body as a major ritual device. If women kept their capacity for more active forms of loving hidden from men behind the guise of "passionlessness," they nevertheless displayed it actively and physically to other women. In what Carroll Smith-Rosenberg has called the "female world of love and ritual" there was no radical disassociation of the body and feelings. Female friends kissed, fondled, slept together without any thought that their relationships might be thought of as purely sexual. As in the early modern period, the body served to express the sense of cooperation and caring that was very much a part (though an increasingly hidden part) of the women's world of the nineteenth century.[113]

Even the white wedding itself served this function, for its symbolism directed attention not so much to the couple—whose love was ritually inexpressible—but to the bride herself. Above all else, the white wedding was a middle-class woman's rite of passage from girlhood to adult status. For the male it was career rather than marriage that established manhood. As we have already seen, men took little interest in and played only a peripheral role in the white wedding. But, for women, the rite was all-important in establishing social status and creating those female support networks which were vital to successful wife- and motherhood. Thus, many of the innovative aspects of the white wedding—the presence of mothers at the wedding, the proliferation of bridesmaids, and (quite recently) the tossing of the bouquet—have little to do with the couple, yet a great deal to say about caring relationships among women.

IX

The new courtship etiquette and the white wedding remained a middle-class phenomenon for most of the nineteenth and for much of the first half of the twentieth centuries. At other social levels, both rural and urban, older understandings of love continued. The kind of rough, demonstrative behavior that had come to be despised by the educated classes and was eventually rejected by respectable working-class adults during the late Victorian period, survived in working-class youth culture well into our own era. It was very much a part of the behavior of boys and girls active in the "monkey ranks" of English industrial towns in the early twentieth century:

> Girls resort to Oldham Street on a Saturday night in nearly as large numbers as the boys. . . . The boys exchange rough salutations with the girls, who seem in no way less vigorous than the boys themselves, and whose chief desire, one would think, was to pluck from the lads' button holes, the flowers which many of them wear.[114]

In rural areas the old love magic was slow to die.[115] Robert Forby noted in 1830 that the rural working girl "still hoards her sixpence, that she may cross the hand of the fortune-teller with silver, and learn the events of her future life; and amongst those of a somewhat higher rank, it is not uncommonly the first thought that occurs to a person who has been robbed, to consult the 'wise woman' or the 'cunning man.' It is, however, a good symptom that this is seldom done openly. They entertain the belief, but are ashamed to own it. . . ."[116]

By the 1850s, most women may have abandoned the traditional magicians, but they had not yet wholly accepted the claims of science. They retained a belief in the unity of the psyche and soma, and were still more likely than men to consult phrenologists and spiritualists for their emotional problems. Many of those practitioners were themselves female; and it was not until the beginning of the twentieth century that the male medical and psychological professions were able to make inroads into the clientele of what they had finally managed to define as useless "quackery."[117]

But even as science celebrated its triumph over superstition, there was abundant evidence of the persistence of love magic. Personal belongings, clothing, and especially body parts, such as hair, continued to be used by working people, particularly young folk, for amorous purposes.[118] The body remained a source of vulnerability as well as power. In the late nineteenth century, rural people often refused to have their pictures taken by photographers because they feared losing something of themselves.[119] Most of the ads for the newly commercialized forms of divination of the turn of the century were directed to women:

> While the servant girl still studies her "Dream Book," her mistress has "Planets of the Month," "Consult the Oracle," or many other books telling her what to do and what to avoid for "luck." Even tea leaf fortune-telling has revived, and Spiers and Pond's, Hamley's, and other large stores have sold "The Nelros' Cup of Fortune" for that purpose.[120]

As late as 1945, note was made in both London and the eastern counties of England of the brisk trade in love potions there. Some of the clients were young girls "who lack the necessary confidence in their own physical attraction or the object of whose love is attracted by another," but another group of devotees were said to be "middle aged spinsters who are desirous of obtaining a husband and go to a witch rather than to one of the matrimonial agencies."[121] Rarely are men mentioned in these accounts, for it was lower-class women's sense of vulnerability, and their desire to create bonds based on something stronger and more enduring than pure feeling, that perpetuated the old rituals even into this supposedly disenchanted century.[122]

X

By the 1920s and 1930s, however, British working-class courtship and marriage were becoming more like the middle-class etiquette. In the postwar years, the chaste period of engagement leading up to a big white wedding became the norm at virtually all class levels.[123] While there have been some changes in recent decades, the symbolism has remained fundamentally un-altered, reflecting contemporary society's tendency to define heterosexual love exclusively in terms of feelings and intimacy. While other, equally valid definitions of love persist, they do not get the same ideological or symbolic validation. Even the Victorian female practice of kissing and touching one another disappeared in a century that defined love exclusively in heterosexual terms and defined all homosocial forms of affection (male as well as female) as signs of perversion.[124] On the other hand, despite recent improvements in women's legal status and earning power, the twentieth century has not vanquished women's dependency on men and on other women. It is not surprising therefore that the white wedding flourishes now more than ever.[125]

I have attempted to show just how strongly the contemporary emphasis on love as feeling and intimacy permeates and distorts historical scholarship. In many respects, historians remain locked into a nineteenth-century view of emotions, one that prevents them from comprehending the full range of human experience. They have ransacked the past for verbal expressions of feeling, but have paid little attention to other notions and representations of loving. Now that other disciplines have begun to explore alternative conceptions of emotions, it is time for historians to begin their own reevaluation. For it is only through becoming more aware of our own preconceptions that we can better comprehend not only the present but also the past.

N o t e s

1. Lawrence Stone, *The Family, Sex and Marriage in England, 1500–1800* (New York, 1977), chapters 6–9; Edward Shorter, *The Making of the Modern Family* (New York, 1975), chapters 3, 4. For other studies centering the change in the eighteenth century, see Philippe Ariès, *Centuries of Childhood: A Social History of Family Life* (New York, 1982); Randolph Trumbach, *The Rise of the Egalitarian Family: Aristocratic Kinship and Domestic Relations in 18th Century England* (New York, 1978), and Roy Porter, "Mixed Feelings: The Enlightenment and Sexuality in Eighteenth-Century Britain," in *Sexuality in Eighteenth-Century Britain*, ed. Paul-Gabriel Bouce (Manchester, 1982), pp. 1–27

2. Alan MacFarlane, *Marriage and Love in England: Modes of Reproduction, 1300–1840* (New York, 1986), Part III. For the rediscovery of love in the sixteenth and seventeenth centuries, see Keith Wrightson, *English Society, 1580–1680* (New Brunswick, N. J., 1982), chapters 3, 4; Ralph Houlbrooke, *The English Family, 1450–1700* (London, 1984), chapter 4.

3. Linda Pollock, *Forgotten Children: Parent-Child Relations from 1500 to 1800* (Cambridge, Eng., 1983), passim.

4. Michael MacDonald, *Mystical Bedlam: Madness, Anxiety and Healing in Seventeenth-Century England* (Cambridge, Eng., 1981), pp. 72–105.

5. Philip J. Greven, Jr., *The Protestant Temperament: Patterns of Child-Rearing, Religious Experience, and the Self in Early America* (New York, 1977). Greven locates three distinctive types of child-rearing, each with its own particular emotional consequences, and only one of which would be described by Stone and Shorter as affectionate.

6. Francesca M. Cancian, "The Feminization of Love," *Signs* 11, no. 4 (1986): 692–709.

7. The literature on nonverbal communication is vast and I mention only the most accessible of the many books on the subject, namely Edward T. Hall, *The Silent Language* (Garden City, N. Y., 1959). My definition of ritual is borrowed from Robert Bocock, *Ritual in Industrial Society: A Sociological Analysis of Ritualism in Modern England* (London, 1974), p. 27, who writes: "Ritual is the symbolic use of bodily movement and gesture in a social setting to express and articulate meaning." Among historians of the modern era interest in nonverbal forms is relatively new. For recent studies of ritual and symbol, see Charles Phythian-Adams, *Local History and Folklore* (London, 1975); Bob Bushaway, *By Rite: Custom, Ceremony, and Community in England, 1770–1880* (London, 1982); on Sweden, Jonas Frykman and Orvar Löfgren, *Culture Builders: A Historical Anthropology of Middle Class Life* (New Brunswick, N. J., 1987); for America, Rhys Isaac, *The Transformation of Virginia, 1740–1790* (Chapel Hill, 1982), and Carroll Smith-Rosenberg, *Disorderly Conduct: Visions of Gender in Victorian America* (New York, 1985); Hans Medick and David Sabean, "Interest and Emotion in Family and Kinship Studies: a Critique of Social History and Anthropology," in *Interest and Emotion: Essays on the Study of Family and Kinship,* ed. Medick and Sabean (Cambridge, Eng., 1984), pp. 9–27.

8. A useful review of recent shifts in the psychological understanding of the emotions is provided by Arlie Hochschild, *The Managed Heart: Commercialization of Human Feeling* (Berkeley and Los Angeles, 1983), pp. 201–22.

9. Ken Plummer, "Symbolic Interactionism and Sexual Conduct: An Emergent Perspective," in Mike Brake, ed., *Human Sexual Relations: Towards a Redefinition of Sexual Politics* (New York, 1982), p. 236

10. I cannot develop in this paper the cultural history of the ideas lying behind these concepts of the body, but instead rely on MacDonald's discussion of humoral theory, *Mystical Bedlam,* pp. 181–96, and Robert Muchembled's analysis of early modern notions of mind and body, contained in his *Popular Culture and Elite Culture in France,* trans. Lydia Cochrane (Baton Rouge, 1985), pp. 71–76.

11. My use of the term *emotionology* is the same as that of Peter N. Stearns and Carol Z. Stearns, "Emotionology: Clarifying the History of Emotions and Emotional Standards," *American Historical Review* 90, no. 4 (October 1985): 813–36.

12. Lawrence Babb, "The Physiological Conception of Love in the Elizabethan and Early Stuart Dramas," *PMLA* 56, no. 4 (December 1941): 1020–55. Also Keith Thomas, *Religion and the Decline of Magic* (New York, 1971), especially chapters 7–9; Muchembled, pp. 71–93.

13. William J. Fieldy, *Strange Customs of Courtship and Marriage* (London, 1961), pp. 56–58.

14. Prior to the nineteenth century *sex* was a term that referred only to gender and

was not understood as a distinct sphere of physical activity. See Raymond Williams, *Keywords: A Vocabulary of Culture and Society*, rev. ed. (New York, 1883), pp. 283–86. Incident reported in *Folk Lore* 17 (1906): 114.

15. John C. Jefferson, *Brides and Bridals* (London, 1872), 1:66.

16. Walter J. Ong, *Orality and Literacy: The Technologizing of the Word* (London, 1982), chapter 3.

17. Notes on this custom, reported in the Ceiriog Valley of North Wales in the nineteenth century, are found in the William Rhys Jones papers, "Folk Lore of the Ceiriog Valley," fol. 82, Welsh Folk Museum; on similar uses of urine, see Muchembled, p. 73.

18. On the uses of body fluids, see John G. Bourke, *Scatological Rites of all Nations* (Washington, D.C., 1891), pp. 216–27.

19. Certain places—caves, bridges, market crosses—were preferred by lovers wishing to have their vows taken seriously. Whether a story was believable or not depended on where it was heard. Something "heard at the church porch" had greater veracity than something "heard at the casement," just as love made public had greater credibility than that expressed in private. On the social context of veracity, see *Reports and Transactions of the Devonshire Association*, vol. 38, 1906, p. 91. On the social context of love tokens, see Peter Rushton, "The Testament of Gifts: Marriage Tokens and Disputed Contracts in North-East England, 1560–1630," *Folk Life* 25 (1986): 25-31.

20. Martine Segalen, *Love and Power in the Peasant Family: Rural France in the Nineteenth Century*, trans. Sarah Matthews (Oxford, 1980), p. 16.

21. Cancian, "Feminization," p. 697.

22. Babb, passim; Thomas, *Religion and the Decline of Magic*, pp. 233–45, 253–54.

23. S. J. Tambiah, "Form and Meaning of Magical Acts: A Point of View," in *Modes of Thought: Essays on Thinking in Western Societies*, ed. Robin Horton and Ruth Finnigan (London, 1973), pp. 199–229.

24. MacDonald, *Mystical Bedlam*, pp. 88–98.

25. Edmund Leites, "The Duty to Desire: Love, Friendship, and Sexuality in Some Puritan Theories of Marriage," *Journal of Social History* 15 (1982): 388–89.

26. MacDonald, *Mystical Bedlam* pp. 195–96.

27. Mary Douglass, *Natural Symbols: Explorations in Cosmology* (New York, 1982), p. 158. For the cosmologies of seventeenth-century peopope, see Thomas *Religion and the Decline of Magic* and *Mystical Bedlam*, and MacDonald's lengthy treatment.

28. This recipe was dated 1642, and was still in active use in the late eighteenth century. Found in Calvert MSS, fol. 13, Institute of Dialect and Folk Life Studies, Leeds University.

29. Miss E. Peacock, "Folklore and Legends of Lincolnshire," MSS, fol. 168, Folk Lore Society Library, University of London.

30. We know more about the "witches" and sorcerers" because they were the ones caught up in the nets of the legal authorities. In fact, almost everyone had magical capacities and used them on occasion. See Thomas, *Religion and the Decline of*

Magic, pp. 240–44; Muchembled, *Popular Culture and Elite Culture,* p. 83. This was also true in colonial America, where magic continued to be practiced by plebeian folk throughout the eighteenth century. See Herbert Leventhal, *In the Shadow of the Enlightenment: Occultism and Renaissance Science in Eighteenth Century America* (New York, 1976), pp. 125, 155–56, 264.

31. Paul Boyer and Stephen Nissenbaum, *Salem Possessed: The Social Origins of Witchcraft* (Cambridge, Mass., 1974), pp. 1–2.

32. Trefor Owen, *Welsh Folk Customs* (Cardiff, 1978), p. 98. Keith Thomas has noted that divining was often an effort "to arrange for the future rather than predict it." *Religion and the Decline of Magic,* p. 243.

33. This argument is presented in detail in my *For Better, for Worse: British Marriages, 1600 to the Present* (New York, 1985), chapter 1. I wish to thank Arthur Mitzman for the discussion of emotional bonding in this period contained in his "The Civilizing Offensive: Mentalities, High Culture, and Individual Psyches," *Journal of Social History* 20 (1987): 663–88.

34. For a discussion of divining on Valentine's Day, see Pierre Alain Genke, "St. Valentine's Day in Britain: The History of a Periodic Custom" (M.A. thesis, Leeds University, 1978), p. 67. Genke notes that this remains a mode of communication and social pressure in Britain today.

35. For a Venetian case, see Guido Ruggiero, *The Boundaries of Eros: Sex Crime and Sexuality in Renaissance Venice* (New York, 1985), pp. 33–35. It may be that in the more patriarchal societies of southern Europe, where age disparity between mates was common, women were more likely to use magic as a means of overcoming their inferior bargaining position. For another example, see Emmanuel Leroy Ladurie, *Montaillou: The Promised Land of Error* (New York, 1979), pp. 32, 296.

36. John Demos, *Entertaining Satan: Witchcraft and the Culture of Early New England* (New York, 1982), pp. 156–65. Muchembled notes that young people were often seen as having magical powers, which the community attempted to harness to its own purposes. He also observes that whether or not a person was thought to be a good or bad witch had to do with the social and spatial context. People would often be accused of practicing black magic by their own village neighbors, but would be considered white magicians by those from outside the village who came to consult them about countermeasures against what they perceived as their own local source of evil. Muchembled, *Popular Culture and Elite Culture,* p. 89.

37. Calvert MSS, fol. 23, Institute of Dialect and Folk Life Studies, Leeds University.

38. Ibid., fol. 66, 96–97.

39. Natalie Davis, "Boundaries and the Sense of Self in Sixteenth-Century France," in *Reconstructing Individualism; Autonomy, Individuality, and the Self in Western Thought,* ed. Thomas C. Heller et al. (Stanford, 1986), pp. 53–63.

40. MacDonald, *Mystical Bedlam,* pp. 98ff.

41. On love knots, Calvert MSS, fol. 27, Institute for Dialect and Folk Life Studies, Leeds University.

42. Ibid., fols. 9, 13.

43. Richard Blakeborough MSS, "Legends of the North Riding," n.p., Center for English Cultural Tradition and Language, Sheffield University.

44. Calvert MSS, fol. 28, Institute of Dialect and Folk Life Studies, Leeds University; also Anna E. Stothard, *The Border of the Tamar and Tavy* (London, 1929), 1:289.

45. *Cymru Fu*, 2 June 1888, p. 192.

46. For additional information on early nineteenth-century conjurers, see Kathryn Smith, "The Role of Animals in Witchcraft and Popular Magic," *Animals in Folklore*, ed. J. R. Parker and W. M. S. Russell (Cambridge, 1978), pp. 104–5; W. L. L. Davies, "The Conjurer in Montgomeryshire," *Montgomeryshire Collections*, 44 (1938): 164–65; Kathryn Smith, "The Wise Man and His Community," *Folk Life* 15 (1977): 24–35.

47. See the case of Roger Lowe, *The Diary of Roger Lowe*, ed. William L. Sachse (New Haven, 1983), p. 27.

48. Trefor Owen, "West Glamorgan Customs," *Folk Life* 3 (1965): 47.

49. Gillis, *For Better, for Worse*, pp. 16–17, 20–21; Beatrice Gottlieb, "The Meaning of Clandestine Marriage," in *Family and Sexuality in French History*, ed. R. Wheaton and T. Hareven (Philadelphia, 1980).

50. This shift is discussed in Gillis, *For Better, for Worse*, pp. 135–42.

51. An early seventeenth-century instance, cited by G. R. Quaife, *Wanton Wenches and Wayward Wives: Peasants and Illicit Sex in Early Seventeenth Century England* (New Brunswick, N. J., 1979), p. 44.

52. F. J. Furnivall, *Child-Marriages, Divorces, and Ratifications in the Diocese of Chester* (London, 1897), pp. xlv, 61.

53. Houlbrooke, *English Family*, p. 78.

54. *Notes and Queries*, 8th Series, 4 (1 July 1893); (12 August 1893): 131.

55. J. D. Chambers, *Nottinghamshire in the Eighteenth Century* (London, 1932), p. 311.

56. Quaife, *Wanton Wenches*, p. 47.

57. William Jones, *Finger-ring Lore* (London, 1898), pp. 155–59; "The Wedding Ring," *Antiquary* 3 (1881): 70–71.

58. Jones, *Finger-ring Lore*, p. 169.

59. For the case of a Gretna Green wedding, where tobacco twist was used, see *Notes and Queries* 7th Series, 4 (22 Oct. 1887): 329; also Claverhouse, *Irregular Border Marriages* (London and Edinburgh, 1939), p. 133.

60. William Gouge, *Of Domesticall Duties* (London, 1622), pp. 198–99.

61. A. Percival Moore, "Marriage Contracts or Espousals in the Reign of Queen Elizabeth," *Reports and Papers of the Associated Architectural Societies for 1909*, vol. 30, pt. 1, pp. 290–91.

62. MacFarlane argues vigorously that there was no such thing as fertility testing in England during this period. See *Marriage and Love in England*, pp. 306–7. See also Peter Laslett, *The World We Have Lost* (New York, 1965), pp. 139–45.

63. From the seventeenth-century account of wedding practices provided by Henry Best, *Rural Economy in Yorkshire in 1641, being the Farming and Account Books of*

Henry Best of Elmswell in East Riding, (Surtees Society, no. 33, 1857), p. 116; also Rushton, "Testament of Gifts."

64. J. Vaux, *Church Folklore* (London, 1894), pp. 91–93.

65. Elizabeth Wright, *Rustic Speech and Folk-Lore* (London, 1913), p. 271; *Church Times,* (24 and 29 June 1898); and *Reports and Transactions of the Devonshire Association* 57 (1925): 128.

66. On similar testing in France, see Muchembled, *Popular Culture and Elite Culture,* pp. 95–96.

67. See Gillis, *For Better, for Worse,* chapter 2.

68. *Admonition to Parliament of 1572,* ed. W. H. Frere and C. E. Douglas (London, 1927), p. 27.

69. For some continental examples, see André Burguière, "The Marriage Ritual in France: Ecclesiastical Practices and Popular Practices," and Nicole Belmont, "The Symbolic Function of the Popular Rituals of Marriage," both in *Religion, and the Sacred,* ed. R. Forster and O. Ranum, (Baltimore, 1982).

70. Richard Blakeborough, "A Country Wedding a Century Ago," fol. 5, Blakeborough MSS, Center for English Cultural Tradition and Language, Sheffield University.

71. W. Crooke, "Lifting of the Bride," *Folk Lore* 12 (1902): 226–51.

72. Blakeborough MSS, "A Country Wedding," fols. 11–12, Center for English Cultural Tradition and Language, Sheffield University.

73. Ibid., fol. 11.

74. Ibid., fols. 13–14.

75. Gillis, *For Better, for Worse,* pp. 70–71.

76. Ginger was said to warm the heart. See *Byegones,* 2d series, p.37.

77. Victor Turner, *Dramas, Fields, and Metaphors: Symbolic Action in Human Societies* (Ithaca, N. Y., 1974), pp. 33–44.

78. Charlotte Sophia Burne, ed., *Shropshire Folklore: A Sheaf of Gleanings* (London, 1883–86), p. 21; *Notes and Queries,* 6th Series, 9 (19 April 1884): 315.

79. Gillis, *For Better, for Worse,* pp. 67–69.

80. There is an immense literature on this subject. While not all rough music was conservative, the function in this case was to restore order. See M. Ingram, "Le Charivari dans L'Angleterre du XVIe et du XVIIe siècle," in J. Le Goff and J. C. Schmitt, *Le Charivari* (Paris, 1981), pp. 251–64. Also Natalie Davis, "The Reasons of Misrule," *Society and Culture in Early Modern France* (Stanford, 1975), pp. 97–123.

81. Gillis, *For Better, for Worse,* pp. 142–60.

82. Ibid., pp. 139–42.

83. Henri Misson, *Memoirs and Observations in His Travels over England (1697)* (London, 1719), p. 183. Even in the villages, those who considered themselves a cut above the rest began to purchase licenses to avoid publicity. See Richard Gough, *The History of Myddle* (Harmondsworth, 1981), p. 112.

84. Quoted in *How They Lived,* vol. 3, ed. A. Briggs (Oxford, 1969), p. 267.

85. On this shift, see Gillis, *For Better, for Worse,* pp. 136–39.

86. For the long struggle against the marriage law, see ibid., chapter 7.

87. Calvert MSS, fol. 31, Institute of Dialect and Folk Life Studies, Leeds University.

88. Ibid., fol. 56.

89. Richard Blakeborough, "A Collection of Valentines," fol. 16, Center for English Cultural Tradition and Language, Sheffield University.

90. Blakeborough, "A Country Wedding a Century Ago," fol. 3, Center for English Cultural Tradition and Language, Sheffield University.

91. From local song, "A Boarding School Miss," originating about 1790 and recorded by Richard Blakeborough in 1875 from a man who had learned it from his mother. Blakeborough Notebook MSS, fol. 43, Center for English Cultural Tradition and Language, Sheffield University.

92. For complete account, see Gillis, For Better, for Worse, pp. 147–50.

93. From Oxford English Dictionary; on similar changes in the meaning of the word sentiment, see Williams, Keywords, pp. 281–82.

94. Oxford English Dictionary; Williams, Keywords, pp. 246, 321.

95. Williams, Keywords, p. 284.

96. Karen Haltunen, Confidence Men and Painted Women: A Study of Middle-Class Culture in America, 1830–1870 (New Haven, 1982), especially chapter 5.

97. For contemporary parallels, see Cancian, "Feminization of Love," pp. 704–5.

98. In the eighteenth century, sensuality was viewed as natural in both men and women. See Roy Porter, "Mixed Feelings," pp. 10–17; also Stone, Family, Sex and Marriage, pp. 528–29. The radical separation of love and sensuality is discussed in Walter E. Houghton, The Victorian Frame of Mind, 1830–1870 (New Haven, 1957), pp. 372–94; and Peter Gay, The Bourgeois Experience (New York, 1984), 1:442–59. On the quasi-religious aspect of middle-class marriage, see Ronald Pearsall, The Worm in the Bud: The World of Victorian Sexuality (Harmondsworth, 1983), pp. 186, 203–11.

99. The immense literature on this is best summarized by Leonore Davidoff, "Class and Gender in Victorian England: The Diaries of Arthur J. Munby and Hannah Cullwick," Feminist Studies 5, no. 1 (Spring 1979): 87–100.

100. Douglass, Natural Symbols, p. 19.

101. On this shift, see Gordon R. Taylor, The Angel Makers: A Study in the Psychohistorical Origins of Historical Change, 1750–1850 (New York, 1974), chapter 6.

102. Cited in Stone, Family, Sex and Marriage, p. 675.

103. G. R. Taylor, Angel Makers, p. 118.

104. See Davidoff, "Class and Gender."

105. Pearsall, Worm in the Bud, p. 165.

106. Dr. Gregory, 1774, quoted in G. R. Taylor, Angel Makers, p. 121.

107. Oscar Wilde, The Importance of Being Earnest, Act 1; on middle-class engagements generally, see Pearsall, Worm in the Bud, pp. 166–67.

108. In the Victorian period, love came to be seen not as a cause of illness but as a cure, a social as well as personal panacea. Marriage was recommended as a remedy

for female hysteria and male masturbatory insanity. See Pearsall, *Worm in the Bud,* pp. 203–12.

109. See Raymond Williams, pp. 320–24; Peter Cominos, "Late-Victorian Sexual Respectability and the Social System," *International Review of Social History* 3 (1963): 18–43, 216–250.

110. The upper classes had begun to abandon the old practices in the eighteenth century. See Gillis, *For Better, for Worse,* pp. 138–39.

111. For more on the world of women, see Leonore Davidoff, *The Best Circles: Society, Etiquette, and the Season* (London, 1973), pp. 49–58.

112. Quotations from Barbara Taylor, *Eve and the New Jerusalem: Socialism and Feminism in the Nineteenth Century* (New York, 1983), pp. 30, 47–48.

113. Carroll Smith Rosenberg, "The Female World of Love and Ritual: Relations Between Women in Nineteenth-Century America," in *Disorderly Conduct: Visions of Gender in Victorian America* (New York, 1985), pp. 53–76. Ellen Ross has found working-class women in late nineteenth-century Britain to have similarly ritualistic relations. See Ross, "Survival Networks: Women's Neighbourhood Sharing in London before World War I," *History Workshop Journal* 15 (Spring 1983): 4–27. Ellen Rothman's description of middle-class courtship in nineteenth-century America shows many features, especially on the women's side, that are clearly ritualistic. See "Sex and Self-Control: Middle Class Courtship in America, 1770–1870," *Journal of Social History* 15, no. 3 (1982): 409–23.

114. C. E. B. Russell, *Manchester Boys* (Manchester, 1905), pp. 115–16.

115. On the practice of personal magic, see Samuel Bamford, *Passages in the Life of a Radical and Early Days* (London, 1905); Joseph Lawson, *Letters to the Young on Progress in Pudsey during the Last Sixty Years* (Stanninglen, 1887); on the importance of ritual in early nineteenth-century trade organizations, see Eric Hobsbawm, *Primitive Rebels* (New York, 1959), especially chapter 9; the role of ritual is further emphasized by E. P. Thompson, *The Making of the English Working Class* (New York, 1963), pp. 418–29.

116. Robert Forby, *The Vocabulary of East Anglia* (London, 1830), 2:397.

117. On women in the British spiritualist movement, see Janet Oppenheim, *The Other World: Spiritualism and Psychical Research in England, 1850–1940* (Cambridge, 1985), pp. 9–10; and Vieda Skultans, *Intimacy and Ritual: A Study of Spiritualism, Mediums and Groups* (London, 1974), especially chapter 4. For America, see R. Laurence Moore, *In Search of White Crows: Spiritualism, Parapsychology, and American Culture* (New York, 1977), pp. 102–29.

118. For examples, see Peacock MSS, fol. 198, Folk Lore Society Library, London University.

119. In the 1870s a white witch in Plymouth struck a photograph so as to remove a spell from the person in the picture. *Reports and Transactions of the Devonshire Association,* vol. 60 (1928), p. 122. For further information on the magic of images, see George Lyman Kittredge, *Witchcraft in Old and New England* (New York, 1929), pp. 91–92. Quotation from "Specimens of Modern Mascots and Ancient Amulets of the British Isles," *Folk Lore* 19 (1908): 288.

120. *Folk Lore* 56 (1945): 289; 57 (1946): 32.

121. For this claim, *Folk Lore* 61 (1950): 265; On the renaissance of ritual among the working classes in the twentieth century, see Gillis, *For Better, for Worse*, chapters 9, 10; for an interesting example of the persistence of magic among West Indians in Britain, see Venetia Newall, "Love and Marriage Customs of the Jamaican Community of London," *Lore and Language* 3, no. 9 (July 1983): 30–43.

122. On evidence of this revival, see Daniel L. O'Keefe, *Stolen Lightning: The Social Theory of Magic* (New York, 1983), pp. 2–11; on the functions of ritual in contemporary society, see *Secular Ritual*, ed. Sally F. Moore and Barbara Myerhoff (Assen/Amsterdam, 1978), passim. The continuity of magical practices in America is also stressed by Eleanor Long, "Aphrodisiacs, Charms, and Philtres," *Western Folklore* 32.

123. Gillis, *For Better, for Worse*, chapter 10.

124. Cancian, "Feminization of Love," p. 694; just how strongly this has affected our evaluation of friendship is stressed by Robert Brain in *Friends and Lovers* (New York, 1976).

125. John Gillis, "Weddings Great and Small," *New Society* 77 (July 1986): 9–11.

5

Anger and American Work: A Twentieth-Century Turning Point

Peter   N.   Stearns

The rise of modern work forms implied, essentially from the outset, a new kind of emotional standard for job behavior. The imagery that accompanied the nineteenth-century separation of work from home suggested rational control of job behavior, with the home as the refuge where emotional expressions could be freer. But work-specific emotional standards were not spelled out clearly during the nineteenth century. At most, vague references alluded to emotions bottled up in business that might trouble domestic tranquillity. The record of actual emotional expression suggests considerable latitude, depending to an extent on one's place in the job hierarchy. It was during the twentieth century in the United States that the implications of a special emotional style for the job were taken up, with particular bearing on anger. The results raise important questions about the emotional experience of Americans more generally.

This essay assesses this vital transition both in work history and in the development of a modern emotional style. The focus of historians concerned with the history of emotion has too long been riveted on the family, or processes, such as courtship, that lead to the family. Without question, families generate and channel powerful emotions, but to view them as the exclusive emotional institutions goes too far toward accepting the modern imagery that contrasts domestic emotionality with "real world" calculation. Neighborhood, school, public recreation and most assuredly work involve emotional expression and motivation as well, and as in the family the standards for emotionality change significantly in these areas over time. The modern history of emotions at work in fact displays a complex linkage with changes in familial standards; the twentieth-century shift in work emotions followed from earlier changes in family emotionology, and in turn impacted on the family in ways that have yet to be fully traced.

From the standpoint of work history, a focus on emotional shifts taps into some familiar benchmarks of change. Heightened discipline and control, building on the precedents of the early industrial factory system; the special focus on personality that was part of the rise of clerical staffs and management hierarchies as white-collar labor burgeoned; the proliferation of personnel experts bent on greasing the wheels of corporate capitalism, all played a role in the emotional transformation of the workplace.[1] But a grasp of how these forces reached toward emotional redefinition, and not simply decision-making processes and speedups of labor that might have vague emotional repercussions, deepens our understanding of how work in the twentieth century continued to change and constrain.

Anger and work have long been associated. A few nostalgic historians, to be sure, have posited an amicable setting for preindustrial labor, assuming that the location of most work in the home transferred the loving sentiments associated with family life to the process of labor. But the preindustrial family was not anger-free, and the family's work relationships often generated more anger than did other aspects of family functioning. Even some of the loving-family apologists have noted that one reason for placing a substantial minority of teenagers as servants or apprentices with other families was a desire to transfer the inevitable tensions of directing an adolescent subordinate to another set of adults. In fact, because the household furnished the essential hierarchy of work relationships, and because anger was often freely used to express and enforce hierarchy in preindustrial society, anger and work were common companions.[2]

The theme of angry abuse of apprentices or servants in the crafts and in farm labor is well known. Benjamin Franklin, for example, found himself "demeaned" more often than he judged compatible with his dignity, in working for his brother. Arguments and beatings were frequent. Family manuals into the eighteenth century assumed that masters would often resort to anger in dealing with their servants, at most warning against excessive physical expression of the emotion.[3] Guild regulations urged that masters should teach apprentices with only "moderate" correction, but they assumed that apprentices might often provoke righteous wrath. Even cheerfulness to customers was not required for economic success, as many producers held a virtual local monopoly for their wares; the surly village miller, like the grumpy artisan master and his equally demanding wife, is a staple of preindustrial folk literature.

This is not a claim that anger was omnipresent in traditional work. Personalities varied. Labor shortages sometimes created additional motives for restraint within the work hierarchy. The main point here is that there were no clear standards regulating the experience of anger on the job, or, as far as the directors of work were concerned, the expression of anger. Subordinates were urged to avoid presumption or ingratitude, which suggested restraint in emotional frankness, but even these guidelines were behavioral, not directed toward inner feelings.[4] A worker, in other words, might be chastised for showing anger but was not explicitly taught to feel guilty about experiencing it. There was certainly no set of standards by which to judge a superior's anger inappropriate. Franklin, again, commented only that his choleric brother was "passionate"; his distaste for his situation was clear, and he ran away, but he suggested no general set of emotional guidelines for the work situation.

Toward the later eighteenth century, Western society began to generate new concern about anger, as witness the invention of new terms such as "tantrum" to designate, and reprove, particular forms of angry outburst. Many families launched a new effort to promote anger control as part of character development,[5] and diaries often recorded this conscious effort in individual lives. But while it was doubtless assumed that anger control would extend to work as well as to other relationships, the link was not spelled out. At the same time, the separation of work from home began to take hold, gradually to be sure; and by the early nineteenth century this produced a clear dichotomy between domestic contexts, where anger control was now uniformly urged, and the public sphere where explicit standards were simply not discussed.

Industrialization may have heightened the amount of anger on the job. This has been argued, for example, in the case of American domestic servants, where a preindustrial sense of equality between mistress and neighbor/servant girl is contrasted with the more rigid, angry hierarchy that arose in the nineteenth century.[6] In the factories and artisan shops, new efforts to spur the pace of work, the tension and noise of unfamiliar equipment, the subjection of growing numbers of adult workers to the supervision of others, and the press of strangers who were colleagues at work could lower the flashpoint for outburst, on the part of workers and managers alike.[7] Here was one key source of the imagery that held work to be a source of tension, home a place of soothing contrast.[8]

It might be suggested that, at least in the Western cultural context, the kind of intense entrepreneurial drive that spurred new business bore some relationship to ready flashes of temper designed to daunt subordinates and enforce some personal space. As we will shortly see, a linkage of this sort, between anger and economic drive, was spelled out in the later nineteenth century. The relationship between anger, individual intensity, and the modern work personality merits further consideration in Western history. Well into the twentieth century, vigorous bosses reacted with unfeigned anger to what they viewed as worker insubordination, sometimes beyond the point of economic or political self-interest. An intensity-anger relationship may apply beyond the entrepreneurial level, as many workers, John Henry–like, learned to vent anger on material objects—still a distinctive anger outlet among

American males (but not females). Deeper probes into past work emotionality, in relationship to wider personality traits, remain desirable. But there were reasons, also, to restrain anger, in the industrial context; indeed the home/work dichotomy recognized the need for self-control at work amid provocations. Managers might need to conciliate vital workers, while factory hands in periodic oversupply might fear for their job if tempers were unleashed. The somewhat greater impersonality of nineteenth-century work, while it could provoke resentments, might also cushion them, as the intensity of traditional relationships, which mixed work hierarchy with co-residence and often involved family ties, lessened.

The impact of industrialization on emotionality at work is thus complex. Not all changes were sudden, in any event. A mood of considerable harmony, for example, pervaded the formal relations between employers and workers in the United States until after the Civil War.[9] Some of the changes that did occur, such as the reduction of personal intensity between owner and worker, may have reduced felt anger. Yet it is tempting to suggest that, at various points, changes in work life stimulated greater anger than had been normally experienced in more traditional work settings, and that much of the anger felt could not safely be expressed. Small wonder that many workers, tired as well as angry, found themselves carrying resentments home, to be taken out, almost against their will, on wives and children.

Yet explicit anger-control standards for work did not change with industrialization itself. Factory owners certainly identified "troublemakers" when they could, but as in previous centuries they were focusing on behavior more than emotional style. Businessmen, though often exposed to new anger control standards in child rearing, did not talk of anger—as opposed to tension, or nervousness—as a work issue. Foremen were given no overt instruction on managing anger, whether their own or their workers'. Indeed, while troublemaking was reproved, late-nineteenth-century United States employers in principle liked the idea of a certain amount of passion on the job, for the idea of channeling anger toward greater work zeal or competitiveness, rather than excising it, was widespread.[10] The channeling idea was a staple in Horatio Alger literature. Even as late as 1919, an industrial engineer could echo this convention, in claiming that scientific management allowed anger to be directed against things, instead of colleagues or supervisors: "Pugnacity is a great driving force. It is a wonderful thing that under Scientific Management this force is aroused not against one's fellow workers but against one's work."[11]

In the absence of explicit standards or efforts at emotional control, the evidence of frequent outbursts, during the nineteenth century, is widespread. Workers frequently quit in anger, or failed to show up for the job.[12] A foreman in a Chicago clothing sweatshop cuts the piece rate. Workers are loudly angry and threaten to leave. The foreman, angry in his turn, says, "Quit if you want to. You are welcome to quit." And five of them do, moving to other jobs until the foreman is replaced. From an employer vantage point, in 1864, many young workers are too quarrelsome and belligerent—with "too much mouth," often walking off "just because they get their back up."[13]

Workers undoubtedly felt more anger than they could safely express. Situations varied, as before; the foreman-worker relationship, particularly, was a crucial variable in nineteenth-century work, depending on the foreman's temperament, as well as on wide economic pressures. But what remains striking is the continuity, during industrialization's first century, of the substantial dependence of workplace emotionality on the personal factors. Anger, as opposed to behaviors that might follow from anger, was not an issue. Factory rules specified behaviors—punctuality, diligence, cleanliness, obedience—not emotions. Workers might bitterly react to a foreman's anger, but they articulated no general set of standards that would hold that such anger was inappropriate; their reactions were personal, ad hoc, and not infrequently the clashes with foremen were treated rather matter-of-factly, as problems to be handled rather than as emotional landmarks. Some foremen were unpleasant, some workers mouthed off, but these were individual occurrences, not issues to be approached through systematic emotional management. At times, one can indeed glimpse expressions of anger that were frankly enjoyed by their authors—particularly supervisors who used their position to chew out subordinates, including child workers, but also workers whose anger carried them into some gesture of defiance. And so, in a century when in the middle class the ideal of domestic anger control gained ground, work remained a setting exempt, bounded by personality and occasion, not by new standards or new guilts.

The one exception to this continuity of preindustrial inattention to work-based emotion—which expressed the fairly obvious primacy of more immediate concerns such as mastering a new technology—was domestic service, where work and home were firmly united. While the potential for anger in nineteenth-century service may have gone up,[14] given new ideas on the part of servants and new demands on the part of mistresses, it is equally interesting that the tension felt concerning anger rose as well. For servants' work was so intimately bound up with home that the growing desire for control of anger in the household, and the growing linkage of femininity with freedom from anger, had an inescapable bearing on work. The preindustrial reliance on emotional laissez-faire, bounded only by an effort to require obedience, no longer sufficed. Hence, as all the household manuals now recommended, mistresses should learn to control themselves. "There is nothing, which has a more abiding influence on the happiness of a family, than the preservation of equable and cheerful temper and tones in the housekeeper." And while a mistress cannot always be happy with her servant, she can "refrain from angry tones," knowing that calm reproof is more effective in winning obedience than a tongue-lashing is.[15] New standards of anger control did not produce a uniform conversion of the actual relationship of servant and mistress, but it is possible that, along with other factors, the tension generated between new standards and actual experience helped cause the declining use of live-in servants toward the end of the nineteenth century.

After 1900, what had already happened in domestic service, in the tentative development of new goals of emotional control, spread to the world of work outside the home, and probably with greater effect. It is this development that opened the clearest new chapter in the modern history of work-based emotionality.

Signs of a concern for the emotional characteristics of work life surfaced, somewhat ironically, with the Scientific Management movement shortly before 1920. Scientific management itself, of course, largely maintained the traditional neglect of explicit emotional standards. It was assumed that rational arrangements in the workplace would further reduce emotional tensions on the job, in part by curtailing the personal element of foreman-worker relations in favor of standardized regulation of both parties; there was no need to address emotions directly. But several of the movement's authors reflected an interesting discomfort with the anger they actually perceived in factories. Frederick Winslow Taylor, thrust onto the factory floor, from a conventional middle-class background, wrote revealingly of his shock at the individual surliness of some workers; this was no small spur to his hope for a "mental revolution" of employers and workers alike.[16] Still more significant were the reactions of Elton Mayo and his associates, in the famous General Electric Hawthorne plant experiments launched in 1927. Mayo's initial intent had been to carry through the early thrust of industrial psychology, in seeking correlations among work arrangements, fatigue or monotony, and worker aptitudes.[17] But he found himself unexpectedly drawn into concern with work-based anger, for he discovered a level of "irritability" that could not be ignored. From this, an emphasis on morale, defined as producing better cheer and less anger in the workplace, became a major focus of the personnel initiatives both at the Hawthorne works and elsewhere. Mayo, like Taylor a product of middle-class upbringing in which anger control was strongly emphasized as the basis for proper domestic life, explicitly wrote a personal unease with angry outbursts on the job—as he put it, the workplace equivalent of a nervous breakdown—into a program for work reform.[18]

Structural developments, as well as personal distastes, provoked the attempt to set explicit anger standards on the job from the 1920s onward. Increases in the use of women workers, during World War I and again from

1940 onward, provoked new concern about anger, as some employers found or claimed to find that a gruffness habitual with men reduced women to tears. Certainly, real or imagined problems with adapting workplace emotionality to the advent of women helped motivate appeals to personnel experts for help, while the longstanding image of an anger-free femininity encouraged reappraisals of job standards when women were involved. Still more fundamental were changes in marketing and in corporate structure. The American economy began to emphasize mass consumerism, with intense competition for sales among retail outlets. A new concern for cheerful salespeople, careful to avoid provocation of vital customers, was a logical product of this transition to new retailing forms. The American economy began to emphasize larger, more impersonal management hierarchies, with a simultaneous new interest in setting standards for anger as part of bureaucratization. The surge of often violent labor protest, from the late nineteenth century onward, inevitably created a new search for more effective mechanisms of social control. Personnel psychology and experiments toward greater harmony sprang up during World War I and with schemes like Henry Ford's Americanization program, and the slightly later growth of attention to emotional control on the job was in part an extension of these initiatives.[19]

The dictates, then, of new competition for consumers, the smooth functioning of corporate bureaucracy, and reduction of class conflict at work all suggested growing attention to the articulation and enforcement of anger control standards. But these large forces must be seen in the more personal context of individuals, such as Mayo, grappling with the uncomfortable dichotomy between emotional criteria at work and those at home, which gave the anger control campaign the shape and intensity that it developed from the 1920s onward. Anger control in this sense was no mere inevitability of advanced social engineering—indeed, it is possible that some strategies were in fact wasteful and distracting to sheer productive effort; it was an attempt to close a real, personal tension that had widened over the previous century, as home discipline and imagery contrasted with the emotional unpredictability of work. Prior emotional standards that urged the incompatibility of anger with good character, though not previously tailored to work, combined with shifts in economic organization to produce an explicit emotionology for the job. Indeed, the concern employers themselves felt at their own anger in response to new unionization may well have entered into the quest for general emotional controls.

And the goal was, without equivocation, a limitation of anger expressed and, as time went on, even felt as part of the work experience. Mayo and his industrial psychologist colleagues produced a clear set of standards in this regard; so did the authors of new manuals for sales work, including Dale Carnegie. From the industrial psychologists: work itself did not generate legitimate anger, but rather served as a target for emotion derived from other sources, particularly domestic situations and unhappy childhoods. Angry workers were "projecting their own maladjustments upon a conjured monster, the capitalists."[20] "It is known that complaints, very often, have nothing to do with the matter complained about."[21] To a point, of course, this was merely translating into the emotional field some commonplaces about the ill-breeding of workers and the blamelessness of industry, though it reversed older images of the home/work dichotomy in making work, now, the place at which emotional smoothness could be expected. But the commonplace had interesting consequences. First, since anger could not really be serious, it could be readily talked away. "Sometimes a worker just bursting with rage at the 'unfairness' of her foreman is able to proceed normally with her work after expressing her feeling . . . and receiving a few words of sympathy or explanation."[22] Workers could easily be embarrassed by their anger, and if forced to repeat their grievance would frequently apologize for having come on so strong. Venting could thus replace serious emotional reaction, or real reform. Further, anger control must be mutual, not merely an imposition on the labor force. Hierarchy could no longer excuse emotional display, and the appropriate emotional standards should cut across the board—just as, in the middle-class home, parental self-control was at least as important as restraint on the part of the child. "Bullying begets bullying,"[23] and in fact the clearest impact of the new emotionology of work was directed at middle-level supervisors, not ordinary workers.

From the sales experts: Customers are not rational, but the salesman must control himself all the more in consequence, absorbing unfairness with a cheerful smile. Dale Carnegie confronts an insulting customer: "By apologizing and sympathizing with her point of view . . . I had the satisfaction of controlling my temper, the satisfaction of returning kindness for an insult. I got infinitely more real fun out of making her like me than I ever could have gotten out of letting her go and take a jump."[24] As on the factory floor, one's own mood becomes irrelevant; the task is to soften up the other guy, the one with the temper out of control.[25] For anger at work is ugly, counterproductive, and unnecessary: "The angry man may himself be the chief victim of his emotion. It incapacitates him from dealing with his problems in a corrective way."[26]

This message spread widely in the 1920s and 1930s. The growing popularity of handbooks such as Dale Carnegie's was matched by the proliferation of personnel officers, armed with a nascent professional literature, one of whose chief charges was the promotion of emotional harmony on the job. The dynamics of twentieth-century bureaucratization and expertise combined with a felt need for codes that would produce a clearer and more consistent emotional climate. Even staid manuals on clerical behavior picked up the theme. Secretarial training books, which before the 1920s had emphasized trustworthiness and responsibility as the key personal characteristics, now turned to temper control. The good clerk would smilingly confront an angry boss, and anyone with a quick temper was "faced with the problem of remedying these defects." "The secretary should never forget that *in order to please people, he needs to exert himself.*"[27] With rare and hesitant exceptions, anger and work did not mix.

The new anger-control campaign went well beyond propaganda. It informed a number of personnel initiatives that took shape from the late 1920s to the 1950s. Indeed, the ability to institutionalize the emotionological distaste for anger differentiated the workplace from the family, where equally strong ideals were harder to put into daily practice. Americans, at least in the middle classes, had long worked on anger through ideas about religion and family, where implementation depended mainly on character formation and personal restraint. Spurred by organizational imperatives above all, but also by a belief that there were ways now to assure that work became a domain of rationality, an emotion viewed as personally and socially undesirable was attacked directly. While control of factory labor continued to spur this effort, it soon became apparent that middle- and lower-middle-class employees were the principal targets, because of their centrality to service occupations and management structures and because class values insisted on emotional conformity.

The spread of industrial relations departments in American business during the 1930s, when 31 percent of all companies maintained such services, and then the further surge during World War II under the sponsorship of the War Industries Board, provided an increasing number of experts eager to undertake the task of defusing workplace anger. The extension of personnel testing also related to the growing concern for the emotional environment at work. Tests for emotional characteristics, including temper control, loomed large, as the range of testing spread out from sheer aptitude assessment. Doncaster Humm, one of the authors of a widely used test to screen troublemakers in the early 1940s, proclaimed that 80 percent of all problem workers had testable deficiencies in temperament, with only 20 percent assigned to jobs inappropriate for their aptitudes.[28]

Still more focused efforts to reshape workplace emotionality, and not merely preach about it, came with the expansion of counseling as an outgrowth of more general industrial relations efforts and the professionalization of personnel experts. These services were expressly designed to provide emotionally cool experts who would intervene between foreman and worker and allow anger to be talked away. A woman janitorial worker in Chicago was caught frequently sleeping on the job, but so abused the supervisor who challenged her, by swearing and showing great anger, that he became afraid to direct her at all. Enter Counseling. The worker poured out her dislike for her present job, her belief that she deserved better; the counselor listened patiently, waiting for her tirade to subside. Calmed, the custodian agreed to work better and admitted that her job was not so bad. And the counselor reminded the foreman to show more tact.[29] Emotional management, not attention to objective conditions, was the key to successful counseling: "You look silly having a temper tantrum at your age."[30] Counselors were meant to be the living embodiment of the belief that anger had no place at work and was usually irrelevant to real work issues. And they were to be role models, willing to listen but without commitment. In what might have served as a slogan for the new emotional style being sought at work, the counselor was to be "impersonal, but friendly."[31]

Counseling services were used not only in cases of outbursts, but in situations where strong emotion might be generated. Counselors often participated in job interviews, in part to judge a candidate's temper control. Interestingly, an initial impulse to use such interviews deliberately to promote anxiety among applicants, as a means of probing character, gave way to a desire for calm: surface cheer should begin at a worker's beginning. Exit interviews also gained in popularity, partly to determine why a valued worker was leaving, in order to identify remediable conditions for the future, but also in part to alter the level of grievance of the departing worker: no one should go away mad.[32]

Even more revealing of the new desire to reshape work-based emotionality was the spread of supervisor retraining in the 1940s and 1950s. Foremen and other on-the-spot managers were to learn new ways of avoiding confrontation, manipulating "surly" workers, and above all controlling themselves.[33] Training courses mushroomed in American companies from wartime efforts onward, with a central emphasis on reshaping authoritarian styles. Foremen were schooled to stop pressing workers so hard, to aid them with problems and allow them to air their feelings before any serious anger could become entrenched. For the foreman's role was being recast. He was no longer, primarily, a technical expert, for these guidelines came from the engineers; rather, he was a human relations manager charged with minimizing frictions and preventing disputes from troubling his supervisors. Some companies made a concerted effort to select genial foremen through personality testing—"is a disappointment more likely to make you angry than sad?"[34]—but even greater hopes were pinned on an ability to reshape existing staff, as the basis for creating a workplace low on grievance and high on harmony. Retraining courses bombarded foremen with examples of the bad old days—foremen who shouted, ignored worker emotions, ridiculed employees in front of others. They provided correct methods of dealing with complaints or mistakes. They introduced role playing, so that foremen would learn the emotions of an angry worker in order to avoid answering in kind. The message was: worker anger, though often unreasonable and unprovoked, was not entirely avoidable. Foreman anger *was* avoidable, part of emotional middle classness, and this, rather than some magic conversion of the entire work force, was the key to the proper emotional atmosphere on the job. Foremen were told the findings of industrial psychologists, that workers asked to repeat complaints three or four times could be made not only to cool off, but to feel silly, often dropping the whole matter.[35] And even where a grievance required some action, the emotional undercurrents could be staunched through the foreman's own self-control: "It is of the utmost importance that the foreman remain cool." "He is sensitive to the feelings of others and exercises restraint in expressing his own."[36]

Retraining, to be sure, was often cursory, even when it carried the standard anger-control message. But exposure to the new goals of emotional management did reach tens of thousands of supervisors in manufacturing firms, banks, and insurance companies, through literally hundreds of retraining programs. And supervisors themselves were apparently eager to learn more about the new approach. A 1944 survey claimed that 80 percent of all foremen wanted some new human relations training.[37] While the intense focus on retraining cooled somewhat after the 1950s, this resulted not from a shift in emotionological goals but from a belief that the old authoritarian syndrome had been penetrated. Supervisors still had to be prepared—the 1960s saw a faddish fascination with the concept of "consideration," designed to connote a surface openness to the worker problems as well as emotional control—but they no longer had to be remade.

The movement to control the emotional context at work spread upward in the managerial hierarchy, in a final guidance program that began in the 1950s and rose to a peak of popularity in the following decade. T-groups, or sensitivity training groups, maintained the basic message of a need for attention to people, and not just production levels. But these group sessions, held typically in more luxurious, tax-deductible surroundings than mere retraining sessions, aimed at younger middle managers with promotion potential. Their focus was on emotion-free communication and on compromise rather than conflict when values or policies were in dispute. Groups met for several days or even weeks, discussing problems in emotional control encountered in past experience and engaging in role playing designed to simulate stressful exchanges within a management hierarchy. T-group participants were in part self-selected, so that angry personalities would not disrupt proceedings. Authoritarian management styles were roundly criticized, as insensitive executives were held to be counterproductive. A key lesson involved learning not to retaliate to hostility but rather to stress the development of more "tender" emotions. The contrived quality of T-group confrontations permitted participants to experience tension without carrying over into outright hostility. The overriding goal was, again, self-control, which in turn would promote rational reactions in others: "Effectiveness decreases as emotionality increases."[38]

T-groups thus embodied most of the anger-control goals that had informed earlier counseling and retraining programs. The purposes were presented tactfully, as managers at this level had to be coaxed, not ordered. And T-groups also showed some characteristic confusion over the emotional climate being sought. On the one hand, the modern executive was urged to become more sensitive to others' feelings, and to let emotions emerge more openly than before lest they fester. On the other hand, there was a strong impulse toward rational oversight of all emotions, and without question the hints at greater emotional freedom were not meant to encompass anger. Greater emotional tolerance was indeed expressly designed to inhibit serious or durable anger. The "real feelings" that sensitive executives might learn to respect were artificially defined to exclude this one basic emotion.[39] And so, while emotional repression was a bad word in T-group circles, precisely such repression was intended where anger was concerned. For T-group members had to go home friends—hopefully, indeed, friendlier than before, and aware that anger was always inappropriate and embarrassing. Emotions were thus basically controllable, and T-groups were designed to promote harmonious feelings useful to the corporate environment and to discourage others: "The rationality of feelings and attitudes is as crucial as that of the mind."[40] Anger, in other words, need not apply. A key hope was that by reducing anger as a weapon in the executive hierarchy—cutting down the table pounding of bosses, the hidden resentments of subordinates—communications would become more open and creative.[41]

More than the earlier efforts to control anger at work, the T-group sessions displayed a revealing confusion about emotions and emotional experience, though a confusion that may have been effective in restyling the executive workplace. With foremen and workers, attention had focused on controlling anger, not in commenting on a larger emotional experience. With the T-groups, and to an extent in the wider American society by the 1960s, anger control goals were maintained but concealed under massive verbiage about openness and spontaneity. At the least, this constituted a heightened effort to distinguish between anger and other, acceptable, emotions, while avoiding direct reference to repression. At most, it was an effort not only to hold anger down but to trivialize workplace emotions generally under a glad-handing guise. While T-group leaders urged participants to get in touch with feelings, as against the sterile constraints of the past, they tended toward fairly superficial emotional exchange; anger was out of place in this context—though because repression was now condemned it was attacked through avoidance—not only because it was disruptive but because it could run deep.

With the decline of the T-group fad, in the later 1960s, the missionary tone of the new emotionology of work came to an end. But this betokened not a shift in goals, but a sense that the need to undo a prior emotional style had passed. Stark recommendations of temper control yielded to more positive, and vaguer, recommendations for consideration and empathy, not because temper control became less important but rather because it was now simply assumed.[42] References to the disruptive effects of anger on problem solving were now made in passing; they did not need to be belabored. Euphemisms such as "inoffensive communications techniques" indeed sought to avoid direct reference to tabooed words such as *temper* or *anger* altogether.[43] But new white-collar employees were certainly told to shun anger, often with dire warnings about anger's impact on health. And in 1970s discussions of assertiveness training anger was still noted, lest forcefulness somehow be confused with flashes of temper; careful distinctions were drawn, and the supervisor who learned assertiveness was also supposed to work on his or her skills of empathy to worker problems, surface friendliness, and the like. A need to learn or relearn some decisiveness was not, then, to imply a new openness to anger.[44]

The decades after the 1920s thus saw the generation and elaborate implementation of new emotional standards for work, focusing on the need to control one's own anger and defuse it in others. Widely popular, and often fairly costly, institutions were established to promote and enforce these same emotional goals. The new emotionology, and its supportive apparatus, aimed particularly at the growing white-collar sector: sales personnel, secretaries, foremen, and middle managers. Interest in controlling the anger of blue-collar workers persisted, but, partly because of residual beliefs in the personality inferiority of this group, attention riveted less on remaking emotions than on managing their expression. Hence the idea that supervisors learn to tolerate worker grievances "even when they are silly."[45] White-collar workers, however, were held to a much stricter emotional ideal, and if this involved change from past standards, then change had to come: "control your emotions—control your remarks—control your behavior."[46] Not only foremen but also go-getter salesmen were urged to learn a new emphasis on courtesy and extrovert friendliness, instead of high-pressure tactics.[47]

Indeed the spread of anger-control standards is above all associated with the rise of white-collar work and the felt need to find internalizable methods of discipline for this growing sector, so that employees would behave properly without constant supervision. Top executives, however, were not so clearly embraced by the new standards. Some openly insisted on a standard of self-control from secretaries that they had no intention of adopting themselves. Others eagerly sent subordinates to retraining sessions or T-groups that they had no interest in attending themselves. And even in theory, some ambiguity remained about the significance, even the desirability, of anger control at the hierarchy's summit. A 1950s survey of management traits thus revealed top managers eager to be pleasant but in a fairly generalized way, whereas middle managers made a particular point of their patience and temper control.[48] Personnel authorities sometimes ruefully had to admit that aggressive executives could still win success, even as their subordinates had learned more temper control.[49]

The exceptions granted to top executives posed some interesting tensions for the anger-control movement at other levels, translating to the corporate environment some of the older inequalities of emotional freedom at work. But the intense campaign directed at the larger white-collar sector involved more than easing the path of a bullying boss. It represented an unprecedented identification of proper and inappropriate emotional styles at work; it represented, also, a substantial modification of the identification of hierarchy with rights to anger, since the middle rather than the lower group was now particularly constrained. In theory, at least, the campaign to manipulate emotional styles at work did for white-collar workers what constraints to a new pace and new sense of time had done for factory operatives a century before, in reshaping key personal habits and responses to the real or presumed needs of a modern workplace.

The new anger emotionology, implemented as well as preached, constituted a vital innovation in the context of twentieth-century work. Did it bring real emotional change as well? We have already noted a key case in which anger-control recommendations and actual performance diverged, at least in part, in the often stormy history of nineteenth-century domestic service. New standards did provoke new guilt, which may have entered into the declining popularity of live-in service, but they hardly engendered literal adherence. Given the impossibility of precisely measuring felt or even subtly expressed anger on the job, either before or after the advent of the anger-control campaign, and given the additional admission of a variety of emotional experiences at work prior to the twentieth century, depending among other things on personality, is there any way to assess the impact of the new standards?

Unquestionably some people exposed to the contemporary emotionology rejected it, sometimes publicly and often in private. As the anger-control campaign took hold, subordinates did not always take kindly to the idea of restraining their response to provocation. A secretary misses a job opportunity when she protests the ground rules, saying to her prospective boss,

"Well, if you are snappy without cause, I'll certainly say something back."[50] Superiors did not always see the need to attend to their charges' tender feelings. One Hawthorne supervisor, after hearing a group of experts explain how fear of fathers could lead workers to hate their foremen, simply observed: "Well, even if it is true, what of it? I still have to direct these birds." More generally, a 1976 survey revealed that 30 percent of all worker grievances derived from harsh, arbitrary supervision. The fact that the line supervisors, as opposed to assignment foremen, were handling more workers than ever before may well have nullified many retraining efforts as far as the most direct treatment of blue-collar workers was concerned, in that some foremen felt too harried to restrain themselves emotionally.[51]

On the other hand, without claiming uniform self-control, it is suggestive that there were no sweeping objections to the new emotionology or expressions of great anguish at goals unfulfilled. Work, already judged an area of rationality, did not produce the kind of literature documenting painful gaps between standards and reality that the effort to reduce anger within families engendered, at various points from the 1750s onward. Studs Terkel's interviews produce an awareness of the need for emotional restraint at work, and pride in moving to this goal, that more directly suggest at least a partial shift in actual emotional experience paralleling the more explicit change in standards. A phone operator discusses the need for "a nice sounding voice. You can't be angry. . . . You always have to be pleasant—no matter how bad you feel." A gas station operator, admitting occasional loss of temper as a "red-blooded American," has learned that customers want a restrained attendant, which he tries to be. A bank teller, also aggravated by customers, knows how to bottle up his anger: "You can't say anything back. The customer is always right." While some younger workers express resentment at the emotional requirements of their jobs, older workers take greater pride in their cool-headedness, if only to avoid giving the bosses another weapon against them. And some middle managers show a still greater internalization of the anger-control goals, like the foreman who deplores the variable moods of his workers not because of direct impact on production, but because of the distance from his cheerful ideal: "If we could get everybody to feel great. . . ."[52] Finally, though less surprisingly, there is evidence that workers have themselves picked up the new emotional standards, heightening or at least formalizing their earlier interest in fair-minded supervision by citing the ideal of restrained, empathic foremen.[53] It was revealing that "cool-headed" became a phrase commonly used in discussing supervisor ratings from the 1950s onward, along with favorable remarks on foremen who knew their "psychology." Thus, inherently impressionistic comparisons of worker comments about their jobs, and their expectations of others, suggest that the new emotionology produced, after the 1950s, a greater awareness of the need for anger control, greater insistence on this control by colleagues and superiors, and in some cases a real desire to make the proper emotional atmosphere at work a high priority. This is not to argue that there was no awareness of anger restraint before the new emotionology, or that restraint is uniformly practiced even in the white-collar sector; and the evidence suggests some division between those who found restraint natural and desirable, and those who practiced it at a cost—a point to which we must return. But the signs of change are present, which is hardly surprising given the vigor with which the new standards have been disseminated.

Studies by outsiders not wedded to the often self-fulfilling paradigms of industrial psychology again confirm the idea of a change in the emotional experience of work, at least since the 1950s. From C. Wright Mills's evaluation of white-collar stress, which involved considerable articulation of the tensions of restraining anger in dealing with subordinates as well as superiors, to Arlie Hochschild's recent evaluation of the pressures toward emotional conformity as part of the training of flight attendants and other service personnel, the theme of emotional manipulation has recurred as part of the assessment of modern work forms. Again, this does not conclusively prove that the manipulation has reached new levels—after all, low-status workers such as servants were undoubtedly pressed to restrain emotional expression in the past, albeit without such explicit rules about what they should feel as opposed to how they should behave; but the consistency of the outsider perceptions is suggestive.[54]

Workers themselves note a change at times. From an older line worker: "You want to know somethin' the younger workers don't even know how to take the crap we took."[55] Despite continued grievances, traditional manifestations of angry clashes with superiors, such as voluntary job changing and absenteeism, have definitely and steadily declined since the 1920–1940 decades, by over 300 percent by the 1970s. While many factors are involved in this trend, including the aging and settling of the work force, it does suggest a reduction in the unrestrained expression of anger—some indication that the encouragement to emotional control plus the provision of counseling services and grievance procedures have affected the emotional experience of work. Most workers—72 percent in one study—claimed to get along well or pretty well with their foremen and based their judgment primarily on the foreman's personality and temperament, rather than fairness or technical competence.[56] Employer valuation of anger restraint as a personal trait among sales and supervisory groups has become steadily more articulate, as reflected in the fact that supervisory personnel themselves have come to rate self-control high, aggression and initiative low among the traits they value and believe are valued by their employers.[57] Middle-level managers in the trade union movement also began to place greater premium on emotional control, in contrast to the give-'em-hell style popular among the older generation. And in business and government some subordinates began to complain, by the 1960s and 1970s, that their employers seemed so worried about doing psychological damage to others and maintaining a friendly reputation that they failed to push through clear policy directives; this was a problem cited particularly on the part of T-group products. A survey of California state agency employees suggested that employers had become so reluctant to criticize that they were no longer able to guide subordinates to improved performance.[58]

Thus the evidence accumulates that real emotional expression has altered in the directions of the new emotionology, though of course incompletely and with considerable possibilities of self-delusion as workers or managers claim a temper control which they fail to exercise in practice. The shift in expressed anger at work predictably lagged a few decades behind the introduction of the new standards; while there is some evidence of adjustment by sales personnel to heightened anger restraint before World War II,[59] for most categories serious indications of change, as opposed to variations resulting from personality differences, emerge only from the 1950s onward. Despite the lag, the change was in many ways rather rapid, as the roughest emotional edges at work came under some control within a few decades and the most stereotyped traditional targets of the control campaign, such as the bullying foreman, dropped from sight in the hortatory literature. Rapidity of change resulted from the fact previous anger control norms had already spread widely in child rearing and family life, so that their extension to work was no total innovation, and from the fact that business leaders threw considerable resources and institutional imagination toward implementing the standards within the world of work. We lack, of course, clear historical models for discussing rates of emotional change, but it seems reasonable to speculate that the shift in the stance toward anger at work ranks among the speedier transitions on record.

The reduction of anger at work, in terms of new standards and some parallel change in emotional expression, raises two final, related issues: How widespread has the impact of this change been, and how stressful has it been in terms of the overall experience of individual workers? Both these issues can only be evoked in the context of a single essay, but both are vital components of a fuller effort to deal with twentieth-century changes in American emotional life.

The difficulty of pinning down or measuring actual emotional change at work, as opposed to the clear emotionological shift, is of course compounded when one seeks to extend a discussion of impact. The marked per capita decline not only of the trade union movement but also of the strike rate in the United States since the 1950s[60] might relate to the effort to discourage anger (and possibly, of course, to a genuine resultant improvement in workplace atmosphere). Of course a multitude of factors are involved in the demonstrable decline of work-based protest, including rising living standards, geographical (and so political) population shifts, and new levels and sources of immigration. But some of the factors commonly cited as contributing to the change, such as the rise of the service sector and the increased feminization of the labor force, in fact relate to the alteration in emotional criteria workers of various types apply to their own job behavior. The simple fact is that work-based protest rates have gone down precisely in the same decades that many workers seemed to be internalizing the message that anger at work was childish and inappropriate. Possible correlation is not proof, but it is conceivable that the new emotional standards have contributed to some sweeping changes in worker behavior—and that the anger-control campaign, as a manipulation of the emotional bases for protest action, has been highly successful. Observers such as Barrington Moore have noted a decline in the expression of "moral indignation" in contemporary United States society, and there may be a direct emotional factor in this decline.[61]

Fascinating also, in terms of extended impact, is the apparent relationship between the efforts at emotional control on the job and a new stage of anger management in child rearing. Deliberate anger restraint had entered the vocabulary of child rearing by the later eighteenth century; in this sense there was no need to accommodate basic strategies to the new work emphasis. But in the later nineteenth century an ambivalence remained, in the sense that child rearing was intended to prevent domestic expressions of anger but not to eliminate the emotion as a spur to adult vitality. Hence middle-class American boys were trained to avoid anger in the home but to retain it, through displacement activities such as amateur boxing, in neighborhood life.[62] This ambivalence, still expressed in the first edition of Dr. Spock, where the utility of anger as a goad to competitive business behavior was specifically noted, began to yield in the 1950s, particularly in corporate management and white-collar families.[63] Parents were advised, and to some extent attempted in practice, to let children talk away any anger not because the emotion was useful or desirable, but because its quick, harmless venting was a vital means of preventing the development of angry personalities. In other words, child-rearing norms began to replicate the same management devices already introduced in the workplace. Anger was bad, but insofar as it could not be prevented, as in workers or children, it should be talked away without result. Dr. Spock, in reproducing this approach in his later editions, revealingly altered his anticipated career futures, from competitive businessmen and farmers to harmonious salesmen and managers.[64]

In other words, the evolution in workplace anger may be a key ingredient in larger changes in American life, in areas as seemingly diverse as protest behavior and personality formation. The point is by no means proved, thought it has been noted in several of the attempts coherently to discuss the directions of emotional change in the twentieth century,[65] but it remains tantalizingly open to further exploration. Indeed changes in emotional needs resulting from new work structures may be the key to wider personality change in recent United States history. Given the novelty of dealing with emotion as an artifact of history, it is impossible yet to know the ramifications of significant shifts, but they may be considerable indeed.

For if anger at work, newly channeled, may have borne some relationship to the personality type successful in nineteenth-century business, so the development of explicit anger control may constitute a decisive shift away from this version, toward a more group-oriented personality structure possibly no less functional, but responding to a much-altered context. The relationship between this kind of emotional control and bureaucratization deserves further emphasis. It is noteworthy that current Western anger standards have moved far closer to those of East Asia, where culture far earlier underwrote a bureaucracy, than was the case even a century ago; continuing differences reflect mainly the novelty of the current Western patterns, as against the more traditional Confucian insistence on careful controls. Thus Americans rank close to Chinese in their distaste for anger as an emotional experience, differing only in their particular zeal to conceal the emotion.[66]

In America, the transformation of the emotionology of anger at work invites consideration in terms of gender, as well as the impact of bureaucratization and the service economy. We have noted the relationship between real and imagined experiences with female personnel in the formation of new anger-control standards at work. The new standards themselves represented, in terms of nineteenth-century ideals, a feminization of workplace emotionality, extending to men the desiderata previously applied to a distinctively feminine personality. Discussions of androgyny, since the early 1970s, have implicitly picked up this point, in arguing for a "liberation" of men from macho anger and aggressiveness. Though the male liberationist attacks on mainstream masculinity bear more on the past than on the present, they feed what is in fact a widespread effort to merge gender ideals of anger on a feminine model, using the workplace as a fulcrum. The coincidence of changes in emotional standards and in the gender balance at work, especially of course in the service sector, fits the wide-ranging implications of the new approach to anger, for women may have prompted wider changes in the general experience of work than is commonly realized.[67]

Evaluation of the campaign to control anger at work must also confront a fascinating dilemma regarding the quality of results. Elements of the campaign are unquestionably distasteful. Workers at various levels have been encouraged to become emotionally more passive on the job. Attention has been lavished on control of the emotional environment that might more fruitfully have been devoted to greater productivity or more coherent protest or both. Some of the loopholes in the control campaign are troubling. The continued tolerance for aggressive personalities at the top of the work hierarchy concurrent with the deliberate effort to encourage embarrassment at anger in middle management belied some of the egalitarian implications (in gender and social class alike) of the anger-control rhetoric. Workers and owners differed in their appraisal of social skills, with the result that executives frequently vacillated in style, opting for temper control as an ideal but yielding to outbursts when the going got rough.[68] Yet anger control was not mere facade. Radical as well as establishment observers have noted a democratization on the job floor, a humanization of personal relations at work if only at the level of surface friendliness.[69] Despite a temptation to blast anger control as the most recent capitalist manipulative device, the benign side cannot be ignored.

But the chief issue, in viewing new work emotionality as part of a larger emotional history, lies in trying to assess the strain that the new standards produced. Particularly if anger control lies at the base of a substantial change in the paradigmatic modern personality, a substantial shift also in characteristic male work style, the question of its side effects looms large. Has change come smoothly, as part of a wider social evolution, or has it been force-fed? C. Wright Mills introduced the concept of "self-alienation" to describe the stress which pressures for conformity, including emotional conformity, produced in white-collar workers. A bureaucrat describes his own emotional dilemma: "You have to keep peace with people at all levels. Sometimes I get home worn to a frazzle over all this."[70] Arlie Hochschild has described (without, however, very clearly documenting) the strains which emotionally managed workers bring from work to personal life, as the injunction to smile no matter what one's real feelings confuses the ability to identify real emotional needs and relationships off the job.[71] Workers, in other words, feel far more anger than they are able to express, not an entirely new dilemma but one which has been exacerbated with the new standards of control and their spread to managerial as well as subordinate ranks. Certainly, the sources of anger at work, both new and old, have hardly disappeared in the later twentieth century, in the form of technological displacements, mobility frustrations, monotony, and personal slights; to the extent that anger becomes more difficult to express, even to admit, than before, the student of emotion logically looks for signs of confusion, and a search for alternative outlets, including the family. One target may be the self, as workers are encouraged to believe that problems, including perceived anger, are their own fault, not legitimately attributable to, or emotionally directable at, other sources.[72] But the attack on workplace anger may also relieve strain for some. It has reduced the putative emotional dichotomy between work and home, modifying the need to shift from aggressive to agreeable as one commutes back to the family. How much this greater theoretical consistency is real, in terms of individual emotional experience, is another subject demanding historically informed inquiry.

The organization of work moved, during the ongoing course of industrialization, from an emphasis on the physical rearrangement of workers and their movements, to concomitant attempts to regulate emotional behavior on the job. Anger, once ignored or even found useful, became the subject of direct attack, with some demonstrable impact on the personal relations and self-perceptions of workers at various levels. The campaign continues, even as the pioneering, retraining phase has ended. Service workers may be warned not only that displays of anger are inappropriate, but that the very experience of the emotion is physically as well as psychically damaging—in a society where health has replaced morality as the touchstone of character. Choleric personalities, once seen as a competitive spice, are now reminded of their mortality, as "cool" joins rational in the recommended work style.[73] The results of the new effort to manage anger are not entirely clear, on the job and most certainly in wider realms of social and individual life, but they may be considerable.

The sweeping change in the emotional standards of work, forming a crucial shift in the direction of a basic emotion, serves as a springboard toward further inquiry in contemporary emotionality understood, historically, as an evolving experience.

Notes

This article is based on data also discussed in sections of Carol Z. Stearns and Peter N. Stearns, *Anger: The Struggle for Emotional Control in America's History* (Chicago, 1986), but with additional reference to several theories of modern personality and other further interpretation.

1. Although twentieth-century work history has received less attention than its nineteenth-century counterpart, several exemplary studies deal with the framework of change within which new emotional guidelines took shape: David Montgomery, *Workers' Control in America: Studies in the History of Work, Technology and Labor Struggles* (Cambridge, 1979); Loren Baritz, *The Servants of Power: A History of the Use of Social Science in American History* (Middletown, Conn., 1960); Susan Porter Benson, *Counter Culture: Saleswomen, Managers and Customers in American Department Stores, 1890–1940* (Urbana, Ill., 1986).

2. For the nostalgic view, Peter Laslett, *The World We Have Lost: England before the Industrial Age* (New York, 1971). For greater realism, Benjamin Franklin, *Autobiography* (New York, 1962), p. 30; see also Stephen Innes, *Labor in a New Land: Economy and Society in Seventeenth-Century Springfield* (Princeton, 1983), pp. 119, 140–48.

3. J. L. Flandrin, *Families in Former Times* (Cambridge, Eng., 1976); Sarah Maza, *Servants and Masters in Eighteenth-Century France* (Princeton, 1983).

4. Laslett, *World We Have Lost*, passim.

5. Philip J. Greven, Jr., *The Protestant Temperament: Patterns of Child-Rearing, Religious Experience and the Self in Early America* (New York, 1977), pp. 111–19; Randolph Trumbach, *The Rise of the Egalitarian Family* (New York, 1978); Flandrin, *Families in Former Times*.

6. Faye E. Dudden, *Serving Women: Household Service in Nineteenth-Century America* (Middletown, Conn., 1983).

7. This was a common theme in worker comment around 1900, at least in Europe; see Adolf Levenstein, *Die Arbeiterfrage* (Munich, 1913) and *Aus der Tiefe, Arbeiterbriefe* (Munich, 1914), passim; also Peter N. Stearns, *Lives of Labor* (New York, 1977), chapter 7.

8. Charlotte Perkins Gilman, *The House, Its Work and Influence* (New York, 1903); Marian Harland, *Eve's Daughter, or Common Sense for Maid, Wife and Mother* (New York, 1882).

9. David Grimsted, "Antebellum Labor Agitation: Violence, Strike and Communal Arbitration," *Journal of Social History* 19 (1985): 1–22.

10. John Foster, *Essays: On Decision of Character* (London, 1982), pp. 67ff. Of course, some industrial-age employers extended serious concern for workers' moral behavior. When this combined with attention to proper discipline, the result could extend—at least in theory—controls over angry behavior beyond the most blatant forms of troublemaking. Thus some railroad concerns sought to control fighting among their workers and gave instructions to foremen on how to settle disputes. And railroads were also concerned about civil behavior to passengers. Still, instruction manuals for workers and supervisors, though sometimes in these cases going beyond material discipline and technical matters, avoid specific comment on emotional style. It may be that growing industrial experience and moral supervisory discipline did gradually alter or affect worker expressions of anger on the job—curtailing fighting, for example, just as on-the-job drinking was gradually reduced. But this aspect of the disciplinary process has not been seriously studied and in any event is at some remove from explicit emotional control. Walter Licht, *Working for the Railroad: The Organization of Work in the Nineteenth Century* (Princeton, 1983), pp. 100–106.

11. L. S. Gilbreth, *The Psychology of Management* (New York, 1919), p. 259.

12. On the emotionality of worker protest, Michelle Perrot, *Les Ouvriers en grève: France, 1871–1890*, 2 vols. (Hawthorne, N.Y., 1974); Stephen Meyer, *The Five Dollar Day: Labor Management and Social Control in the Ford Motor Company, 1908–1921* (Albany, 1981).

13. Daniel J. Elazar, ed. "Working Conditions in the Early Twentieth Century: Testimony," *American Jewish Archives* 21 (1969): 163; L. G. Lindahl, "Discipline

100 Years Ago," *Personnel Journal* 28 (1949): 246. See also Tamara K. Hareven and Randolph Langenbach, *Amoskeag, Life in an American Factory City* (New York, 1978), p. 352.

14. David M. Katzman, *Seven Days A Week: Women and Domestic Service in Industrializing America* (New York, 1978); Daniel E. Sutherland, *Americans and Their Servants: Domestic Service in the United States from 1800 to 1920* (Baton Rouge, La., 1981); see also Leonore Davidoff and Ruth Hawthorn, *A Day in the Life of a Victorian Domestic Servant* (Winchester, Mass., 1976); Theresa McBride, *The Domestic Revolution: The Modernization of Household Service in England and France 1820–1920* (New York, 1976).

15. Catharine E. Beecher, *Treatise on Domestic Economy* (Boston, 1841; repr. 1970), pp. 122, 134, 139–40.

16. Robert F. Hoxie, *Scientific Management and Labor* (1915; repr., New York, 1966) August M. Kelley; *Shop Management* (New York, 1911); Frederick W. Taylor, *The Principles of Scientific Management* (New York, 1911); Judith A. Merkle, *Management and Ideology: The Legacy of the International Scientific Management Movement* (Berkeley and Los Angeles, 1980).

17. Early industrial psychologists like Hugo Münsterberg, in claiming to be able to improve worker selection, did discuss "secondary traits" such as belligerence, but their primary concern was with intelligence and other measurable aptitudes. The rise of industrial psychology thus facilitated but did not fully determine the ultimate concern with work emotions. Hugo Münsterberg, *Psychology and Industrial Efficiency* (Boston, 1913), pp. 128, 205; Mary Smith, *Handbook of Industrial Psychology* (New York, 1944); David Nelson, *Management and Workers: Origins of the New Factory System in the United States, 1880–1920* (Madison, Wis., 1975), p. 37.

18. Elton Mayo, *The Human Problems of an Industrial Civilization* (New York, 1933), pp. 84ff.; F. J. Roethisberger and William J. Dickson, *Management and the Worker* (Cambridge, Mass., 1941), pp. 180ff.; Walter Dill Scott, R. C. Clothier, S. B. Matthewson, and W. R. Spriegel, *Personnel Management: Principles, Practices, and Point of View* (New York, 1941).

19. Nelson, *Managers and Workers,* p. 152; John B. Miner, *Personnel Psychology* (New York, 1969), p. 194; Stanley M. Herman, *The People Specialists* (New York, 1968), pp. 245ff.

20. Harry W. Hepner, *Human Relations in Changing Industry* (New York, 1938), p. 96.

21. Nathaniel Cantor, *Employee Counseling: A New Viewpoint in Industrial Psychology* (New York, 1945), p. 64.

22. Annette Garrett, *Counseling Methods for Personnel Workers* (New York, 1945), p. 71; see also Baritz, *Servants of Power.*

23. C. S. Slowcombe, "Good Technique in Negotiating," *Personnel Journal* 14 (1935): 49; see also Lester Tarnopol, "Personality Differences between Leaders and Non-Leaders," *Personnel Journal* 37 (1958): 57–64; Miner, *Personnel Psychology,* p. 194; Erwin H. Schell, *The Techniques of Executive Control* (New York, 1934), p. 101.

24. Dale Carnegie, *How to Win Friends and Influence People* (New York, 1940),

pp. 2, 27, 68, 70, 156; R. C. Borden and Alvin Busse, *How to Win a Sales Argument* (New York, 1926), p. 7.

25. C. R. McPherson, "Kid Gloves vs. Iron Fist," *Personnel Journal* 43 (1964): 43; R. A. Eman, "Three Ways to Humanize Your Handling of Workers," *Personnel Journal* 33 (1952): 62; Rexford Hersey, "Self-Analysis Quiz for Supervisors and Executives," *Personnel* 24 (1948): 454–74; Harvey Stowers, *Management Can Be Human* (New York, 1946), p. 94.

26. Ordway Tead, *Human Nature and Managers* (New York, 1933), p. 40.

27. Edward Kilduff, *The Private Secretary* (New York, 1915), pp. 50, 57; see also later editions to 1935; see also Margery W. Davies, *Woman's Place Is at the Typewriter: Office Work and Office Workers, 1870–1930* (Philadelphia, 1982), p. 95. The routinization of claims of emotional control as part of professional competence in industrial psychology can be traced through standard textbooks (Hepner, *Human Relations*) and journals.

28. Garrett, *Counseling Methods for Personnel Workers;* Baritz, *Servants of Power,* passim; Joseph Tiffin and E. J. McCormick, *Industrial Psychology* (Englewood Cliffs, N.J., 1965), pp. 90, 188; Theodore Hewlett and Olive Lester, "Measuring Introversion and Extroversion," *Personnel Journal* 6 (1928): 352–610; Doncaster Humm, "Skill, Intelligence and Temperament," *Personnel Journal* 22 (1943): 80–90; Herman, *People Specialists,* pp. 245ff.; R. A. Sutermeister, "Training Foremen in Human Relations," *Personnel* 20 (1943): 13.

29. Roethisberger and Dickson, *Management and the Worker,* p. 542; Helen Baker, *Employee Counseling* (Princeton, 1944), p. 40; William R. Spriegel et al., *Elements of Supervision* (New York, 1942), p. 116; Cantor, *Employee Counseling,* p. 66.

30. Garrett, *Counseling Methods,* pp. 120, 151ff.

31. Baker, *Employee Counseling,* p. 40; Garrett, *Counseling Methods,* p. 120.

32. Paul Johnson and J. C. Bledsoe, "Morale as Related to Perceptions of Leader Behavior," *Personnel Psychology* 26 (1973): 48–49.

33. Lester Tarnopol and Julia Tarnopol, "How Top-Rated Supervisors Differ from the Lower-Rated," *Personnel Journal* 34 (1955): 332; see also Sutermeister, "Training Foremen," p. 13, and Miner, *Personnel Psychology,* p. 194.

34. "The Humm-Wadsworth Temperament Scale," *Personnel Journal* 13 (1934): 322; on the evolution of testing to screen out hard-driving supervisors, and specific programs as in Pillsbury Mills, see M. L. Gross, *The Brain Watchers* (New York, 1962); William H. Whyte, Jr., *The Organization Man* (New York, 1956), pp. 140, 276ff.; Robert M. Guion, *Personnel Testing* (New York, 1965); Ludwig Huttner and D. M. Stone, "Foreman Selection," in *Personnel Psychology* (1958); Laurence Siegel, *Industrial Psychology* (Homewood, Ill., 1969), p. 165; John D. Cook, S. J. Hepworth, T. D. Waller, and P. B. Warr, *The Experience of Work: A Compendium and Review of LYP Measures and Their Use* (New York, 1981).

35. Edwin Fleishman, "Leadership Climate, Human Relations Training and Supervisory Behavior," *Personnel Psychology* 6 (1953): 205–22; Baritz, *Servants of Power,* pp. 164ff.

36. Sutermeister, "Training Foremen," p. 13; Brian Kay, "Key Factors in Effective Foreman Behavior," *Personnel* 36 (1959): 28.

37. W. B. Dominick, "Let's Take a Good Look at the Foreman's Job," *Personnel* 21 (1944).

38. Burt Scanlan, "Sensitivity Training: Clarification, Issues, Insights," *Personnel Journal* 50 (1970): 549; see also Thomas Greening, "Sensitivity Training: Cult or Contribution?" *Personnel* 41 (1964): 22–25; Edgar Schein and W. G. Bennis, *Personal and Organizational Changes through Group Methods* (New York, 1965), pp. 286–96.

39. Scanlan, "Sensitivity Training," pp. 549–52.

40. Chris Argyris, *Interpersonal Competence and Organizational Effectiveness* (Homewood, Ill., 1962), p. 137.

41. Ibid., pp. 174ff., 255ff.

42. Burt Scanlan, "Managerial Leadership in Perspective," *Personnel Journal* 58 (1979): 168–71; D. H. Brusch, "Technical Knowledge or Managerial Skills?" *Personnel Journal* 58 (1979); Charles C. Smith, *The Foreman's Place in Management* (New York, 1946), p. 119.

43. Otto Altorfer, "Emotional Job Fitness," *Personnel* 52 (1975): 33.

44. S. R. Siegel, "Improving the Effectiveness of Management Development Programs," *Personnel Journal* 60 (1981): 771–73.

45. George D. Halsey, *Handbook of Personnel Management* (New York, 1947) p. 270; see also Spriegel et al., *Elements of Supervision*, p. 116.

46. W. E. Baer, "Do's and Don'ts in Handling Grievances," *Personnel* 43 (1966): 30.

47. Tiffin and McCormick, *Industrial Psychology*, pp. 188ff.; C. Wright Mills, *White Collar: The American Middle Class* (New York, 1952) p. 184; Scott et al., *Personnel Management;* Borden and Busse, *How to Win a Sales Argument;* Laurence Siegel, *Industrial Psychology*, pp. 347–57; Susan Porter Benson, "The Clerking Sisterhood: Rationalization and the Work Culture of American Saleswomen in Department Stores, 1890–1960," in James Green, ed., *Workers' Struggles, Past and Present* (Philadelphia, 1983), pp. 107–16.

48. Lyman W. Porter and E. E. Ghisells, "The Self-Perception of Top and Middle Management Personnel," *Personnel Psychology* 10 (1957): 397–407.

49. W. H. Leffingwell and E. M. Robinson, *Textbook on Office Management* (New York, 1950, p. 386; see also Rensis Likert, *New Patterns of Management* (New York, 1961); Brusch, "Technical Knowledge or Managerial Skills?"; see also D. K. Hardesty and W. S. Jones, "Characteristics of Judgement of High Potential Management Personnel," *Personnel Psychology* 21c (1968), where high-potential executives scored average or below in interpersonal relations; Mary C. H. Niles, *Middle Management: The Job of the Junior Administrator* (New York, 1941), pp. 72–93.

50. Davies, *Woman's Place Is at the Typewriter*, p. 146; see also pp. 155–210.

51. Roethisberger and Dickson, *Management and the Worker*, p. 349; see also Harvey Swados, *On the Line* (Boston, 1947), pp. 24, 48, 169, for a judgment that overt anger remains a basic feature of assembly-line work. But see also, on evidence of

change, D. A. Fleishman and E. F. Harris, "Patterns of Leadership Behavior Related to Employee Grievances," *Personnel Psychology* 15 (1962); David Katz et al., *Productivity, Supervision and Morale among Railroad Workers* (Ann Arbor, 1951), p. 33; Woodruff Imberman, "Letting the Employee Speak His Mind," *Personnel* 53 (1976): 12–22; C. A. Turner, *A Practical Manual of Effective Supervision* (New York, n.d.).

52. Studs Terkel, *Working* (New York, 1974), pp. 32, 81, 260, 285ff., 547.

53. Roethisberger and Dickson, *Management and the Worker,* p. 212; Tiffin McCormick, *Industrial Psychology,* pp. 188ff.

54. Mills, *White Collar,* p. 184; Whyte, *Organization Man;* Arlie Russell Hochschild, *The Managed Heart* (Berkeley and Los Angeles, 1984).

55. Sar A. Levitan and W. B. Johnston, *Work Is Here to Stay, Alas* (Salt Lake City, 1973), p. 66.

56. John S. Ellsworth, *Factory Folkways: A Study of Institutional Structure and Change* (New Haven, Conn., 1952), p. 204; Theodore V. Purcell, *The Worker Speaks His Mind on Company and Union* (Cambridge, Mass., 1953), pp. 188–230; Levitan and Johnston, *Work Is Here,* pp. 67–68; Jai Ghorpade and J. R. Lackrits, "Influences behind Neutral Responses in Subordinate Ratings of Supervisors," *Personnel Psychology* 34 (1981): 511–22; P. J. Andersini and M. B. Shapiro, "Women's Attitudes toward Their Jobs," *Personnel Psychology* 31 (1978): 23; Charles W. Walker and Robert H. Guest, *The Man and the Assembly Line* (Cambridge, Mass., 1952), pp. 92ff., 143; Leonard Goodwin, "Occupational Goals and Satisfaction of the American Work Force," *Personnel Psychology* 22 (1969): 313–25.

57. M. D. Makel and A. J. Schuh, "Job Applicant Attributes," *Personnel Psychology* 24 (1971): 48–49; W. K. Graham and J. T. Calendo, "Personality Correlation of Supervisory Ratings," *Personnel Psychology* 22 (1969): 483–87; K. R. Student, "Changing Values and Management Stress," *Personnel* 53 (1976): 48–55.

58. E. L. Miller, "Job Attitudes of National Union Officials," *Personnel Psychology* 19 (1966): 395–410; A. H. Cochran, "Management Tigers and Pussycats," *Personnel Journal* 50 (1971): 524–26; C. J. Lilley, "Supervisors Don't Criticize Enough," *Personnel Journal* 31 (1952): 209–12.

59. Benson, "Clerking Sisterhood," passim.

60. *Analysis of Work Stoppages* (U.S. Department of Labor, Bureau of Labor Statistics Annual, 1941–80), passim; *Strikes in the United States, 1880–1939* (U.S. Department of Labor, Bureau of Labor Statistics, 1937), passim. The pattern of rising numbers of strikes per decades that prevailed from the late nineteenth century to the 1950s has thus been broken, with a brief interruption after 1965, and the post–World War II peak in number of strikers has never been equaled. Specific strike rates over most issues, such as labor organization, likely to generate or reflect particular anger have dropped off with particular rapidity, and have of course fallen even more markedly on a per capita basis. For a fuller analysis of the indicators of anger control, as well as the institutionalization of the anger control campaign, see Stearns and Stearns, *Anger,* esp. chaps. 5 and 8.

61. Barrington Moore, *Injustice: The Social Bases of Obedience and Revolt* (New York, 1978), pp. 500–502. On a cautionary note, various works on protest by Charles

Tilly warn against including emotional factors as a basis for action, as opposed to more measurable features of political structure and opportunity.

62. On the American ambivalence, W. Lloyd Warner, *American Life: Dream and Reality* (Chicago, 1962), p. 108; Stearns and Stearns, *Anger;* Jerome Kagan, "The Child in the Family," in A. S. Rossi, J. Kagan, and T. Hareven, eds., *The Family* (New York, 1978), p. 395.

63. Daniel Miller and Guy Swanson, *The Changing American Parent* (New York, 1958), p. 143 and passim.

64. Benjamin Spock, *The Common Sense Book of Baby and Child Care* (New York, 1946), pp. 204, 252; Michael Zuckerman, "Dr. Spock, the Confidence Man," in C. Rosenberg, ed., *The Family in History* (Philadelphia, 1957), pp. 179–208.

65. Abram de Swaan, "The Politics of Agoraphobia: On Changes in Emotional and Relational Management," *Theory and Society* 10 (1981): 359–85. See also Richard Sennett, *The Fall of Public Man: On the Social Psychology of Capitalism* (New York, 1978); and the relationship between the anger-control findings and Christopher Lasch's partially compatible discussion of shifts in modal personality.

66. Shula Sommers, "Adults Evaluating Their Emotions: A Cross-Cultural Perspective," in Carol Malatesta and Carroll Izard, eds., *Emotions in Adult Development* (Beverly Hills, 1984), pp. 319–38; see also, on comparative emotional standards, William Goode, "The Theoretical Importance of Love," *American Sociological Review* 24 (1959): 38–47.

67. Joseph Pleck and Jack Sawyer, eds., *The American Man* (Englewood Cliffs, N.J., 1974); Marc Fasteau, *The Male Machine* (New York, 1974).

68. George Thornton, "The Relationship between Supervisory and Self-Appraisals of Executive Performance," *Personnel Psychology* 21c (1968): 441–55; Hal Pickle and Frank Friedlander, "Seven Societal Criteria of Organizational Success," *Personnel Psychology* 20 (1967): 165–78; James H. Mullen, "The Leadership Dilemma in American Business," *Personnel Journal* 40 (1961) 290–94.

69. de Swaan, "Politics of Agoraphobia."

70. Mills, *White Collar*, p. 184; Whyte, *Organization Man*, p. 152.

71. Hochschild, *Managed Heart*, passim.

72. Swados, *On The Line*, p. 169.

73. Hochschild, *Managed Heart;* Meyer Friedman and Ray H. Rosenman, *Type A Behavior and Your Heart* (New York, 1981), pp. 17–24 and passim.

6

Meanings of Love:
Adoption Literature and Dr. Spock,
1946–1985

Judith Modell

I. Introduction

*F*or forty years Dr. Spock has been telling American parents how to take care of their children and how to "be" parents. In the process, Spock conveys a model for parental love; the behaviors and expressions exchanged between parent and child constitute a blueprint for feelings of love. *Baby and Child Care* has been a best seller since its first paperback appearance in 1946, and Dr. Spock is the book "all parents" in the United States use.[1] There are also books for adoptive parents in American society. These manuals, like Spock, first came out in the post–World War II period and have been appearing ever since. My essay compares the model for parental love set forth in adoption books with that conveyed in the "bible" of American child rearing, Dr. Spock. The comparison will illuminate not only a cultural view of adoptive parent-child relationships but also the assumptions underlying a Spockian model for parental love.

My assumption is that Spock represents the prevailing cultural model for parental love in late-twentieth-century American society. Instructions, comments, reassurances to the parent in *Baby and Child Care* constitute a model for love to which adoption books, sharing the same cultural premises, respond. From the first edition in 1946 to the recent 1985 edition, Spock has explicated the "meaning" of love in terms that are by intention comprehensible to all parents.[2] Adoption manuals, emphasizing the "normalness" of adoptive parent-child relationships, accommodate the Spockian model to the adoptive situation. As I show, however, the fact that an element—a biological connection with the child—is missing entails revisions of Spock that importantly distinguish the meaning of parental love in adoption texts from that in *Baby and Child Care*. The revision suggests there are competing models for parental love in American society. If so, this raises more general theoretical

151

questions about the implications of presenting people with alternative models for what are deemed "basic emotions." Do alternative models result in different emotions? Do adoptive parents love their children differently?

My paper is about cultural constructs, not about behaviors. I do assume these constructs pattern the behaviors and consequently the feelings people have as parents.[3] Constructs for parental love, whether presented in an "idealized" or a "realistic" form, serve as mechanisms for experiencing, and often evaluating, emotions on the part of parents. Parents, in other words, perceive and feel love through the standards presented in child-rearing books. In the case of Spock, and of adoption manuals until recently, the constructs are presented to and embraced by a largely white, middle-class population. These versions of parental love assume certain socioeconomic and demographic conditions (e.g., a small family).[4] In Spock, the assumptions changed remarkably little over a forty-year period.

The prescriptions in child-rearing manuals provide a "model for" parental love, in a Geertzian sense. Culture models, Geertz explains, "have an intrinsic double aspect: they give meaning, that is, objective conceptual form, to social and psychological reality both by shaping themselves to it and by shaping it to themselves."[5] Models, in other words, both reflect and create psychological reality. A similar perspective underlies my analysis of the textual material in Spock and in adoption manuals. I further assume that the construct for parental love in these books does not relate directly to the sociocultural context or to contemporaneous theories of emotion and the self but rather is filtered through the responses of readers, the predilections of the authors, and a cultural pattern for following instructions. Such factors are hard to delineate, and remain implicit in my argument that Spock's formulation sets parameters that other manuals have followed over the years. Since the first edition in 1946, Spock's "common sense" instruction books have let American parents know how they should feel toward their children and also how to know they are "feeling right." Adoption manuals responded to this persuasive program of child rearing, and discussions in those books reveal the strength of a particular, persistent cultural model for parental love. Child-care manuals do not directly reflect or create an emotional climate; they do determine the interpretation individuals make of their responses, in this case to being parents and having children—feelings culturally named "love."

Spock is a classic—"THE source book for several generations of parents," reports the back cover of the 1985 edition accurately. There is no comparable "classic" book for adoptive parents; the back cover of one optimistically calls it "the Spock for adoptive parents."[6] Instead there are many adoption texts, written by diverse authors, including adoptees, adoptive parents, and "experts." For this paper, I have selected adoption texts that would have been readily available (e.g., paperback editions), and that were textually accessible and obviously directed to "ordinary" adoptive parents. Adoption books from a particular period tend to share themes and tone, so that generalizations can be made. Product of an era, and sensitive to social and cultural conditions, to theories of child development, and to adoption policies, adoption books tended to voice the same points of view whether written by a social worker, an adoptive parent, or, on occasion, an adopted individual.[7]

My method is textual analysis, an interpretive reading of the manuals. In reading, I assume meanings are communicated by various elements in the text, from individual words to the pervasive tone of voice—conveyed through vocabulary, grammatical structure, "plotting," and illustrative examples. Few of the texts defined parental love in so many words. Spock never does, and only one or two adoption books made the attempt. "Love, if its illusive mystery has to be defined for consumption by a Univac, is an emotion engendered by one person in another which will ultimately result in an unselfishness uncongenial to the human animal."[8] Given the elusiveness of definitions of emotional concepts in American culture in general, metaphors, images, and symbols become significant delimiters of meaning.[9] I assume such metaphorical constructions are understood—at some level—by readers of Spock and of adoption manuals. Metaphors, in these texts, draw upon fundamental cultural concepts,[10] incorporating a good deal of what is "understood already" in order to delineate the meaning of parental love.

Child-care manuals uphold a wider cultural and social structure, transmitting patterns of behavior and belief through a set of prescriptions for the parent-child relationship.[11] In the pages of all five editions of *Baby and Child Care* lie the values and ideologies of a distinctively American cultural system, with the resulting "recreation" of generations of Americans—parents who will raise their children to fit into the dominant structure of the surrounding context.[12] The Spockian model for parental love, in other words, incorporates American views of the family, of gender roles, and of the development of an individual—and the model has proved to be remarkably durable. As I show, Spock does recognize changes in the family and in the social context of the American family as institution, but his model for the love expressed within that family remains extremely consistent. One might argue that the model maintains a stability of feeling in order to counteract this very flux in the conditions of child rearing. Moreover, in its conservatism the Spockian model assumes a particular kind of parent-child relationship: the Spockian model is based on a mother's physiological tie to her child.

In contrast with the substantially unchanging Spock, adoption literature has changed noticeably over the past four decades. For a variety of reasons adoption manuals have been especially sensitive to circumstances and have necessarily stretched the model of parental love expressed in their pages. Changes in these texts partly reflect changing theoretical analyses of the meaning of love in a socially constructed parent-child relationship and partly reflect developments in the institution of adoption itself (e.g., shifts in the criteria for adoptive parenthood). In a society in which biology determines parent-child love,[13] "social" parenthood becomes a matter of concern. Such concern has led to self-conscious probings into the feelings involved in this kind of relationship, and a sense of diversity in the expressions of love that stems from alertness to the diverse ways of "having" a child socially. (Having a child biologically has recently shown the kind of radical change that may, in the future, prompt a further shift in understandings of parental love.) Theories about kinship, family, and the bond between parent and child thus have played a part in adoption manuals, but tailored to the assurance perceived as needed by parents entering into a "contracted" relationship with a child. Shifts in practice, too, influenced what was said about parental feelings in adoption books. For instance, the encouragement of noninfant and mixed-race adoptions in the 1960s drew the discussion of parental love in adoption books away from the Spockian model. At other times, adoption practice that attempted to replicate the biological family (e.g., placing children in families where they would look like the adoptive parents) brought the adoptive model closer to the one outlined in the pages of *Baby and Child Care*. Currently in the 1980s, the model for adoptive parent love shows pronounced differences from Spock. Furthermore, the new adoptive model is shaped by and shapes changes in the wider social and cultural context, anticipating revised cultural views of the emotional content of relationships altogether.

Dr. Spock has received some scholarly attention as a cultural document,[14] adoption literature practically none. The latter, addressed to parents who lack a culturally defined essential ingredient of parenthood—birth and blood connection with the child—can cast light on the assumptions that structure love for "normal" parents in American society. In a society where instructions for feeling have become a major enterprise, instructions for the nonconventional situation distinguish the features ordinarily not marked in instructions for the conventional situation. Child-care manuals, in describing behaviors, "instruct" parents on how to love a child. Adoption manuals embed descriptions of behavior in the context of a bond between parent and child that has been formed, not by nature, but by contract and law. The instruction in feeling, consequently, contrasts in some part with what is presented in child-care books that assume a biological bond. Adoptive texts present a more distinct version of "the attitudes or standards that a society, or a definable group within a society, maintains toward basic emotions and their appropriate expression."[15]

In the following pages, I compare adoption literature with Spock, outlining the models for parental love in these manuals and noting the changes both in content and in tone of presentation. My discussion of the historical and theoretical contexts of Spock and of adoption manuals is based closely on the textual material in these instruction books. That is, I assume that the content of the texts reveals the trends presumed to be significant in the sociocultural as well as in the theoretical context of their writing.[16] What emerges conclusively from the comparison is the biological basis of the Spockian model, and specifically the significance of a physiological link between mother and child. In Dr. Spock, parental love is maternal love—and this holds true for five generations of American parents. The cultural importance of biology and of motherhood represented in Spock posed a problem for adoption texts, and the problem was solved in various ways in the decades from 1940 to 1980. I discuss the ramifications for the meaning of parental love of responses to a Spockian model in adoptive texts. In my conclusion, I suggest that adoption literature sets forth a model for parental love that, in moving away from biology and from motherhood, suits 1980s concepts of the family and the self more adequately than does Spock.

II. Parental Love: Defined

Spock's model for parental love is a conservative one. The changes he made in each new edition (quite self-conscious changes) were effectively changes in the letter and not the spirit of the law. The conservatism stems from an apparent conviction about the importance of continuity (a "loving parent raises loving children") and from the implicit grounding of his model for parental love in maternal love: how a mother loves a child sets the parameters for how a parent loves a child. In addition, "how a mother loves a child" in Spock reflects cultural definitions of motherhood. In American culture, "[k]inship is the mother's bond of flesh and blood with her child, and her maternal instinct is her love for it."[17] Spock's model in *Baby and Child Care* draws from and perpetuates what might be called a "mainstream" or, in a Spockian phrase, "common sense" understanding of parental love in American society. Compared with Spock, as I show, adoption literature takes a more radical stance, one that by the 1980s tests cultural assumptions about love that presuppose a necessary conjunction of physiological bond, motherhood, and love for a child.

In modern Western society, prescriptions for parental love have traditionally been based on interpretations of mother love. More precisely, to the extent that cultural meanings of love involve nurturance and expressiveness, these traits have been assumed to be consonant with maternal instinct.[18] Fathers played a part, an instrumental role in bringing up a child, but paternal duties and responsibilities did not provide the meaning of parental love. Culturally, role is not feeling—though feeling may be introduced into the role, as today's literature on parenthood indicates (e.g., a father can be "nurturing" in his parental role). Love is an emotion, and not (simply) a role. And this emotion has, for a variety of cultural and historical reasons, been ascribed to women as parents.[19] Discussions of changes in the expressions of love, and in the behaviors that indicate love, focus on the mother, including the mother who assigns care to someone else (whether the someone else be wet nurse, nanny, or father). Thus, whether or not children received "less love" in earlier centuries becomes a question of whether or not mothers gave less love.[20] Likewise, studies that inquire into the complex relationship of behaviors, expression, and "real" feeling focus on what mothers (and women) do and say about having children.

Spock inherits a legacy evident in scholarly writings and in conventional assumptions; his book also contributes substantially to the comprehension and transmission of this legacy from one generation to another. All five editions of *Baby and Child Care* define parental love in terms of maternal love by utilizing diverse references to a cultural concept of nature. In this section, I show how "nature" works to define love in child-rearing texts, as well as the modifications of a shared cultural concept in adoption books. In American culture, nature is a complex symbol; its multiple meanings can be manipulated to convey culturally acceptable but not precisely identical definitions of parental love.

Adoption books inherit the same cultural tradition as Spock: an emphasis on motherhood that inserts physiology, maternal instincts, and feminine traits into a model for parental love. From the initial appearance of manuals for adoptive parents, in the Second World War period, through the 1980s, adoption texts have revealed the significance of birth and of motherhood for cultural interpretations of parental love. Over four decades, and despite different motivating purposes (e.g., the perils of nonagency adoptions; the dilemma involved in telling a child about adoption, etc.), adoption books have had to grapple with an inherent contradiction: parental love is culturally linked to pregnancy, birth, and associated changes in the mother, and yet the adoptive parent, who lacks these features, is presumed to love the child thoroughly. Adoptive parents do not have the experiences that culturally seal the bond to the child, making the commitment of the parent absolute and enduring. And so adoption texts have to replace physiology with symbols that are equally convincing representations of bonding, permanence, and commitment. The problem elicited several solutions from the 1940s to the 1980s, primary among them an expanded interpretation of the "natural" in parent-child love and, as well, a set of references to the other contractual relationship in American society presumed (until recently) to be permanent and lasting, marriage. Both strategies had important and what I call radical implications for a model of parental love. Expanding the meaning of nature freed parenthood from motherhood; social not biological traits constituted parental love. Turning to marriage resolved issues of choice, contingency, and performance, issues that are left unformulated in the ordinary Spockian model for parental love.

A concept of nature is the central metaphor in Spock and in adoption texts. In diverse forms, nature provides an interpretive framework for parental love in American culture: parents "naturally" love their children. Metaphor is necessary, because love and other emotional concepts "are not so clearly delineated in our experience in any direct fashion and therefore must be comprehended primarily indirectly, via metaphor."[21] Nature itself is a polysemic symbol, so that various aspects, various cultural connotations, can be selected, depending on the content and the purpose of a particular text.[22] Moreover, in books about having children, nature is not only descriptive but also prescriptive; nature indicates not only how parents do feel but how they should feel toward a child.

Adoption texts, like Dr. Spock, draw on a concept of nature to symbolize permanence and lastingness, traits that in American culture distinguish parental love from other emotions. Nature represents the enduring continuity characteristic of parental love, a commitment beyond law and contract, beyond "lessons" and instructions. Adoption books and Spock equally assume there is something fundamental and unchangeable in parental love, and this abstract quality can be well represented by the cultural connotations of nature. References to permanence and rootedness are especially stressed in adoption books while, not unsimilarly, in Spock nature reminds parents of the existence of parental feelings "before" and "beneath" the expressions and behaviors that demonstrate those feelings.

Because Spock has delineated the prevailing cultural model for parental love, it is important to look more closely at the significance of nature in *Baby and Child Care*. Spock uses the concept of nature in a universalistic sense, to signify permanence and continuity, but also in several specific senses. Nature in *Baby and Child Care* over forty years refers to "instinct" and to an idea about the parental self I have called *character*. In the end, the specific meanings interact with one another, and are subsumed under and reinforce the broader meaning of nature. This reference to the natural in parental love is fundamental and persistent in Spock, justifying a manual—a paradox I discuss below—and defining an emotion, a feeling, that exists in individuals outside personal, cultural, and historical circumstances.

On the second page of chapter 1 in the 1946 edition, the following paragraph appears. "It may surprise you to hear that the more people have studied different methods of bringing up children the more they have come to the conclusion that what good mothers and fathers instinctively feel like doing for their babies is usually best after all. Furthermore, all parents do their best job when they have a natural, easy confidence in themselves. Better to make a few mistakes from being natural than to do everything letter-perfect out of a feeling of worry."[23] The passage appears, unchanged, in each subsequent edition. The word *instinct* as used—what good mothers and fathers instinctively feel like doing—has a conventional meaning in Spock, with a stronger bias toward maternal instinct than is evident in the quotation. *Character* is more difficult to pinpoint; I use the word to cover what Spock means by having a "natural, easy confidence" and "being natural." I will begin by outlining the role of instinct in parental love, a point on which *Baby and Child Care* is evidently conservative.

Even in the "updated" 1985 edition, instinct is related to the "moving and creative experience of birth."[24] Linked to a physiological change, instinct remains attached to "mother" and this in spite of revisions throughout the preceding three editions directed toward playing down the role of the woman as parent. The 1985 edition includes the father, the stepparent (Spock was one himself by then), and the "caretaker" in the child's world, but it simulta-neously exalts the experiences of pregnancy and birth for determining a "parent's" behavior toward the child and feelings about the child. Spock expresses as much sympathy in the 1985 as in the 1946 edition for the new father who lurks about the hospital and then the house with nothing at all to do.[25] But it is on the subject of feeding that the Spockian emphasis on maternal instinct becomes clearest. In 1985, mothers "tell of the tremendous satisfaction they experience from knowing that they are providing their babies with something no one else can give them, from seeing their devotion to the breast, from feeling their closeness."[26] This is really just a rewording of the 1946: "she's giving him something real, something that no one else can give him."[27] Breast-feeding in all editions becomes a kind of "charter" for the love given the child forever afterward. Breast-feeding represents nurturance that is natural—Spock does not say "hormonal"—and thereby epitomizes the ideal parent-child relationship. "In this sense, breast-feeding does wonders for a young mother and for her relationship with her baby. She and her baby are happy in themselves and feel more and more loving to each other."[28] Spock's paean to breast-feeding in 1985 also suggests the persistence of an ideal family, in which mother can be at home (and is physiologically able) to provide the child with "something that no one else can give him." The absolute importance of the feelings that accompany breast-feeding, crucial to the expression (and consequent existence) of parental love, would seem to outweigh Spock's otherwise timely recognition of changed family circum-stances—working mothers, child-rearing fathers, and the increasing use of day care.

Thus, although in one sense the mother herself is less "primary" than she was in 1946, in another sense mother's feelings remain just as primary in

1985. In 1946 breast-feeding is presented, at least at the beginning of the chapter, in a casual fashion, creating a context in which "bottle feeding," though "unnatural," is not terrible for the child.[29] Fathers (and others) could assume feeding duties. In that edition, however, they did not often do so. The flexibility bottle feeding potentially introduces, allowing either parent to express love through feeding the child, is lost under the general emphasis on the mother and the not-so-subtle assumption that this will be a mother who stays home. The emphasis and the assumptions did not change in the 1957 edition: "Feeding is a baby's greatest joy, by far, and it's good for him to link this with his mother's presence and his mother's face."[30] Nor does 1968, despite Spock's own public radicalism, bend the model of parental love toward father and away from traditional notions of motherhood; on page 72 of that edition "breast feeding is natural." It was not until the 1976 edition that Spock evidently responded to changes in American culture and in the audience he addressed. Through the late 1960s and early 1970s, Spock had come under fire for sexism, and the 1976 manual deliberately answered such attacks. He noted in the preface: "The main reason for this 3rd revision (4th edition) of *Baby and Child Care* is to eliminate the sexist biases of the sort that help to create and perpetuate discrimination against girls and women."[31] He began to give father, and others, more of a part in child rearing, though, as I show, with mother's love still the map for the feelings expressed toward a child and the guarantee of a child's proper development. Despite the presence of new figures, in the 1976 edition the "how" of being a loving parent continued to be modeled by a mother's natural feelings for the baby.

A closer look at the role of the father in the five editions of Spock can clarify the point. The father is present and active in every version of *Baby and Child Care*. Yet, though his role in child rearing changed over the forty years of publication, his expression of parental love hardly changed at all. Spock does not imply that a father cannot love a child or, especially with the 1976 edition, cannot nurture a child, but rather that the expression of this love differs from a mother's. And this difference, I think, underlines the importance of mother's instincts, of her natural bond with a baby, and of her special feelings for her child. In the first three editions (1946, 1957, 1968), father seems clumsy and uneasy with the child; his instinctive behavior leads him to tease, roughhouse, and generally "pal around" with his child. And Spock cautions, in 1985 as he had earlier, that for young children, "a father who is pretending to be a bear or a prizefighter really becomes one for the time being. This is usually too much for a small child to take. So rough-housing should be mild and good-natured and brief."[32]

More to the point, the 1985 "father as parent" is described as "responsible and capable."[33] He should participate in "management" of the children and not be afraid to demonstrate what Spock calls "leadership," by which he means discipline. "The father who avoids the leadership role simply forces his wife to discipline for two."[34] Between 1946 and 1985, the father is transformed from a clumsy outsider and occasional onlooker as mother takes care of the baby into a participatory and dutiful parent. But he lacks the instincts mother has, and continues to muddle his way through various situations. An illustration that appears in each edition vividly expresses this persistently clumsy fatherhood. In the 1985 version, a young black father watches helplessly as his child hurls food to the floor.[35] Through these and similar incidents, father is shown as not knowing instinctively what to do for (and with) the baby. Even when he is present as an active parent after 1976, father still holds a less prominent place in the behaviors and expressions that demonstrate love to the child. Descriptions of responses to prolonged crying, an outburst of roseola, a refusal to go to sleep all implicitly assume a mother's instincts at work in 1985 as much as in 1946.

"Furthermore," Spock writes after advising parents to follow their own instincts, "all parents do their best job when they have a natural, easy confidence in themselves." This "natural, easy confidence" in oneself is what I cover with the word *character*. "Trust yourself" are the famous first words of the first chapter of every *Baby and Child Care*. And all subsequent chapters continue the advice. Be yourself, Spock says, act "naturally" and don't worry too much about what the "experts" say. The message to parents, then, is "act in character." In effect, I am treating the word character as a representation of being yourself and acting confidently: a "good parent," in the words Spock uses. He does not quite mean by this the nineteenth-century idea of character—moral worth and goodness—though he occasionally approaches this understanding in, for instance, the 1968 edition, when he advises parents to be concerned about the "state of the world" and not just the state of the child. And, too, the main purpose of the manual is to guide individuals into being "good" in the role of parent. (The moral connotation of character is more explicit in Spock's descriptions of what the child, properly loved, will become: virtuous, outgoing, and responsible; grown up, he—and after 1976 she—has a good character.) Even less, in communicating the message to a parent to be yourself and to act in character, does Spock imply the contemporaneous meaning of character: idiosyncratic personality. Advised to act themselves, Spockian parents are not expected to demonstrate strange, unusual, or even especially pronounced "characters."

Personal idiosyncrasies are subsumed under the character of parent. Moreover, in the Spockian context, parental character assumes maternal traits as defined by American culture. The nonidiosyncratic and somewhat flat but constantly concerned parent much more reflects a stereotype of mother than of father. If the figures who perform parental roles over four decades do change in the text, the ideal character of these parents does not, and it is character that lays the foundation for expressions of love in *Baby and Child Care*. Illustrations indicate what this "character" involves in day-to-day behavior, and confirm the stability over time of Spock's concept. To cite just one example: In the 1946 edition there is a picture of a young woman in a dress and an apron shaking her finger at a toddler engaged in pulling a lamp onto his head. The same picture appears in 1985, except that now the woman has long, loose hair and is wearing jeans. "Firmness," Spock explained in 1968, "keeps them [children] lovable. And they love us for keeping them out of trouble."[36] The gentle guide and firm companion turns out, time after time, to be the woman in the pages of *Baby and Child Care*.

The Spockian concept of character in fact depends upon conventional mid-1940s gender socialization processes in American society. To borrow a cliché, *Baby and Child Care* assumes that it is "second nature" for women to be mothers. Parental character, according to Spock, is given, ascribed, a matter of inherent traits. And, in an American cultural context, this means parental traits are mother's traits, unchanged over four decades. Spock does recognize that it may be more or less difficult to demonstrate these traits, depending upon circumstances. By 1976 he discusses the problems of raising a child in poverty or in a single parent household, but it is also clear that exactly because of the pressures of changing circumstances, the model of love based on maternal instinct must be sustained.

A concept of nature also appears in the manuals written for adoptive parents from 1946 through the present. And, on the face of it, nature has the same meanings in adoption books as in Spock, referring to the instinct and the character of a "good" parent and, more abstractly, to the permanence and absoluteness of parental love. There are also variations in the significance of these words, so that instinct and character do not mean exactly the same thing in adoption books as they do in *Baby and Child Care*. In addition, the variations in meaning suggest the extent to which these concepts changed, as writings on adoption responded to changes in the social and the cultural contexts of the institution. Increasingly, instinct and character in adoption books lost their Spockian, and cultural, association with motherhood and woman-as-parent.

Adoption texts have a different history from that of Spock. While equally addressing parents and, importantly, equally assuring parents of their ability to love a child (to be loving parents), adoption manuals also possess distinctive features. For one, these manuals are dealing with a social institution—the transfer of a child from one parent to another—that has a history of its own. For another, adoption books are written by an array of "experts," from doctors through social workers to adoptive parents and adopted individuals. Discussions of parental love reflect changes in the institution of adoption (for instance, the availability of infants for adoption), in the perspectives of the authors (adoptive parents do not always agree with trained personnel), and in societal expectations for family and parent-child relationships. There is also a continuity in adoption texts, as these manuals respond to a cultural model for parental love conveyed preeminently if not exclusively in Dr. Spock.

Nature as a concept that stands for the significant features of love for a child occurs throughout writings on adoptive parenthood. Nature represents the permanency, absoluteness, and nonjudgmental quality that distinguishes parental love from other emotions in American culture. And adoption manuals, like Spock, claim that the expression of such love is "instinctive." For adoptive parents instinct cannot be linked to pregnancy and birth. Adoption texts consequently minimize the biological connotations of the word, a shift that actually serves two purposes. By eliminating biology as one referent, adoption books confirm the ability of the adoptive parent instinctively to be a loving parent; the same verbal maneuver also eliminates the birth mother from the adoptive situation, since a biological connection no longer underlies the instinct to care for a child. The latter point is typically subdued, and the former stressed. "The bond which instinctively ties a mother to the baby she has carried and borne is lacking at first in the adoption situation. A bond that is equally strong can, and does, grow as the mother and father feed and care for their adopted child."[37] Instinct refers to the urge to take care of an infant, to feed, fondle, and protect a child. Instinct in this sense is equally "available" to fathers and to mothers, is a human rather than a gender-linked trait. Either parent can perform tasks instinctively; instinct refers not to physiological processes but to responses to a child. "The mother and father who care for a child, who listen for his voice and try to interpret what he means, who comfort him, soothe him, feed him and play with him, discover for the first time what it is to be parents. They do not become parents by virtue of conception and birth alone. They grow to be parents, just as the infant grows to know what parents are."[38]

Through the years, a few adoption books even claimed that the adoptive mother had an advantage over the biological mother. In the 1970s, an adoption expert could write: "One advantage you, as an adoptive mother, have over the new biological mother is that you are physically well and strong."[39] Not having had the debilitating experience of birth, the adoptive mother is portrayed as better able to act on her own inclinations and to be herself with the child. Changes in the institution of adoption itself led to a further distancing of instinctive love from pregnancy and birth. In adoption books written during the 1940s and 1950s, when babies were not only the desirable but usually the actual adopted population (at least in nonrelative adoptions), parental love could be tied to feelings for an infant, to the gestures and expressions appropriate for a newborn baby. In decades of so-called baby shortage, when few applicants could count on receiving an infant (and when, correspondingly, adoption experts wrote of the virtues of noninfant adoptions), the model for love was modified. Adoption books responded to a trend that began in the 1960s and continued through subsequent decades: babies were less frequently the adopted population, and older children as well as those with special needs more frequently the children entering adoptive families.[40] Manuals followed practice, and while maintaining the instinctive basis of love, freed that from responses associated with nurturing and caring for an infant. The instinctive feelings arising from contact with a vulnerable and helpless being were recast for the "new adoption." Parental love then might be described in terms of, for example, "heroic energies" and "enormous doses of patience."[41] Nothing in these altered descriptions, however, implied anything but an unconditional commitment to the child.

Underneath the different descriptions of parental feelings, one element did hold steady in adoption books and this element sounded a strong echo of Spock. A parent's love for a child is portrayed as a distinctive emotion regardless of its origin, and the distinguishing quality is an absolute, unswerving attachment coded, in an American context, by nature used metaphorically. Post-1960s adoption literature extended the metaphor to fit a "new" adoptive family, but without relinquishing its core meaning. The persistence of the metaphor, and its continuities from Spock to adoption manuals, suggests that in American culture adoptive and biological parents are presumed to love a child in exactly the same way. The parent by law, no less than the parent by blood, loves unquestioningly and nonjudgmentally: an instinctive response to the child. The feelings experienced by a parent are the same, whether the child entered the family by birth or by social contract. In adoption manuals, furthermore, this assertion of similarity assured the parent not bound by blood to a child that love would flow from contact. Being yourself and acting in character, these books went on to note, expressed love to the child. "Affection and protectiveness are conveyed by parents to their child even before words have any meaning. . . ."[42]

Character here is connected to the idea of developing love for a child, acquiring the feelings that constitute parental love. The notion of learning to love a child, as it appeared in adoption books of all four decades, casts further light on the model for parental love in American culture. The idea of learning also illuminates the changes in this model, at least for adoptive parents, from 1946 to 1985. Avoiding the attribution of parental love to a biological bond, adoption texts utilize language that suggests love can be learned and achieved. An implicit accompanying assumption, incidentally, is that a biological parent who has relinquished a child can "unlearn" love for the child. Partly a response to the missing ingredient, pregnancy and birth, the idea of learning emphasizes the significance of developing one's nature as a parent in the process of caring for a child. Like the meaning of instinct, too, the meaning of character in adoption books avoids an association with one sex.

The basis for inserting an idea of learning into "acting yourself" as a parent is linked to the contractual origin of the relationship, to the necessity of applying for a child, and to a culture pattern shared by Spock and evident in his "How to be Natural." The outstanding fact about adoption, in American society, is that an individual has to qualify as a parent, has to meet certain requirements in order to have a child. Whether adopting through an agency or independently,[43] every adoptive parent has been asked to show what he and she is "like" as a person. This is a process of demonstrating character, whose precise requirements have changed over the decades but whose necessity has not. A beginning in the need to demonstrate one's character cannot but affect descriptions of the feelings one can expect to have toward an adopted child. Adoption books, over the years, have been remarkably clever at juxtaposing the initial experience with the anticipated experiences that indicate "you have learned to love a child not your own."

During the 1940s and 1950s babies were available and adoptive parents qualified easily. Petitioners did not have to be wary about describing their (potential) parental characters. This ease disappeared in subsequent decades and the expectations for qualifying as a parent also shifted. Adoption manuals presented a revised view of parental character, reflecting not only a "baby shortage" but also the perceptible frustration of individuals who had to demonstrate parental traits when other people "just had babies." A vivid representation of the change appeared in portraits of the typical adoptive parent: no longer a perfect parent and increasingly one with flaws and insecurities of her or his own. In 1947, an adoption text could say without prejudicing the decision to adopt: "In general, it is probably true that men and women who seriously consider the adoption of a child are people of more than ordinary emotional depth, greater than common seriousness in their relation to life and to each other, more than usual conscientiousness. . . . They are able, consciously, to examine their own feelings and to seek the full expression of those which are deepest, perhaps finest."[44] This virtually perfect parent had already learned love. Twenty-five years later the message was different: social workers "aren't looking for perfect parents. . . . Instead they are seeking applicants who have the desire and the potential to become good adoptive parents."[45] The road to adopting a child was no longer smooth; correspondingly, the task of bringing up a child was portrayed as more difficult, requiring practice and enormous doses of patience.

Whatever the demands and the detail of the qualifying process, this had to fit into the discussion of loving an adopted child. Adoptive parents read that they could anticipate learning to love a child not biologically their own, and that they would acquire a parental character as they interacted with, nurtured, and fed the child. But this was always said with a caution: Love might not happen automatically, the feelings that constitute that emotion might not be immediately detectable. Well before Spock talked about a possible delay in a mother's discovery of love for her child,[46] adoption manuals saw such delay as a distinct possibility in the relationship between parent and child. A 1947 manual struck a typical note of warning: "Both parents and child need to get acquainted, to grow close to one another in understanding and affection."[47] With a sense of realism connected to the deliberateness of an adoption proceeding, adoption books told of parents who did not define their responses to the child as love or "act natural" in their relationship with the child. This represents a quite different perspective from that of Spock, whose basic tone of confidence—trust yourself—persisted from one edition of *Baby and Child Care* to the next. For adoptive parents, unlike Spockian parents, loving a child could be difficult without threatening the child or the parent-child relationship. And if occasional reports in adoption books about the struggle to love a child warned away some potential adoptive parents, overall the message that love might be hard was encouraging inasmuch as it acknowledged diversity in the experience of an emotion.

The claim that parental traits could be acquired, love for a child learned, and the emotions constituting love gradually recognized had as a corollary, in adoption books, a less homogenous parental character than appeared in *Baby and Child Care*. The figures who represent typical adoptive parents do not seem so flat or one-dimensional as do the parents in Spock. Nor are they conventionally maternal: in adoption books the traits associated with being a mother do not so clearly define the traits associated with being a parent. An emphasis on learning removed the feelings constituting parental love from those experienced by a mother who has given birth to the child, and allowed for both a wider panoply of emotions and for a diversity of expression of these emotions. That meant, simply, that parents in adoption books could have more idiosyncratic characters than Spock permits. Nurturing and protective instincts, adoption texts say, must be tended and "grown" into love by the adoptive parent of either gender. Being a woman does not make it easier, and does not (as in Spock) present the program for both mother and father. What adoption manuals and Spock do share is an assumption that parental feelings are continuous with how the child arrived in the family. In Spock, birth flows into a loving response on the part of the mother. In adoption manuals, the process of qualifying as a parent sets the foundation for learning how to love a child.

There is, however, a problem with the idea of acquiring parental character. Learning to love a child does not accord with the absoluteness and inevitability embedded in the metaphorical usage of "nature" in these child-rearing books. Learning implies a role and set of behaviors achieved by an individual and performed under certain conditions. But culturally, parental love is unconditional, an inherent trait rather than a learned pattern of behavior. Adoption books, then, had to handle an implicit contradiction between the assertion that anyone could learn the traits of a loving parent and a cultural assumption that parental love developed inevitably, naturally, and without regard for particular circumstances. A learned love suggests contingency, not the essential givenness presumed of parental feelings. To counteract an impression of impermanence, adoption texts turned to the other contractual relationship in American society that was supposed to be noncontingent and permanent, marriage.[48]

Adoption books borrowed images from literary and psychological interpretations of marital love in order to delineate the bond in adoptive relationships. The borrowed images changed as views of marriage, and marriage itself, changed in the decades between World War II and the 1980s. But new images retained the original, core meaning of continuity and commitment. The analogy to marital love had a special force in books on adoption; the significance of the concept was immediately comprehensible to readers and marriage itself was directly relevant to becoming an adoptive parent. In the process of applying for a child, individuals have to think about their own marriage. In some instances, petitioners only qualified as parents if they were married (and not contemplating dissolving that relationship); in other instances, especially with new policies in the 1960s and 1970s, applicants were asked to explain why they were single if they were and, by implication, the nature of their sexuality.[49] Regardless of its precise role, marriage remained central to the process of applying for a child.

References to marriage in books written for adoptive parents could be startlingly direct, in some cases barely metaphorical. Adoption books talked about love-at-first-sight, a honeymoon, and an adjustment stage. Of these, the first—love-at-first-sight—was both the most powerful and the most modified trope. In the immediate post–World War II period in the popular imagination, and to an extent in scholarly literature on marriage, love-at-first-sight communicated the inevitability of the relationship: people "fell" in love. Furthermore, passionate love became the test for true emotional bonds between members of a family. "Romantic love became the test [for family affections]. It was a passion for another person so great that one was singled out from all others as the only fully satisfying object in the world."[50] These connotations characterized use of the phrase in adoption literature of that era. Love-at-first-sight proved the parent and child were meant for one another. A 1946 text claimed that "Whatever may be true in other emotional relationships, love at first sight is real enough between foster [i.e., adoptive] parents and children," privileging the parent-child love above marital love, and adding "And you may not fall in love according to plan, even though the plan is yours."[51] The relationship between adopting parent and adopted child, like passion, was uncalculated. The connotation of inevitability persisted when, ten years later, love-at-first-sight was presented as variable and chancy—not all parents fall in love. "While many couples 'fall in love' with their new child at first sight, others find the first meeting an unexpectedly upsetting experience."[52] Those who do fall in love are permanently attached to the child. And ten years after that, somewhat paradoxically, falling in love was seen to "take time." "Our caseworker told us not to worry. 'It takes time to fall in love' is the way she put it."[53] Love-at-first-sight sealed the bond between parent and child. The image remained an appealing one in adoption books through the 1970s, after it had faded from discussions of marriage. By the late 1970s, however, love-at-first-sight began to disappear from adoption literature too, in books written by adoptive parents as well as by experts in the field of adoption. The disappearance occurred for several reasons, among them the elimination of love-at-first-sight from cultural views of marriage; the de-romanticizing of marriage made love-at-first-sight a less effective metaphor for parent-child relationships. A shift in the institution of adoption, too, changed notions of parental love; the rise in numbers of older children, special needs children, and stepchildren in the adopted population undercut an implicit premise of love-at-first-sight—adopting an infant. And, finally, the textual change reflected a change in the surrounding emotional climate, toward a presumably more realistic view of feelings and the nature of interpersonal bonds. By the end of the 1970s, falling in love in adoption as in marriage manuals implied delusion, blindness, and naïveté, an unsound basis for a permanent commitment. So, in 1985, a typical text quoted a social worker: "People see a picture of this blonde, blue-eyed little girl . . . and they'll immediately fall in love with her. They'll assume she's a bouncy, happy little girl, only to find out in reality that she's perhaps been sexually or physically abused. . . ."[54]

But love-at-first-sight had conveyed a culturally important quality of parental love, and that could not disappear entirely from adoption texts. The metaphor was replaced by another, one that carried the same sense of inevitability and absoluteness: a metaphor of fate or destiny. "I've been told by many other adoptive parents that they, too, feel their adopted child was predestined to be theirs."[55] Fate, like falling in love, responds to a perceived contradiction between the contingency of adoption, an arranged parenthood, and the permanence that defines parental love. Being fated, like falling in love, meant the bond was sealed.

Falling in love, and later fate, described one part of the adoptive relationship. There was more to the marriage analogy than that, further delineating the elements in a model for adoptive parent love. References to marriage
conveyed the notion of stages in a relationship between parent and child.
(The idea of stages complemented that of learning to love a child, though the
two were not necessarily explicitly linked in adoption literature; the gist of
the two presentations was the same: relationships between parent and child
evolved over time.) In this, the "honeymoon" played a key part, and was
borrowed quite directly from conventional accounts of a honeymoon in
marriage. Occurring at a different time—before, not after, legalization of the
contract—a honeymoon in adoption accomplished the same purposes for
adoptive parent and adopted child as it did for newly married husband and
wife. According to adoption manuals, the honeymoon was a lovely interlude
when the child and the parent were on their best behavior. The baby in the
1940s and 1950s, and the child in later decades, is portrayed as sweet,
contented, and charming, while the parent is unfailingly affectionate and
gentle. The child's special sweetness is not explained, but the parent's behavior is, in terms of the appreciation she or he feels at having a child at last.
And, in a startlingly direct analogy, the adoptive honeymoon is said to
provide the physical foundation for emotions and responsibilities crucial to
an ongoing relationship. Adoption books describe the honeymoon stage in
phrases that evoke an intense sensuality between parent and child, through
bodily contact. The gestures expressing intimacy are available to the adoptive
father and the adoptive mother equally.

Spock also writes about a sensual element in contacts between parent and
child, and every edition of *Baby and Child Care* reminds fathers as well as
mothers of the importance of holding and fondling a child. The 1976 and
1985 editions are more daring in suggesting that the sensual responses of a
parent toward her child resemble sexual feelings. This may be true for either
parent but, Spockian, it is most true for the mother. In *Baby and Child Care*
heightened sensuality comes with breast-feeding. Breast-feeding uniquely
establishes intimacy between parent and child—a mother and her child. In
the updated 1985 edition, Spock adds that the mother's intense sensual
feelings for her baby often make a father jealous; but, says Spock in his
customary comforting tone, that's natural.[56] Adoption books recognize and
praise sensuality but scrupulously avoid any suggestion of sexuality, in this
instance being more conservative than Spock and bowing to the traditional
American denial of an erotic component in parent-child love.[57] Adoption
texts are here operating within cultural parameters, accepting the assumption that blood ties rule against a sexual relationship whereas a social
contract does not. The same assumption allows Spock to describe breast-
feeding as sexual, knowing it will not become "sex" but will substantiate a

mother's love for her baby.[58] Within the cultural context, then, no natural taboos against sex exist between an adoptive parent and adopted child. In fact, very few adoption books suggest there is any sex in the family at all, a delicacy that may also reflect concern that marital sex is a reminder of the adoptive couple's infertility. Books published during the 1950s offer a slight exception; in that era of romantic love[59] references to the mother's and father's feelings for one another conveyed the general lovingness in an adoptive family: "The affection that flows between them [husband and wife] creates an atmosphere in which the child's emerging personality can flourish."[60]

Even when love-at-first-sight dropped from the comparison of adoption and marriage, references to the honeymoon remained important in discussions of an adoptive parent-child relationship. And true to its original meaning, the honeymoon did not last any longer in adoption than it did in marriage. The presumption in adoption literature was that the physical intimacy represented by a honeymoon would last, creating a solid grounding for parental love. In adoption texts that used the metaphor, the honeymoon also represented a stage in the growth of love; a honeymoon marked the transition from initial enchantment to the routine of bringing up the child. After the honeymoon, fondness and affection are embedded in the chores of day-to-day life, taking on a different cast than they had in the first stage of the parent-child relationship.[61] After the honeymoon, life settles down to normal, though assurances to adoptive parents of how easily this was supposed to happen changed over the four decades. Smooth sailing went away in the 1960s. A typical touch of reality appears in the following statement from a 1969 book by an adoptive father: "[Y]ou don't love him yet for what he is; now there he stands by the kitchen table: hostile, remote, immovably implanted in his imperious determination not to budge ever, not ever."[62] Simultaneously, the lack of smoothness in parent-child love was interpreted as proof of its naturalness. In the struggles of daily life, adoptive parent and adopted child are acting just like a real family.

Just like a real family: the bias throughout adoption literature has been to diminish the difference between adoptive and biological families. The metaphor of nature in adoption books argued the point and, as well, defined the feelings that characterize interactions between any parent and a child. A natural feeling, the love a parent has for an adoptive child begins to sound as inherent and inevitable as the love a biological mother has for her child. "Nature" conveys the essential ingredient of parental love, the feeling that binds any parent to her or his child without question and without judgment of the child's performance. Still, and almost defensively, the strength of the contracted relationship had to be brought home and it is for this reason that adoption books drew on an analogy with marriage, the other contracted love relationship in American society. Like a parent-child bond, marriage was culturally viewed as lasting, an enduring solidarity. Using references to marital love to delineate the bonds between adoptive parent and child also highlighted the assumptions in a Spockian model for parental love: the significance of physical intimacy and sensual bodily contact for sealing the bond between parent and child, the importance of total commitment to the child, and (in later Spock) the idea that love developed over time and through the routines of ordinary upbringing.[63] When attitudes toward marriage in the United States changed, adoption texts accommodated their use of the metaphor, dropping love-at-first-sight but maintaining the idea of a honeymoon and of "normalcy." Love-at-first-sight was replaced by a notion of fate and inevitability: the relationship between parent and child in an adoptive family was as "given" and "uncalculated" as that between a biological parent and child.

Permanency, absoluteness, and inevitability are the key words. In adoption literature from 1946 through the present, whatever else changed, the idea that parental love is a perfect and lasting commitment did not change. The consistency from decade to decade demonstrates the strength of a cultural model for a particular emotion. The model is persuasively outlined in the pages of *Baby and Child Care* and the emotion defined for generations of American parents: parental love is a feeling experienced by a parent for a child and the feeling exists apart from the behaviors performed by either. Parental love is not a socialized but a natural emotion. And this is no less true of the parent-child relationship that originated in a legal contract than of the relationship originating in a biological event. Feelings of love experienced by a parent, in other words, exist "beyond" the social, beyond the exigencies of role and duty. Parental love is not supposed to shift with the chores of the day. When descriptions of love became less romantic in adoption manuals of the 1970s and 1980s, the essential quality of absoluteness remained—even if patience, not passion, formed the commitment. This element of the Spockian model did not drop from the pages of adoption manuals, even as these distanced the meanings of parental love from the Spockian ideal of motherhood, pregnancy, birth, and breast-feeding.

Another similarity between adoption books and Spock lay in the role of the child in precipitating parental emotion. Spock's model left little room for the child; not being judged, the child hardly has to do anything to elicit love from a parent. A child is recipient not creator of the love felt by a parent, an adoptive as much as a biological parent. To have a child create love would put a burden on him (or her) that, judging by child-rearing texts, is unacceptable in American culture. *Baby and Child Care* presents the cultural model, but gradually, as adoption itself changed, adoption books stretched its parameters. With an "older" population of adopted children, texts changed the description of how love came about; the child played a greater role, not through her or his actions but through the personality he brought into the new family.

Yet adoptive parents who first read adoption manuals and then read Spock would not detect a discrepancy in what they were supposed to feel toward a child. They might, however, appreciate the wider scope given to the evolution of this feeling by writers on adoption. Not having a biological bond or a known blood tie makes a difference; in books written for their situation, adoptive parents read that love can be learned, parental traits acquired, and the stages to a real family feeling be followed. All of this frees love, in adoption texts, from the association with woman and with motherhood that is apparent upon close reading of Spock.

On all levels, from the marked connotations of "nature" to the use of a marriage metaphor, the model of love for adoptive parents was presented as virtually gender free. The initial commitment to a child was described as instinctive, without suggestion of a physiological grounding for this instinct in pregnancy and birth. Similarly, an emphasis on learning to love a child and acquiring the traits characteristic of a "good" parent freed the emotion from an association with woman as parent. Over time the prose in adoption manuals changed, indicating a growing reaction against a cultural pattern that equated parental love with motherhood. The shift in image, for instance, from falling in love to being fated accorded more recognition to a male parent: in American culture men do not "fall in love" with babies but they can be destined to be fathers. Falling in love as a concept had also presumed an infant; changes in the adoptable population complemented revisions in theories of parenthood and family relationships to modify the model of love in adoption books. Bemused enchantment was not appropriate for an older child or a stepchild.[64]

Simultaneously, by the late 1960s, another metaphor dropped out of adoption literature. Analogies between feeling pregnant and anticipating an adopted child were no longer used to underline the "realness" of the relationship. In 1969 an adoptive father used the analogy, in the process converting pregnancy into a gender-free mood of excitement and distractedness. "The change [to thinking about being a parent] is indeed like a pregnancy; you will find to your embarrassment that you are showing exactly the same symptoms of mood and behavior. Hours of idle dreaming; total and constant preoccupation with the little life now so tenuously and mysteriously joined with your own. . . ."[65] For writers and readers of books on adoption, parental love was natural but not maternal.

And, as the concept of nature indicated, parental love was enduring and solid whatever its origin and whatever the form of its expression to the child. Established in a different way, adoptive parent love was yet as natural as the love felt by a biological parent—the culturally right kind of love for children. With their "natural" family established, adoptive parents could turn to *Baby and Child Care* for help with the details of bringing up a child and could use the guide for expressing parental love available to all parents in the United States.

III. Parental Love: The Outcome

Baby and Child Care is a manual for the expression and the demonstration of parental love. "How to be natural," a subheading on page 7 of the 1985 Spock, explains why there is a manual if to be a "good and loving" parent means "following your own inclinations." Instructions are needed in order to be natural. The book reflects a cultural assumption that one learns to be oneself and develops character in order to act spontaneously. The apparent contradiction between being instructed and "trusting yourself" creates a tension that runs through all editions of Spock and is never resolved, partly because it is central to Spock's purposes in writing a child-rearing manual and partly because the tension is unresolved in American culture.[66] What may be most remarkable about *Baby and Child Care,* in fact, is its author's comfortable, and cultural, acceptance of the fact that people must learn how to be natural.

The contradiction between being natural (acting yourself) and learning how by consulting experts and following instructions is not unique to Spock or to the domain of parental love in an American context. Historically, appreciation of the natural has coincided with an effort at control, at taming the wild and civilizing the savage. Nature appreciated in American culture is nature ruled, and turned to productive uses. In the case of child-rearing manuals, the concept of nature contains several referents: from one perspective, the child is a natural being who has to be trained and civilized; from another perspective, the process of child rearing should be natural even if that means imposing rules on the parent. This last is the perspective evident in Spock and in adoption literature. Spock's child is never purely natural but always "naturally sociable." His is not the child of Rousseau; the child in *Baby and Child Care* is ready to join the forces of civilization and is on occasion more sociable than his parents. Nature in Spock refers to the parents' behaviors, to their instincts and character, and to the lovingness that will ensure the child's "flourishing" and growing naturally into a good adult. For the parent to be natural, she or he must learn to be comfortable with an array of feelings, to judge their "value" for the child, and to assess their impact on the child's development. It is a measured and rule-abiding naturalness, if you are a parent in a Spockian world. Spock, of course, did not create the milieu in which instruction allows you to be yourself. *Baby and*

Child Care responded to an existing cultural context and, surpassingly well, to the consequent anxiety attendant upon child rearing in American society.

Historically the process of bringing up children has had a moral component in American culture, though the content of the precepts changed from decade to decade. *Baby and Child Care* took on the significance of child rearing in a special way, addressing the fear of failure in American parents who experience the pressure to "bring a child up right." According to Spock, "You're happy and excited, but, if you haven't had much experience you wonder whether you are going to know how to do a good job."[67] Instructions and advice tell how to do a good job and thereby provide a comforting structure for expressing oneself as a parent.

In a very broad sense, then, the contradiction between nature and "expert" guidance is resolved, at least for individuals. Because so much is culturally assumed to rest on proper child rearing, it is comforting, not contradictory, to have the process bound by rules and the reassuring advice of an expert. Parents, Spock realized and reiterated, must be guided through the possible pitfalls of the process. And while Spock admits there might be demand for a manual directed entirely at the parent's needs,[68] his basic goal is to build parental confidence for the sake of the child. To an extent, this focus on the child's flourishing well-being is shared by adoption manuals. Adoption books, however, also address the needs, insecurities, and anxieties of the parent, assuring adoptive parents of their ability to be natural and loving with an adopted child. But, in the last analysis, what the child will become— how he will grow up—is the main justification for adoption manuals by experts and by parents, just as it is for *Baby and Child Care*.[69] In this section, I compare the content and the implications of a focus on outcome, on the adult product of "good" child rearing, in Spock and in adoption literature further to delineate the model of parental love in each. To anticipate: the adult growing up under Spockian guidance remains consistent from decade to decade; there is little change in the posited personality and associated behaviors. By contrast, adoption literature produces a diverse "product" over the years, as it had a diverse parent. Adoption books seem more sensitive to changes in the social and cultural context in discussing the goals of child rearing than does *Baby and Child Care*. And yet there are similarities: the ideal outcome in each is a loving adult who can, and will, raise loving children.

Spock should, obviously, be discussed first. The seven hundred pages of detailed instruction in each edition are unified by what can be called a dominant theme: indulgence versus strictness, otherwise phrased as "being casual" versus inhibiting one's responses to a child. The balance between these foci changed from one edition to the next without genuinely altering a model for love based on "being natural." As I have mentioned, the concept of nature in Spock refers to parental behaviors and to the "climate" created by the parent in order that a child flourish. How much attention the parent paid and how much she could let the child's nature take its own course constituted probably the most substantial revision in *Baby and Child Care* from the 1946 through the 1957 and 1968 to the "updated" 1976 and 1985 versions. The clearest shift from being casual to exerting control occurred between 1957 and 1968, though a metaphorical shift in 1957 anticipates the change: "In automobile terms, the child supplies the power but the parents have to do the steering."[70] In 1946 imagery, the child's nature required only a nurturing environment.

By the 1968 edition Spock came to see the necessity of limiting the demonstration of love. The commonsensical 1946 edition gave way by then to a definitively sterner edition in which parental love was monitored rather than uninhibitedly expressed. And "common sense" was dropped from the title. Spock wrote in the 1968 preface: "THE PRINCIPAL CHANGE THAT HAS OCCURRED IN MY OWN OUTLOOK on child rearing has been the realization that what is making the parent's job difficult is today's child-centered viewpoint. . . . I mean the tendency of many conscientious parents to keep their eyes exclusively focused on their child, thinking about what he needs from them and from the community, instead of thinking about what the world, the neighborhood, the family will be needing from the child. . . ."[71] The 1968 parent who followed Spock would be obliged to regulate the child more deliberately than was the case for the 1946 parent. In 1946 scheduling the child was entirely a matter of choice; for instance, on the subject of weaning Spock advised: "take it easy and follow his [baby's] lead."[72] In the post-1968 editions, scheduling becomes a way of giving children "a feeling that they are in this world not for their own satisfaction but primarily to serve others."[73] Toilet training should occur at eighteen months instead of "whenever," and the child should be told to put on a coat rather than reminded about the cold weather. Other examples could be cited; the emphasis evidently does shift, and parents are explicitly warned of the dangers of succumbing to a child's every demand. The warning is for the child's and for the parent's sake. "In other words, parents can't feel right toward their children in the long run unless they can make them behave reasonably, and children can't be happy unless they are behaving reasonably."[74] In the last three editions of *Baby and Child Care* it is clear that the parent who devotes herself to a child loses a sense of herself, and cannot "act in character"—be naturally loving.

Furthermore the child does not thrive. She (as the by then "aware" Spock would have it) becomes anxious, locating her anxiety in "bogeymen or witches or robbers or dogs or dinosaurs or polio or lightning, depending on her age. . . ."[75] Or worse, because with ramifying consequences, the child will be spoiled. A wonderful word bequeathed by *Baby and Child Care* to generations of parents, spoiled reveals a great deal about the Spockian model for parental love. Above all, and persisting from edition to edition, a parent's love is supposed to facilitate the flourishing of a child's being and not "spoil" the development of her natural good spirits. I discuss the outcome of parental love more fully below, but here it is important to note that "spoiling" in the post-1968 editions of Spock became the prime symbol for parental love gone awry. A few mild paragraphs in 1946 treat spoiling as easily remediable.[76] "We aren't as scared of the danger of spoiling," the pediatrician notes.[77] The preface to the 1957 edition suggests the emergence of second thoughts: "If you are an old reader of this book, you'll see that a lot has been added and changed, especially about discipline, spoiling, and the parents' part. . . . Since then [1946] a great change in attitude has occurred, and nowadays there seems to be more chance of a conscientious parent's getting into trouble with permissiveness than with strictness. So I have tried to give a more balanced view."[78] And in 1968 the spoiled child becomes slave driver: "If she continues to give in, he realizes after a while that he has his poor tired mother under his thumb and he becomes increasingly disagreeable and tyrannical in demanding this service."[79] The texts concentrate less on explaining why spoiling happens than on the consequences, for the parents' feelings of love and for the child's personality. Parental love gone awry feels wrong to the parent; she becomes less easygoing, casual, and self-confident in the relationship. "The mother can't help resenting such an unreasonable attitude and she gets to dislike him [the child] heartily. But these emotions are apt to make her feel guilty, and besides, she doesn't know how to get out of the jam."[80] The child with a tense and resentful parent cannot develop into his naturally outgoing, gregarious, and imaginative self: "Your baby is born to be a reasonable, friendly human being";[81] all you have to do is "let him." Spoiled, the child becomes selfish, narrow, timid, and unloving—"in fact, everybody dislikes them [spoiled children] for their selfishness."[82]

Actually, there is some hint at the why of spoiling in later editions. In 1985 Spock wrote: "But some parents are more easily drawn into spoiling than others—for instance . . . parents with too little confidence in their own worthiness who become willing slaves to a child and expect her or him to be all the things they felt they never could be; parents who have adopted a baby and feel that they have to do a superhuman job to justify themselves; parents who have studied child psychology in college. . . ."[83] How do the advocates of adoptive parents—adoption manuals—respond to the "spoiling" versus "being firm" issue? In the 1940s and 1950s the issue of spoiling was rarely tackled. (Discipline is mentioned, perhaps not surprisingly, only in chapters on adolescent adoptees.)[84] Given the terms of adoption, in which a social contract rather than a blood tie linked parent and child, all expressions of love were assumed to be significant for sealing the bond with the child. And, of course, during the immediate postwar period Spock himself was indulgent about spoiling, a part of the context for authors of adoption manuals.

By the mid-1950s, however, adoption books no longer presumed that love would flow generously; authors began to prescribe love. "There is now quite conclusive evidence that babies need loving just as much as feeding," warned an expert in 1959.[85] The significance of love for sealing the bond with the child appears in these later texts in the form of instructions to "devote yourself" to the child. In another 1959 statement parents were told that adoptive children "need extra of the good things all children should have," evidently referring to affection, not material goods.[86] Ten years later the adoptive parent received advice to ignore, at least for a few months, spouse, other children, and routine activities for the sake of a newly adopted child. "Do you give him preference over your other children, not to mention your dog and your husband? The answer is yes."[87] Absolute devotion "secured" the child, attaching her to the family as well as providing her with psychological stability.

What Spock called spoiling became desirable in adoption books, and the "slavish devotion" he counseled against was portrayed as a natural response to the adoptive situation. By the 1970s, adoption books were telling adoptive parents: "As you grow to love this special little person, you give of yourself completely. You become almost a slave to your child—conscious of his every need, his every desire. You lovingly, willingly, devote your life to him. . . ."[88] The passage reads like an implicit critique of Spock; it also reflects a contemporaneous theoretical position on the importance of demonstrative love for cementing an adoptive parent-child relationship. The same author goes on to say, "yet you have absolutely no guarantee of ever getting anything in return."[89] Devotion is for its own sake and for the sake of the child, not in expectation of any "return."[90] An emphasis on devotion also confirms, indirectly, the importance in American culture of the biological connection between parent and child. With that connection a parent can be, in Spock's words, "matter of fact" and "casual." Without it, she must devote herself to the child in order to establish a long-lasting love. By the end of the 1970s, adoption literature had reached a consensus on the point: the adoptive parent must "decide that love, and commitment, will have to do it."[91] Publications of the Child Welfare League of America, which instruct the social workers who instruct the parents, put love in terms of a right: "It is every child's right to receive love."[92]

As in Spock, much of the discussion of demonstrations of love in adoption literature has to do with what the child will become, the outcome of expressions of parental love. Advice on how to act with a child, on how to demonstrate love, is geared toward turning the child into a particular kind of adult. American society places an enormous burden on parental love—a cause and a consequence of the remarkable outpouring of child-rearing manuals. Parental love creates the adult. And as natural as the expression and existence of love should be, the product must be a cultivated and socialized adult.

Descriptions of this socialized adult in Spock and in adoption manuals have some similarities, but also some important differences. In both, the good outcome of parental love is a secure and loving adult. In Spock, this adult can further be characterized as the American of his time—or, accurately, the Spockian "ideal" American: creative, innovative, joyous, trusting, and idealistic.[93] Varying only slightly in the specifics, each edition continues the project of perpetuating an American personality. Arguably all child-rearing manuals create the culturally appropriate personality, but Spock allows comparatively little room for diversity and for change in this personality. He does say "love the child for what he is," but entirely so that the child will grow up to be "friendly" and "reasonable," not idiosyncratic or unusual. "The child who is appreciated for what he is, . . . will grow up with confidence in himself, happy," Spock wrote to parents of the 1960s.[94] The details of difference are minor; the child who grows up according to the 1985 Spock will, like the child of the four previous editions, be genial, gregarious, and concerned about others.[95] The discussion of socialization into gender roles further reveals the basic conservatism of a Spockian outlook.

In spite of revisions to counteract sexism,[96] *Baby and Child Care* raises "women" and "men" with sex-related roles and personalities. A part of the Spockian project was not just to raise "good" adults, but to raise adults with clear gender identities—to be good mothers and fathers.[97] In 1946 and 1957 raising good mothers and fathers was easy: parents treated girls like girls, boys like boys. "This is the time when the boy acquires much of his desire to be cooperative with men, brave in danger . . . just as his father is. This is the age when a girl is inspired to be helpful in the house, devoted to babies . . . just as her mother is."[98] In fact in those two editions the Spockian baby was generically male and the main discussion of a girl baby occurred in the context of gender socialization: "a friendly father plays a different but equally important part in the development of a girl. She won't exactly pattern herself after him, but she gains confidence in herself as a girl and a woman from feeling his approval. I'm thinking of little things like approving of her dress. . . ."[99] In 1976, to avoid sexism, Spock deliberately introduced girl babies and the pronoun "she" throughout the text: "your baby, say it's a girl" became a litany. Simultaneously, the discussion of gender socialization became more awkward. To be "equal," girls and boys should be treated exactly the same way—given the same jobs and the same toys.[100] What happens, then, to how girls learn to be women? The 1976 (and to a lesser extent the

1985) edition waffles around, alternating advice to give girls trucks with reminders of the boy's adventurousness and "greater need to explore the outside world." In the 1985 edition the dilemma is slightly eased by a vague assumption that gender "will work out," and that the main purpose of parental love is to produce a loving and sociable adult. "Since there is no such thing as a 100 percent identification with one's own sex, it's better to let children grow up with the mixture of identifications, attitudes, and interests that have developed in them, as long as they can accept comfortably what they are. . . ."[101] But other paragraphs scattered through the 1985 version emphasize the need for a boy to identify with his father, a girl with her mother. "A boy doesn't grow spiritually to be a man just because he's born with a male body."[102]

Adoption manuals treat the outcome of parental love in some of the same ways that Spock does, but also with important differences. A successful outcome in adoption texts is the secure and loving adult of *Baby and Child Care*. In terms of specific personality traits, however, adoption texts do not describe an "ideal" American or a particular kind of woman and man. In fact, adoption books rarely discuss gender differences, except almost inadvertently in descriptions of the stereotypical adopted baby: a blue-eyed, blond-haired girl.[103] Issues of identity and of security overwhelm that of gender. "Your child can be just like you," adoption books tell adopting parents. The phrase meant several things, from a psychological identification between parent and child to a visible resemblance, a sharing of features. "In adoption you take a child not born of you, not related to you, and not known to you, into your home. As you care for the child day by day—attend his needs, his wants—you grow to love him, to understand him, and to care about him as a special person. Soon he becomes part of you—a very important part of your life, your family, your very being."[104] Written in the 1970s, these sentences represent "just like you" as identity: the child becomes a part of you, a oneness that is culturally assumed to characterize parent-child relationships. The phrase "just like you" embeds a notion of identity that indicates the success of a loving upbringing. The secure adult is like the adoptive parent.

Adoption books also treated "just like you" more simply. In every era, some books asserted that eventually an adopted child would visibly resemble her adoptive parents. Such resemblance included emotional as well as physical traits, a likeness extended to mean "fitting" the family. There were differences in how resemblance was described, depending on when a book was written, on the policies current in adoption, and on the general context in which family and relationships were being discussed. For those who wrote, and read adoption manuals in the 1940s and 1950s, resemblance could literally mean "looking like," and a child could be expected to share physical features with his adoptive parents. This was not fantasy or wishful thinking, since these were the decades of "matching," when experts in adoption made strenuous efforts to match a child with the potential parents, choosing an adoptive family with features, coloring, and ethnic and religious background that matched the birth family's. So, especially in those years, despite the official proclamation that parental love did not depend on a blood tie, adoption agencies nevertheless attempted to replicate blood ties through physical resemblance between parent and child. The attempt to copy nature underlines the contemporaneous weight of a biological model for parental love.

In subsequent decades, matching dropped from formal adoption policy,[105] partly because matches became difficult when there were not enough adoptable children to go around and partly in response to a general liberalizing of attitudes about race and ethnicity in the family. Yet even then adoptive parents were assured that a child would acquire their characteristics and gestures, and would begin to "look like you" after all. From this point of view, love created a physical bond where none had existed before. "As in all children, you will eventually begin to discover family traits in your Asian child. The eerie part will be that the traits are yours."[106] Above all the child fit into the family, and, in the conventional phrase, "reflected" his upbringing. "Andy is the Matthews' [adopted] eight-year-old son—tall and blond as is Vicki, and outgoing—his mother's son. . . ."[107]

Descriptions of the growing-up child in adoption literature point to the importance of love for identifying (binding) parent and child. And as in Spock, "being just like you," whatever the particular details, preeminently meant being loving: a loving child grows up in a loving family. "He learns to love by being loved."[108] Similarly, Spock notes about well-brought-up women and men: "[T]hey also love children because they remember being loved so much by their parents in their own childhood."[109] Parent and child are alike in being loving, in an adoptive as in a biological family. Earlier I noted that several adoption books claim there is no "reward" for slavish devotion to the child, but in a sense there is a reward: with love, the child grows up to be just like you, sharing gestures, temperament, and likes and dislikes—just like a "real" child.

Lovingness from generation to generation, identifying parent and child, is an equally strong notion in Spock and in adoption literature. But the idea carries an extra significance in books on adoption. In an adoptive parent-child relationship, the transmitted trait of lovingness proves the absolute and permanent connection between parent and child and, as well, demonstrates the love expressed in the child-rearing process. While physical resemblances make the tie visible, the loving nature shared by adoptive parent and adopted child indicates the tie is fundamental and "real." Adoption texts use both the specific just-like-you and the general characterization of "loving" to assert the permanence of a relationship between parent and child begun in law. The adult who has grown up in an adoptive family, by his or her personality proves that adoptive love is as natural as the love expressed in a biological family.

IV. Conclusion: Diverging from Spock

Adoption literature cannot break entirely away from the Spockian model for parental love. From 1946 to the present, the model in *Baby and Child Care* has reflected and perpetuated assumptions that are fundamental in American culture. These assumptions have to do with the qualities and the consequences of a parent's love for a child. Cultural assumptions, and especially those concerning emotional concepts, are not ordinarily expressed in so many words: they are "just assumed." Dr. Spock's manuals begin to outline and to explicate assumptions about parental love, but still largely indirectly, through numerous specific instructions, an amount of "sermonizing" (telling a parent what is good, what bad), and tone of voice. The various elements gain meaning from an overriding interpretive framework based on the use of "nature" as a symbol for parental love. Furthermore, in Spock nature elides into the traits and behaviors culturally associated with women and with mothers. Parental love remains, in the spirit if not the letter of Spock, maternal love. And for this reason I have described the Spockian model as a conservative one.

Adoption texts, too, utilize a concept of nature to delineate parental love. But in these texts nature accumulates cultural connotations that weaken the emphasis on mother and on feminine traits evident in Spock. Nature, in adoption books, represents the absoluteness and noncontingency culturally assumed to distinguish parental love from other emotions. And in these books for adoptive parents nature cannot imply blood, birth, or, by extension, motherhood—or they would lose their audience. Revised to eliminate references to biology, nature retains the important connotations of permanence and absoluteness. For the adoptive parent who finds it in a manual, a concept of nature signifies the inevitability of parent-child relationships and counteracts the note of contingency struck in an adoption proceeding, with its "chance" of getting a child. Adoption manuals address the need on the part of an adoptive parent to know that her (or his) love is as given and as permanent as that of any parent.

"Nature" in adoption texts constitutes a response to the missing biological link between parent and child, while simultaneously conveying the absoluteness of the bond against the chance of the placement. From a certain cultural perspective, adoption in American society is an odd business: an individual petitions for a child, is judged qualified (or not) as a parent, and can change her or his mind at several points before the child actually appears in the household. Adoption is "odd" because this kind of apparently conscious calculation of parenthood does not suit American understandings of what it means to become and to be a "real" parent. (An adoptive parent can return the child, even after legalization, and though this happens rarely, when it does it makes a dramatic statement about the difference between biological and "contractual" parents.) Even if planned, a biological baby is not—at least is not supposed to be—consciously decided upon along the way. "Soon you're going to have a baby," Spock says on page 1 of the 1985 edition, gliding over the decision.

The issue of contingency and, linked to that, of choice in parenthood remained important in adoption manuals from the 1940s through the 1980s. Treatment of the issue, however, was not directly related to a historical period, neither to the social and cultural context nor to the policies embraced by adoption workers. Differences in dealing with the matter of choice in adoptive parenthood seem largely attributable to the theoretical framework and the personal experience of the writer of a manual, though both theory and experience might be influenced by the context of adoption. In the 1940s and 1950s the metaphor of love at first sight, and the delineation of parental love in terms of a "fall" into love, eliminated the question of choice; these images argued that commitment to the child was uncalculated and inevitable. Falling in love minimized the element of choice at the time the child was first seen, an effect gained equally by the newer metaphor of fate and destiny. But falling in love and fate did not handle the whole problem of the selective process by which an adoptive child came into a family. The problem of choice in adoptive parenthood remained, coming up especially in discussions of how to tell the child about adoption.

"Telling" is a central subject in virtually all adoption books: when and how do you tell your child he's adopted?[110] For nearly three decades what was called the "chosen child story" dominated adoption manuals. There were various versions, but the gist went something like this: a wife and husband really want a child, are judged to be fit parents and shown a number of babies (often only photographs of babies), finally choosing the one they like best of all. In 1951 a social worker described the advantage of the chosen child story: "His growing comprehension that his parents adopted him because they wanted him very much ensures support to the child. . . ."[111] Wanted, the child is "secured." In the 1970s and 1980s, books on adoption still had titles like "Chosen Children" and "Families by Choice."

Over time there was also a change, and some writers of books for adoptive parents began to doubt the advantages of the chosen child story. The story suggested selection, a process of deciding about the child that does not accord with the absoluteness of parental love. Chosen once, the child could later be un-chosen, no longer wanted. The chosen child story also implied performance; having won his parents' approval at first encounter, the child had to keep on doing things to maintain their approval. As writers on adoption probed the implications of the chosen child story, it became evident to some that the story contradicted cultural assumptions about a parent-child relationship, in which looking for and choosing a child play no part.[112] In addition, the idea of a chosen child was seen by many as putting an unfair burden on the child. Love should be a child's "right," not his responsibility. These writers warned that the favored story, rather than producing a feeling of being wanted and loved, produced anxiety and insecurity in the so-called chosen child. The story has by no means disappeared from the pages of adoption books and is staunchly defended by experts, parents, and adoptees as the best way to tell about adoption. Those on the other side, who reject the story, consider it not only risky for the child's feelings of being loved for himself, but also a lie. From the latter point of view, adoptive parents do not have, and never have had, a choice about the child they will be given.

These writers argue that the chosen child story be replaced by "fact." With impetus from changes in adoption and in cultural attitudes toward roots, knowing your ancestry, and freedom of information, adoption texts of the past fifteen to twenty years increasingly advise parents to tell adopted children the truth about their adoption. A change in adoption theory, this also reflected a change in adoption practice (when older children and children from abroad composed the adopted population it became hard not to tell the child a truth he probably knew already, and these adoptions influenced attitudes toward infant adoptions), but no change whatever in the ideal emotional underpinning for the parent-child relationship. "Obviously, it is best to tell the whole truth: yes, you are adopted and, yes, you are really my child. Yet, there are still many adoptive parents who have never realized that love and history are what build families."[113]

There is no apparent consensus on what "the whole truth" means. The point was to provide the child with complete information about the circumstances of his adoption and with details about the background of his birth family—without identifying any members of that family. Most adoption books of the late 1970s and early 1980s advise parents to provide a child with knowledge of his blood ties and genealogical roots. The biological bond of a child to his birth family, known but never by law enacted, is presumed to cement the social bond of a child to his adoptive family.[114] Not fully explained, the idea seems to be that with knowledge of his biological identity, the child can form solid and enduring social relationships. With knowledge of his ancestry, too, the child is complete and there are no missing pieces (gaps and holes, say adopted individuals) to mar the development into an adult who will be secure, confident, trusting, and loving.

The view that the child should be given information about her or his biological background reflected changes in the institution of adoption as much as it did changes in theoretical assumptions about the adoptive family and about parental love. The weight of these changes can be gauged by the fact that even where the chosen child story remained the preferred way of telling the child about adoption, the advice to provide a full "blood" history emerged with equal strength. The decade of the 1980s does present a new picture of adoption. The stereotypical, and for years ideal, adoption of an unrelated infant occurs more rarely and instead a child often arrives in an adoptive family with a long, independent history as well as with a clear biological background. The adopted child of the 1980s brings distinct patterns of behavior and characteristic traits to relationships in his adoptive family. Correspondingly, adoptive parents are advised to attend to these given elements of the child's personality in order to establish the loving responses that underlie a parent-child tie. Building on ideas that traditionally appeared in guides for adoptive parents, recent texts add an emphasis on the child's nature that had previously not been dwelt upon in literature for adoptive parents. These contemporaneous adoption manuals construct a model for adoptive parent love that incorporates a substantial (in both senses of the word) component of the child's being. Learning to love a child means learning to love an individual with an evident identity of his or her own. Establishing a natural parent-child relationship involves accommodating to the nature, the biological heritage, of the child.

And so, in its movement forward—including biology in the model for love between parent and child—adoption literature seems to be moving back, toward Spock. This is not entirely the case. Biology in recent adoption books, like nature throughout, is used metaphorically. With meanings close to but not exactly the same as those associated with nature, biology in adoption texts represents roots and realness, an essential aspect of the adopted person's identity. Moreover, biology also stands for "blood" and thus complements "law" for inserting the child into a family (in the dichotomy of American kinship outlined by David Schneider).[115] In effect, biology as a metaphor represents the basis for a solid and permanent relationship, replacing love-at-first-sight and fate for linking the child to his social family.

Like earlier metaphors in adoption literature, the concept of biology draws upon conventional cultural connotations and marks some features while omitting others. Primarily, biology stands for a solidity and integrity in the adopted child that creates the foundation for loving relationships throughout his lifetime, not least with his adoptive family. Biology becomes a matter of identity and the potential for a flourishing of self, a subject virtually all child-rearing manuals address. The word does not refer to specific inherited traits or to details of genealogy. As used, biology belongs to the adopted child and does not imply a connection of birth to a particular parent. The suggestion of a physiological tie is present only in the generalized sense of birthright and ancestry. Biology refers to what the child is, an essence that incorporates blood ties; biology does not, in adoption books, refer to being a member of a blood family. This focus is of a piece with contemporaneous cultural notions of identity in American society in which, for instance, ethnicity is a matter of shared traits rather than of membership in a particular group. So, too, in adoption manuals biological connections become important in the identity of the child rather than as a link to identifiable kin.

In stressing select cultural meanings of biology, adoption books continue their traditional effort at eliminating references to pregnancy, birth, and motherhood. Biology becomes un-Spockian. The tie of birth is not the significant component and the birth mother not the significant factor in the adopted person's biological identity. Moreover, with this new emphasis on biology the adoptive parent also loses her importance, another un-Spockian maneuver. A child's development no longer depends, to the extent it had earlier, on the expressions of love by a parent. While still important, parental love loses the be-all and end-all bearing on outcome it had in adoption books until quite recently. No longer is parental love the sole determinant of an adoptee's adult personality; biology plays a part, lifting the burden from parental feelings and the demonstration of those feelings. With less of the outcome of growing up attributed to the expression of love, parents are relieved of the Spockian charge that they are responsible for the child's development into a good and genial adult. And given the social and psychological contexts of child rearing in American society, relieving the parent means relieving the mother.

In a corresponding but more subtle change, the child herself has an effect on the love expressed, and felt, by the parent. Not because the child does something to win love—this is still anathema in American culture—but because in possessing her biological background, the child achieves a security that contributes to the responses on the part of a parent. Parental love sounds more mutual than it did in earlier adoption books, more reciprocal than a "right" of the child's. Used metaphorically, biology in adoption books constitutes a revision, not a reflection, of the cultural model for parental love that held sway in all five editions of *Baby and Child Care*. This does not mean, it should be noted, that adoption books advocate anything but fully and "naturally" loving the child. Devotion is still used positively in manuals for adoptive parents, but without the idea that this kind of lovingness ensures a particular course toward adulthood on the part of a child. The adopted child now brings a full measure of her own nature to the "climate" of upbringing.

With the 1985 edition, Spock appointed a successor. "As I neared my eightieth birthday, I realized this revision of *Baby and Child Care* might be my last chance to work closely with a successor and ensure a smooth transition. . . . Dr. [Michael] Rothenberg and I see eye-to-eye in virtually all respects. . . ."[116] Quite possibly, having lasted for forty years, the model for parental love in Spock will last through successive revisions. But of course one cannot know. Nor can one know what may be the impact of the alternative model beginning to emerge from the pages of adoption manuals. This model, drawing on selected cultural connotations of "nature," retains the traditional qualities of parental love, permanence, and absolute commitment. In this sense, adoptive parent love is not totally distinguished from the American interpretation of "real" parent love. At the same time, adoption texts edit the connotations of nature in such a way that traditional assumptions about parental love are tested, primarily the association with a physiological bond between mother and child. The edited model, in adoption manuals, resembles views of love implicit in other 1980s cultural documents, including statistical reports on behavioral changes in the family, on family arrangements, and on the placement (custody) of children. These, like more theoretical statements, argue for the "social" and volitional quality of love, linking commitment and permanence not to something "given" but to something enacted, situational not fated.

Adoption books deal with social birth and parenthood by contract. To the extent that a concept of social birth represents a contradiction, inconsistent with cultural interpretations of the parent-child bond, adoption manuals have traditionally had to deal with "difference." In some periods, differences between adoptive and biological families were minimized, though never entirely ignored, in adoption texts. In other decades, including the 1980s, difference has been emphasized and the model for adoptive parent love adjusted accordingly. Treatment of the difference reflects contemporaneous psychological theory as well as conventional views of the family and of emotions in the family. Contingency, conditionality, and choice increasingly enter the discourse on love; in sharing this perspective, adoption books suggest that parent-child love may no longer be culturally distinct. Parental love may be losing the "absolute" and privileged position it has traditionally held in American culture—and continues to hold in Spock. Adoption books in the 1980s convey a model for parental love whose outcome will be a loving generation, but with a different experience of love.

Might one speculate, then, that the adoptive will replace the biological model for parental love? Might one even go so far as to predict that Spock will lose its cultural hegemony? *Baby and Child Care* has been so rooted in

American parental consciousness that it is hard to imagine the complete disappearance of the comfortingly chunky paperback. An alternative hypothesis is that Spock, revised, will incorporate the changes presaged in the pages of adoption manuals—resulting in a radical revision of the American cultural model for parental love.

Taken as a whole, the durability and largely unreflective quality of the Spockian idea of natural maternal love remain in many ways the strongest impression of the parental emotionology of the past forty years. Spock preserves the concept amid some changes that might have jostled it, such as new concern about spoiling and sexism. During much of the same period adoption literature sought various accommodations to apply as much of the natural love model as possible to an obviously different—in some ways uncomfortably different—setting. Ideas of love at first sight or a honeymoon may not have prevented some feelings that emotionally adoption was second best, but they did allow considerable application of the dominant model to the adoptive setting. Changes in adoption trends, and a possibly growing gap between Spockian emotionology and the actual emotional experience even of nonadoptive mothering, do raise some questions about the future of an unaltered Spockian model, questions that deserve to be explored over time precisely because so many parents, including adoptive parents, seem to have been affected by the imagery of natural maternal love for so long.

Notes

1. The official title of Spock's book, *Baby and Child Care,* has become interchangeable with the word *Spock.* I have followed that convention in my paper, and mark the few references to the man himself.

2. New editions appeared in 1957, 1968, 1976, and 1985, each with a short introductory preface by Spock.

3. Peter N. Stearns with Carol Z. Stearns, "Emotionology: Clarifying the History of Emotions and Emotional Standards," *American Historical Review* 90 (1985): 813–36.

4. The class bias of child-rearing books has been discussed elsewhere; for one example, see Daniel Miller and Guy Swanson, *The Changing American Parent* (New York, 1958). The diversity in Spock's audience comes partly from the distribution of *B&CC* throughout the world. Translations, however, do not always capture the uniquely reassuring tone of voice that is a Spockian hallmark; see Lynn Z. Bloom, *Dr. Spock: Biography of a Conservative Radical* (New York, 1972), p. 342.

5. Clifford Geertz, "Religion As a Cultural System," in *The Interpretation of Cultures* (New York, 1973): 93. An alternative version of the relationship between constructs and feelings can be found in Nancy Chodorow, *The Reproduction of Mothering* (Berkeley and Los Angeles, 1978) chap. 2, and in Arlie R. Hochschild,

"The Sociology of Feeling and Emotion," in M. Millman and R. M. Kanter, eds., *Another Voice* (New York, 1975) pp. 280–307.

6. Jan deHartog, *The Children: A Personal Record for the Use of Adoptive Parents* (New York, 1969).

7. In the case of Spock, I have drawn much of my evidence from the 1946 and the 1985 editions; I mention revisions in the middle three editions when these are particularly significant for my argument. In the case of adoption, I have avoided books written for special circumstances, e.g., the adoption of handicapped children; I have also not referred to books that focus on getting, rather than bringing up, a child.

8. "Univac" refers sarcastically to agency criteria for qualifying as an adoptive parent. The definition comes from a 1960s book on adoption, deHartog, *The Children*, p. 258.

9. George Lakoff and Mark Johnson, *The Metaphors We Live By* (Chicago, 1980).

10. Ibid., p. 22.

11. The role of child-care manuals in American society has been discussed in several places; e.g., Robert Sunley, "Early Nineteenth Century American Literature on Child Rearing," in M. Mead and M. Wolfenstein, eds., *Childhood in Contemporary Cultures* (Chicago, 1955), pp. 150–167, and Halbert Robinson et al., *Early Child Care in The United States of America* (New York, 1974).

12. Spock did become critical of American society in the late 1960s, but within well-limited parameters, as I show below.

13. David Schneider, *American Kinship* (Englewood Cliffs, N.J., 1968).

14. Michael Zuckerman, "Dr. Spock: The Confidence Man," in C. Rosenberg, ed., *The Family in History* (Philadelphia, 1975), pp. 179–207; and Nancy P. Weiss, "Mother, The Invention of Necessity," *American Quarterly* 29 (1977): 519–46; Lynn Bloom's *Dr. Spock* (1972) is a semischolarly, semipopular biography of Spock.

15. Stearns and Stearns, "Emotionology," p. 813.

16. *Baby and Child Care* and adoption manuals originated in the same milieu, product of the surge of "expertise" and of self-conscious improvement programs that came in the aftermath of World Warr II. Spock's enormous and instant popularity partly explains the subsequent publications of a new edition per decade. The case of adoption is different; the formation of policy and the training of social workers specifically in adoption (and foster care) remained haphazard and thus the publication of manuals compensatory—in fact, a good many adoption books are written by adoptive parents who view themselves as the "real" (and perhaps only) experts. Mary Kathleen Benet, *The Politics Of Adoption* (New York, 1976).

17. Schneider, *American Kinship*, p. 107. In a later book, Schneider points out that the association of maternal instinct and mother love—as well as the association of "flesh and blood" with relationship—is an entirely cultural, and historical, phenomenon. In *A Critique of the Study of Kinship*, Schneider argues that conventional American assumptions about motherhood, about parent-child relationships, and about family have inadvertently determined anthropological studies of kinship, so that anthropologists construct theories of kinship based on "flesh and blood" con-

nections important to them but not important to their informants. David Schneider, *A Critique of the Study of Kinship* (Ann Arbor, Mich., 1984).

18. Jerome Kagan, "The Child in the Family," in A. Rossi, J. Kagan, and T. Hareven, eds., *The Family* (New York, 1978), pp. 33–56; Chodorow, *The Reproduction of Mothering;* Schneider, *American Kinship.*

19. Elizabeth Badinter, *Mother Love: Myth and Reality* (New York, 1980); Chodorow, *The Reproduction of Mothering.*

20. See the discussion in Stearns and Stearns, "Emotionology," pp. 821–25.

21. Lakoff and Johnson, *Metaphors We Live By,* p. 85.

22. Carol MacCormack, "Nature, culture and gender," in C. MacCormack and M. Strathern, eds., *Nature, Culture and Gender* (New York, 1980), pp. 1–24.

23. Benjamin Spock, *The Common Sense Book of Baby and Child Care* (New York, 1946), p. 4. The title became *Baby and Child Care* for the 1957, 1968, and 1976 editions; in 1985, co-authored, the book was called *Dr. Spock's Baby and Child Care.* In all further citations, I use only date of the edition and page number.

24. 1985:79.

25. 1946:15; 1985: 34.

26. 1985:105.

27. 1946:33.

28. 1985:106.

29. 1946:33.

30. 1957:117.

31. 1976:xix.

32. 1985:391.

33. Ibid., 53.

34. Ibid., 55.

35. 1985:347. Incidentally, this illustration accomplishes another purpose, granting *B&CC* a racially wider audience, though not an economic spread—this black father appears thoroughly middle class. Spock took the illustrations seriously as information, and argued with the publisher for his first illustrator, Dorothea Fox; Bloom, *Dr. Spock,* chap. 6.

36. 1968:23.

37. Jane Rowe, *Yours by Choice: A Guide for Adoptive Parents* (New York, 1959), p. 31.

38. Florence Rondell and R. Michaels, *The Adopted Family* (New York, 1951), p. 3. This does not mean adoption books have invariably advocated dual parenting. Books of the 1940s and 1950s, a product of their times, assumed mother would be home with the child. The difference from Spock lay in distinguishing her behaviors as a parent from those that came from "being a woman."

39. Colette Dywasuk, *Adoption: Is It for You?* (New York, 1973), p. 132.

40. There is not perfect agreement on the meanings of these terms. "Older" usually refers to over one year; "special needs" refers, generally, to children with problems that can range from behavioral disorders to substantial physical handicaps.

41. Edmund Bolles, *The Penguin Adoption Handbook* (New York, 1984), p. 31, and Fred Powledge, *The New Adoption Maze* (St. Louis, 1985), p. 273.

42. Rondell, *The Adopted Family*, p. 25.

43. Independent adoptions are arranged by a third party, for example a doctor or lawyer, and subsequently legalized in court.

44. Lockridge, *Adopting a Child*, pp. 32–33.

45. Dywasuk, *Adoption*, p. 114.

46. 1976:25.

47. Lockridge, *Adopting a Child*, p. 187.

48. Schneider, *American Kinship*, p. 97.

49. Since the late 1960s single applicants are supposed to be given full consideration as adoptive parents, but chapters in 1980s adoption manuals on "how to beat the system" suggest this may not be the case.

50. Miller and Swanson, *Changing American Parent*, p. 199.

51. Frances Lockridge, *Adopting a Child* (New York, 1947), p. 43. In the 1940s and 1950s the word *foster* referred to adoptive parents before they had legalized the adoption.

52. Rowe, *Yours By Choice*, pp. 102–3.

53. Claire Berman, *We Take This Child* (New York, 1974), p. 77.

54. Fred Powledge, *The New Adoption Maze—and How to Get Through It* (St. Louis, 1985), pp. 20–21.

55. Dywasuk, *Adoption*, p. x.

56. 1985:105–6.

57. Schneider, *American Kinship*, p. 38.

58. Assumptions about the taboo created by biological relatedness have crumbled in recent years, with increasingly reported cases of parent-child incest. Adoptees who have located birth parents also report on the strong sexual attraction to a blood relative; Modell, "In Search," *American Ethnologist* 13 (1986): 646–61.

59. Miller and Swanson, *Changing American Parent*.

60. Rondell, *The Adopted Family*, p. 56.

61. As described in adoption literature, the adjustment period coincides with the time adoptive parents are expected to "forget" the contractual basis of their parenthood.

62. deHartog, *The Children*, pp. 50–51.

63. Spock is more ambiguous on this point than are adoption books, and my sense as a reader is that he never wholeheartedly supports the idea of a "gradual" love.

64. The inappropriateness of falling in love with an older child or a stepchild may also stem from the suggestion of sexuality in these cases, still an ordinarily tabooed subject in adoption texts.

65. deHartog, *The Children*, p. 21.

66. See Zuckerman, "Dr. Spock." In pointing out the many contradictions in *B&CC*, Zuckerman argues that cultures rarely resolve their contradictions but rather learn to live with them.

67. 1946:3; cf. 1985:127, which describes the mother "anxiously" looking for "signs of failure."

68. 1985:22; unchanged since 1946, the 1985 statement ignores the number of books on emotional well-being American parents had access to by the 1980s.

69. Since the midtwentieth century, adoption itself has been justified as being "in the best interests of the child" and not as an institution for providing children to those who do not have any.

70. 1957:333.

71. 1968:xvi. Spock himself denied this was a change from "indulgence" to "discipline," claiming the first edition never advocated indulgence but was misunderstood by readers who had only more rigid child-rearing guides for comparison; Bloom, *Dr. Spock*. Presumably he means he has only made a change from the "child-centered" to the "community-centered" parent, though this is not at all clear and, in any case, would influence the ways in which parents were instructed to express love.

72. 1946:183; this is just one example.

73. 1968:16.

74. 1985:24.

75. 1985:425.

76. 1946:102–03.

77. 1946:114.

78. 1957:1.

79. 1968:192.

80. 1968:192.

81. 1946:19.

82. 1985:401.

83. 1985:248.

84. E.g., Florence Rondell, *The Adopted Family*.

85. Rowe, *Yours by Choice,* p. 75.

86. Ibid., p. 127.

87. deHartog, *The Children,* p. 94.

88. Dywasuk, *Adoption,* p. 80.

89. Ibid.

90. Paradoxically, the un-Spockian advice to devote yourself to a child tended to assume a Spockian family: a mother at home with the time to devote to a child, though this is not stated explicitly in books by social workers or by adoptive parents—who seem to ignore the sheer number of hours devotion requires.

91. Berman, *We Take This Child,* p. 54.

92. CWLA, *Standards for Adoption* (New York, 1978), p. 8.

93. These adjectives appear on one page of the 1985 edition (p. 18).

94. 1968:5.

95. 1946:147, and cf. 1985:44.

96. 1976:xix.

97. Spock knew the anthropological literature (and probably heard a great deal from one of his first "mothers," Margaret Mead), and realized he was talking about a culturally and not a biologically determined gender identity.

98. 1957:332–33, referring to the ages 3 to 6.

99. 1946:255. Spock was influenced by Freud, and *B&CC* was an important popularizer of Freudian theory; to an extent, then, the Spockian emphasis on male-female differences stems from psychoanalytic theory that remains constant despite the

ostensible attention paid to social and cultural changes by *B&CC*. Freudian interpretations of sex-role development continue to appear in the "nonsexist" 1976 and 1985 editions.

100. 1985:47.

101. 1985:48.

102. 1985:390.

103. My impression is that in the 1940s and 1950s, the stereotypical baby was invariably a girl; later, with the adoption of older, international, and special needs children, pronouns suggested a more even gender distribution for the typical adopted child.

104. Dywasuk, *Adoption*, pp. 68–69.

105. From my interviews with adoptees now in their twenties, it seems apparent that some kind of matching continued to be an informal policy among those who arranged adoptions and, almost certainly, still is.

106. deHartog, *The Children*, p. 219.

107. Berman, *We Take This Child*, p. 9.

108. Dywasuk, *Adoption*, p. 14.

109. 1985:23.

110. For the past forty years, probably a majority of adoption agencies have advised telling, fearing the consequences if the child found out "some other way." This does not of course mean parents have to tell, and reportedly many adoptions are still kept secret from the child. Personal communications.

111. Rondell, *The Adopted Family*, p. 22.

112. Jane Collier, M. Rosaldo, and S. Yanagisako in *Rethinking the Family*, 1982.

113. Edmund Bolles, *Penguin Adoption Handbook*, p. 212.

114. Laws about contact between birth parent and relinquished child vary from state to state, and are currently under debate.

115. In the 1968 and 1980 editions of *American Kinship*.

116. 1985:xiii.

7

The Rise of Sibling Jealousy
in the Twentieth Century

P e t e r   N .   S t e a r n s

"A proper amount of this passion [jealousy] is most desirable in both romantic and conjugal love."[1]

"We may even blight and blacken our happiness by jealousy, which is really an admission of our own inferiority, of our own cowardice and conceit."[2]

The twentieth century has been a busy period in the history of American jealousy. The partial breakdown of previously assigned gender roles and women's domestic confinement, plus the increasing overtness of sexuality, have combined to create a host of new opportunities for active experience of the emotion. A commercial environment that encourages emotion-based striving to match the standard of living of others, a work and school environment that promotes rivalry, enhance opportunities for jealousy and kindred envy. Yet, while unquestionably responding with intense jealousy to the occasions provided by growing infidelity, divorce, competition, and even stepparenting, Americans have also, during the twentieth century, become more uncomfortable with the emotion than ever before. The handling of jealousy—how to view it in others, how to judge it in oneself, even whether to admit it fully—constitutes one of the more interesting tensions in modern American emotional life. While elements of the tension antedate our time, with some possibly inherent in the emotion itself, there is little question that the twentieth century has seen the addition of important new ingredients, both in the contexts in which jealousy can be experienced and in the definition of what jealousy is.

Some aspects of jealousy may be instinctive, or at least so inevitably rooted in early childhood that its outcropping is fundamental. We will see that many twentieth-century Americans, while deploring its existence, came to believe in a kind of inevitability, though at less than an instinctive level. Darwin and many post-Darwinian psychologists, such as William James, claimed that jealousy was an animal instinct. Darwin held that even insects expressed jealousy, along with anger, terror, and love; one of the first thorough American definitions urged that jealousy reflected "something very deep and universal in human nature."[3] Post-Freudians such as Melanie Klein have posited a primitive envy, rooted in infant resentment of dependency on the breast, preceding even Oedipal conflicts, from which jealousy flows.[4] Yet whether instinctive or not—and one must also note the extraordinary variations in the intensities of at least certain kinds of jealousy, for example in twentieth-century American responses to sexual promiscuity—there is little question that jealousy for practical purposes roots also in a social context, and constitutes something of an emotional hybrid. It depends on interpersonal situations for incidence and expression, and most cultures have fairly specific guidelines concerning what it is "worth" being jealous about. Jealousy itself seems to blend fear of emotional loss, often with anger at the prospect of loss and/or the rival who causes it, and sometimes with grief at the prospect. Because of both its social and its hybrid qualities jealousy is particularly open to cultural definition and, perhaps, to significant, even rapid, change, not only in the emotionology applied to it by available pundits but in the actual experience of the emotion itself. An instinctual substratum there may be, but a focus on social context and on historical change will capture a great deal of what the emotion is in real life.

Ironically, however, jealousy has not received a great deal of attention in recent decades from researchers who approach emotion from a social vantagepoint, and it has been effectively ignored by the new brand of historians concerned with emotional change. Despite the hosts of opportunities to include considerations of jealousy in treatments of courtship, family life, love, or anger, the surface of the subject has not been scratched. Yet precisely because of what we already know about the history of emotions in Western society over the past several centuries, jealousy seems an obvious candidate for attention. To the extent that it involves anger, jealousy was likely to come under increasing attack, as a cause of undesirable friction in what should be delectable relationships. Insofar as it reflects love or a need for love, however, jealousy could hardly be scorned entirely. On both counts, the positive and the negative, the treatment of jealousy had to receive serious scrutiny as part of an appropriate emotional definition of family life—and it demanded considerable complexity as well.

This essay focuses on a particular facet of the recent history of jealousy—the identification and management of jealous rivalry among young siblings—in the United States in the twentieth century. It emphasizes the middle-class experience, which is most open to investigation and, perhaps, most sensitive as a barometer of change. It argues that the twentieth century saw important new dimensions in what many Americans came to believe (wrongly) was a tragically inherent part of family life; that these innovations can be explained; and that the result, significant in itself, allows some insight into the wider experience of jealousy, among adults as well as children, in the same period.

Jealousy has undergone two major shifts in modern Western history. During the seventeenth and eighteenth centuries, when so many emotional standards were being rethought, the emotionology of jealousy was changed in at least two respects. First, the emotion was narrowed to focus almost exclusively on personal relationships, and particularly on relationships where love might be expected to prevail. Jealousy had long been seen as an ingredient of romance, to be sure, but it had also maintained a somewhat separate meaning in its application to defense of power and honor.[5] This latter application was progressively withdrawn, and with it, gradually, use of the word "jealous" as signifying an approved combination of zeal and possessiveness in defense of rights or dignity. As honor-based codes yielded in the face of more commercial relationships, it was obviously possible in fact for nonromantic jealousy to find new spurs, in rivalries for wealth, prestige, and bureaucratic position. Interestingly, however, whatever the emotional reality, the term *jealousy* was rarely directed at these situations, with more neutral and emotion-free words like competition being used instead.

Along with the narrowing of jealousy to personal relationships came a growing, though not entirely uniform, tendency to see the emotion as antithetical to true love. This latter required constancy,[6] or perhaps (in some nineteenth- as well as twentieth-century formulations) mutual freedom, and in either case unselfish devotion to the other. Jealousy, involving possessiveness and also anger and other unattractive emotions, was a perversion of love and potentially its destroyer. With this shift, once common efforts to distinguish between "normal" jealousy, which could be good and useful, and excessive or pathological forms tended to fade from usage, though they did not disappear entirely: for what was bad, was bad regardless of degree.

These early modern changes in jealousy standards, both of which require further exploration, undoubtedly worked into widespread consciousness gradually and unevenly. De facto efforts to use jealousy to enhance love have hardly died off in the twentieth century, and in parts of the United States a jealousy-linked concept of honor lasted well into the nineteenth century. But the changes did have increasing effect, as witness the most common definitions of love and their contrast—oddly unnoticed heretofore—with chivalric codes wherein intrinsic jealousy had been assumed as part of love's toils. The narrowing of jealousy to emphasize love relationships had largely been accomplished, at least outside the South, by the midnineteenth century in the United States, at least in emotionology. The purely negative evaluation placed on jealousy in contrast to love moved somewhat more slowly. While marriage reformers in the nineteenth century zeroed in on jealousy explicitly, blasting its equation of love with property, more mainstream standards remained a bit ambivalent. Revealingly, jealousy was not directly invoked to defend marriage, but some writers proudly noted love's exclusive qualities. Most family emotionology, however, sought to promote a loving marriage without jealousy. As Mrs. E. B. Duffy wrote in 1873, in *What Women Should Know*, the "truest, purest, highest form" of love is a "strong, unselfish affection blended with desire," an ennobling affection that contrasted with the baser passion of jealousy.

A complete modern history of jealousy must deal more fully with the narrowing and increasing condemnation (or avoidance) of jealousy, including the almost certain lag between actual emotional control, especially where sexual jealousy was concerned, and the dominant emotionology. This essay, focused on a second change, does not pretend such complete coverage. It is however vital to realize that by 1900 the first set of changes had produced an emotionology bent on seeing jealousy strictly as a function of personal interaction and rather firmly set against any positive role for jealousy in true love.

The second major shift in the modern history of jealousy in the United States worked from the first set of changes, in deepening the condemnation of jealousy but also applying it to relations among children. This shift was more focused than the first set of changes, and more easily transferrable into emotional reality. It rested, however, on the negative evaluation of jealousy already current, while trying to incorporate the treatment of jealousy into basic childhood socialization. This second change gained increasing momentum from the 1920s onward. It brought concern for jealousy home, quite literally, to many Americans, as the first, more abstract shift had perhaps not fully done, and made jealousy the object of repression as well as reproval. Though ignored to date by historically informed students of emotion, it constitutes a clear case of recent and ongoing change in emotional context, rivaling in significance some of the better-studied instances of the seventeenth and eighteenth centuries. And the key to the second shift lay in a dramatic new perception of jealousy among siblings.

American parents in the nineteenth century do not seem to have been explicitly concerned about jealousy among their children. References to the subject of childish jealousy are striking in their absence.[7] Parents and parental advisers might discuss various failings of children, from precocious sexuality to sloth to carelessness with property, but jealousy simply did not make the list. The phenomenon was known, of course, and children themselves learned a relevant vocabulary. Letters by sisters in the middle-class Hills family abound with references, as siblings carp at each other's purchases, receipt of letters from their mother ("I thought it very strange you should have written Emily first . . ."), and so on. "I suppose Papa told you of how jealous I was when I heard you are going to allow Emily to go to the Phi Psi musical for it did not seem at all like you to let a *child* like her go to any such things." "I am very jealous of Emily for I think she has more than her share of gaiety when I am away." But an idea that emotions such as this merited any particular notice, much less parental action or criticism, is oddly missing. Missing also is any record of jealous reactions by very young children, as on the birth of a new baby.[8]

Indeed letters like those of the Hills sisters suggest precisely that middle-class parents had *not* worked to banish jealousy. To twentieth-century eyes, the poutings of the Hills sisters seem like the scribblings of four-year-olds (were they magically or tragically literate), expressing sibling rivalry in the starkest form short of violence. Yet these laments to mother about feeling jealous because sister got a letter first were being penned by a twenty-year-old, who clearly had not been taught, as Americans were to be taught in the following century, that jealousy, even if experienced, should be veiled more cleverly lest one be labeled childish. They compare oddly, for example, with the deliberate efforts to "outgrow" jealousy reported as standard from roughly age eleven onward, in the midtwentieth century, by Gesell and his colleagues. They also contrast with abundant nineteenth-century interest in dealing with anger among children, in the family context and as part of character formation. Unlike anger, jealousy seems to have been a nonissue.

The same negative finding about nineteenth-century concern over childish jealousy applies to virtually all the popular child-rearing manuals before the very end of the century. John Abbott, to be sure, mentioned the possibility that a girl might refuse to share a bed with her sister (in which case obedience must be insisted upon), but the word jealousy was not used and the context, focusing on proper parent-child relations, had little to do with judgments of sibling emotions. Marion Harland described situations in which a girl might well have been jealous of her brother's privileges, and the favors granted him by a sexist father, but again overt jealousy was neither described nor invoked. Jacob Abbott talked of childish boasting and its immaturity, urging that parents avoid punishment for this but guide toward more mature behavior—an approach suggestive of twentieth-century tactics on jealousy; and he wrote widely on how to handle disputes among children, with use of dolls and calm mediation. He may thus have been writing about situations resulting from jealousy, but he was not writing about jealousy itself, at least explicitly, and when he turned to emotions that needed atten-tion, such as childish fears, jealousy was simply not listed.[9] Christian man-uals urged that children be taught to work together (by their sixth year, argued one such in 1919, they should be "habitually cooperative"),[10] and obviously general invocations of Christian goodness, obedience to adults, respect for the property of others and generosity may have embraced the problem of jealousy. Again, however, it is striking that the emotion was not mentioned, even as an illustration of original sin or, in milder treatments, an example of the barriers posed to desired virtues.

Family manuals in fact manifested consistently high expectations about the importance and normality of brotherly or sisterly feelings. Wishful thinking surely entered into this picture, but it was noteworthy that no inherent or common impediments to the ideal were mentioned. Even adult advice manuals included sections on utilizing good relations with brothers or sisters, and the image of a large group of siblings engaged in a common activity, such as music, was a frequent one. Among younger children ungoverned temper might briefly cause flareups, even violence, but jealousy did not enter the picture and there was no durable tension under any other label. A sister strikes her younger brother in T. S. Arthur's 1856 manual, but she is immediately sorry: "She had no animosity against her little playmate; on the contrary, she loved him dearly." Lydia H. Sigourney, noting that parents can help soothe competition and compose differences, urged that this would build on a fraternal love "planted deep in the heart," which "seldom fails to reveal itself." Many authors noted how frequently siblings grouped together (respectfully) to plead the cause of one of their number against parental discipline. The image of an older brother or sister aiding his younger kin cropped up frequently, with a rare admission that a younger child might be "jealous" of this kind of authority.

Catharine Sedgwick's popular manual conveyed the common view. Children in a large family grouped together. A new baby was "an object of general fondness." Jealousy was nonexistent. Its possibility came up only in young adulthood, when two brothers loved the same girl. Even here, however, the earlier "home cultivation of affections" had produced a "glare of fraternal love," which allowed the brothers to master "the most selfish and exorbitant of the passions." This view of a loving, envy-free childhood obviously set implicit standards against jealousy, but this was not done with any sense of a common emotional problem in early childhood that must be combatted, in contrast to other emotional issues, such as temper (or indeed jealousy in siblings as young adults), where high standards were also asserted but against recognized if unfortunate impulses.[11]

To be sure, Bronson Alcott in 1837 (but in a context wider than explicit child-rearing advice) briefly mentioned the possibility of a "moment of jealousy" in which a child, frustrated at her older sister's receiving a picture, said she hated her father, who responded by getting a picture for her too but also pressing her to understand that it was better to give than to receive. The jealousy—and this is an unusual use of the term in talking about children in the nineteenth century—was "understandable" because "she is a very little girl"; no huge crisis was involved. Alcott quickly moved on to other illustrations of mastering appetites. Lydia Child, in her popular manual, wrote nothing at all about jealousy and very little about siblings. She did talk about children's propensity to quarrel and urged that brothers and sisters should be kind. "Any slight rudeness, a want of consideration for each other's feelings, or of attention to each other's comfort, should be treated with quite as much importance as similar offenses against strangers." Again, quite apart from the implicit quality of any reference to jealousy, the tone was matter-of-fact, with no indication of a major problem under consideration, and the author quickly went on to note how sisters often helped each other.[12] Indeed, predominant literary treatments of siblings in nineteenth-century America, such as *Little Women* or the widely popular Rollo series (featuring Rollo aiding his sister), joined the family manuals in stressing easy sibling harmony.[13] As late as 1904 an incident that a quarter century later would be invoked with howls of anguish, was virtually brushed aside in another popular manual. Mrs. Theodore Birney describes a child biting her baby sister, without apology; the advice to parents is to strike the girl "lovingly" in the same place, to show her it hurts and to bring home the suffering of the baby, "of whom, in her baby way, she was very fond." End of lesson, with no portents of dark passions that must be leashed.[14]

Jealousy, then continued to be played down, in some cases well into the twentieth century. If mentioned at all, it was usually treated in passing, and certainly never given a specific section of its own, as became commonplace in manuals by the later 1920s. It was, to be sure, interesting that the few examples cited referred to sisters, doubtless a reflection of an expectation that girls should behave better than boys but possibly resulting also from girls' greater domestic dependence and confinement and their proneness to sibling tension in early childhood. Nevertheless, one could sum up the evidence on actual family life, as reported by participants, or suggested in family advice or portrayals in the nineteenth century, without mentioning sibling jealousy as a perceived issue.

Why was this so? Surely, as already implied, a part of the explanation results from different kinds of labeling, with parents noting quarrels or obedience issues that by the twentieth century would be seen as instances of sibling rivalry. The fact that nineteenth-century views of children sometimes used a broader brush does not mean that specific emotional issues went entirely unperceived. And in insisting on docility, generosity, or politeness, or simply on emotional restraint and self-mastery, parents may well have been combating the effects of jealousy. At the same time, particularly between 1830 and 1870, widespread middle-class belief in the innocence of children may have inhibited comment on jealousy, though here one must add that the subsequent willingness to discuss various passions, not only sex but also anger, did not produce a commensurate recognition of jealousy.

Some parents may indeed have found jealousy so natural that it did not merit comment. Others, in the spirit of John Locke, may have welcomed some jealousy, on grounds that it could spur children to achievement. The growing hostility to jealousy among adults, as leading to "profligacy and ruin," a passion that Tennyson had written could "make earth Hell," may have spread slowly, like some other ingredients of the emotionological transformation of the seventeenth and eighteenth centuries.[15] Certainly some ambivalence about jealousy, as a source of danger but also a useful spur to love, must have lingered, and this could color reactions to childish emotion. Note also that what little perception there was of early childhood jealousy in the nineteenth century judged it more as rivalry for power than as competition for affection; hence the focus on jealousy of younger against older. This reflected remnants of the more traditional, honor-linked definition of jealousy and may on these grounds have seemed more normal or even quietly useful to adults, and less threatening to the loving emotional ideal of the family.

Most striking, however, is the probability that serious nineteenth-century concern about jealousy, though very real, associated the emotion primarily with sexual maturity, not with childhood. This was the case with G. Stanley Hall,[16] who largely condemned jealousy—placing his comments in a section on juvenile criminality—but referred its source to puberty not, as in twentieth-century parlance, to earlier childhood experience. Indeed, in nineteenth-century emotionology generally, jealousy was a passion to work on as part of becoming adult, under the spur of sexual urgings. Appropriate control might be prepared by more general character building and self-mastery in childhood, though this link was not specifically drawn. Childish jealousy in itself, whether noted or not, was incidental, not an explicit problem. And parents, in their silence on the subject, seemed to agree.

The fact seems to be that an explicit effort to include repression of jealousy in childhood socialization came surprisingly late—later, for example, than attempts to reduce or divert childish anger once this emotion was redefined and reproved. Ideas about jealousy and concerns about childhood—amid a welter of diverse approaches and contrasting degrees of severity or indulgence—did not mix in the nineteenth century. One result would be a considerable amount of naïveté, and no little shock, when the problem was newly identified in the early decades of the twentieth century. The idea of jealousy flowing from child to a sibling baby was especially unprepared by nineteenth-century thinking.

Only at the very end of the century can a change of tone be noted, amid what was still predominant neglect; only then did the idea of sibling jealousy begin hesitantly to emerge as a specific entity. The first popular manual to take up the theme was Felix Adler's *Moral Instruction of Children*, in 1893. Adler talked about inequalities among brothers or sisters resulting in "ugly feelings in the hearts of the less fortunate," unless parents were carefully evenhanded. He moved beyond invocations of generosity specifically to urge children to "be more eager to secure the rights of your brother than your own. Do not triumph in your brother's disgrace but rather seek to build up his self-respect." Parents who did not get to the root of children's quarrels might promote an "incipient hatred" of brothers, despite the fact the love should form the basic center of family life. Here was the kernel of what would become, three decades later, a veritable flood of concern about sibling relationships. But Adler's approach was transitional, as he continued to emphasize childish innocence and scattered his remarks about brotherhood rather than concentrating them in a powerful single section, with elaborate tactical advice bolstering the central message.[17] In the same turn-of-the-century years, an early psychological article on jealousy—not, to be sure, a popular item—talked clearly about jealousy among young children, citing among other things Helen Keller's autobiography, in which she lamented her loss of "only darling" status at the birth of her sister, and the violent reactions that resulted.[18] Again, however, the overall approach to sibling relationships as a breeding ground for jealousy remained somewhat tentative. Many advice manuals persisted in ignoring the subject and even academic assessments often played down the possibility of serious emotional tension.

American embrace of sibling jealousy as a preeminent fact of family life, particularly on the arrival of a newborn, dates from the late 1920s, at which time it quickly became a staple topic. From this point onward, at least until the 1960s, child-rearing manuals uniformly contained comment, and usually anguished comment, on the importance of dealing with this aspect of emotional interaction. Basic emotionology was involved as well, beyond the management of a particular phase of family development. Early childhood became the focal point of an attack on jealousy, the juncture at which this facet of emotional character was made or broken. The contrast with the nineteenth century was simple but fundamental: childhood, and indeed early childhood, became for the first time the key battleground in the campaign against jealousy, and the negative evaluation of jealousy became more unambiguous than ever before.

Appropriately enough in terms of standard setting, one of the first salvos in a new war on children's jealousy came in a widely cited government publication on child rearing, by D. A. Thom, published in 1925. "Few emotions are experienced by man which from a social point of view are more important than jealousy," Thom warned: and jealousy takes root in early childhood, preventing happiness and possibly causing violence. "The jealous person becomes an object of dislike. Often he develops the idea that he is unjustly treated or persecuted, and all too frequently this idea causes uncontrolled resentment and disastrous results." So parents should attend carefully to jealousy in their children, doing all they can—and Thom had a few suggestions along lines of impartiality—to prevent it. A more complete set of tactics emerged from the Children's Bureau in 1930, again under the heading "Nobody likes a jealous person. A jealous person is never happy." Fortunately, appropriate tactics on the arrival of a new baby could stem the tide: "Tony was happy again. Now he loves his baby brother. He is not jealous anymore."[19]

Standard privately authored manuals for parents eagerly picked up the theme. The Child Study Association of America, in 1926, while briefly acknowledging jealousy's potentially useful role in spurring competition—and so "speeding up the wheels in the business world"—came down clearly on the side of repression. Jealousy was normal, but if left uncontrolled "so intense that little but harm can come from rousing it in its more primitive forms, and that even in the higher form of rivalry and emulation greatest caution must be used." If a child's jealousy works to hold back his siblings, "There is no limit to the depths to which he may sink." "Children who quarrel because of jealousy . . . are in a serious state. This type of quarreling should be treated at once by getting at and doing away with the cause of it."[20] So much for the unspecific approach of the past century or more: jealousy must now be isolated from other childish attributes and given focused attention. Dorothy Canfield Fisher, one of the most prolific writers for parents during the interwar years, turned to the problem of jealousy by 1932. The emotion was infantile but not easy to outgrow, yet it could readily distort adult relationships. Parents had a serious responsibility in helping children through the emotion, for the family context was where jealousy began. Failure to staunch jealousy was "a severe indictment of the family." Yet too many parents deliberately encouraged competition among siblings. "In inciting their children to rivalry . . . parents may be wrecking their chance of present and future happiness."[21]

There were, to be sure, some alternative voices on the subject of childhood jealousy, particularly during the 1920s and 1930s. A minority of advice manuals simply avoided the subject, as in the older tradition. Watsonian behaviorists mentioned jealousy but tended to downplay it, predictably arguing against any idea that it was instinctive and claiming, correspondingly, that a few simple tactics would prevent its emergence. Avoidance of too much mother love was the key, for parents caused whatever jealousy there might be.[22] More interesting still, and more durable, was an undercurrent of belief that jealousy might in fact be useful, at least in appropriate doses, by spurring achievement. This quite logical line of argument, similar to beliefs about channeling boys' anger to purposes that would serve in adulthood, occurred in a few manuals that attempted to reduce the dominant tone of anxiety about sibling jealousy and also, occasionally, as an inconsistent note in treatments largely set against the emotion. Thus jealousy might encourage young children to learn from their older brothers and sisters—though it should never be used deliberately to motivate. Or, more positively, "To outdo each other, each [child] puts forth more energy, to gain adult recognition." After all, the competitive spirit was fundamental in American society, and it was too much to ask children to love one another. Jealousy, in sum, might have "character-building and creative uses."[23]

This was not, however, a very common approach. Unlike the idea of channeling anger, which received widespread support until the 1940s, jealousy was seen by most commentators as too dangerous to try to use. In fact, in the dominant emotionology of the period from the late 1920s until at least 1960, jealousy required more concerted repression than any other childish emotion. Revealingly, individual manual writers who had not identified the theme of jealousy in early work, prior to 1930, such as Dorothy Canfield Fisher and Gladys Groves, converted to vigorous concern in their later writings, recognizing the importance of this emotional issue but also, implicitly, its novelty as well.

Hostility to jealousy was not itself new, for the redefinition of love to exclude jealousy had occurred, at least on the adult emotionological level, considerably earlier. What was novel in the twentieth century was the intensity of the attack on the emotion and its focus on early childhood. These innovations had several ingredients in turn. Guidance experts and many parents themselves reported a growing anxiety about the direct results of sibling rivalry in the family. Jealousy was dangerous. It might, and some argued that it normally would, lead to attacks, even murderous attacks, on a new baby. Jealousy, unchecked on a new sibling's arrival, would spoil a brotherly or sisterly relationship well beyond babyhood, to the disadvantage of the children involved and the disruption of the larger family. "Unless the parents recognize that jealousy will normally appear, and are prepared for it, strong feelings of hostility often develop which continue to make life miserable for both children over many years." Jealousy, quite simply, contradicted the emotional goals long since advocated for family life, and many authorities cited the shock parents experienced on witnessing the hatred with which a new baby might be greeted. Yet, authorities were now arguing, jealousy among siblings was inevitable. Indeed, insidiously, it was more likely to be present when concealed than when manifested in overt acts of violence. This was a subtle emotional monster, whose existence must now be assumed. "The child whose jealousy is not as easy to recognize suffers more and has greater need for help."[24]

Furthermore, jealousy was not simply a problem during childhood years. It could become a permanent liability to personality, unless attacked during those years. "If he [the child] does not have the right kind of help, his personality may be damaged. Unfriendly, disagreeable, self-conscious adults show these traits because of unsolved jealousy problems in their childhood." Sibling rivalry "indelibly stamps personality and distorts character."[25] It became, indeed, a conventional piece of wisdom that jealous adults were defective, and that their defects stemmed from childhood jealousy improperly handled. "A prolonged state of jealousy is a symptom of retardation in emotional development and shows itself along with other evidences of emotional immaturity." Unchecked, jealousy could lead to unhappy people, bad marriages, homosexuality, criminality, the works—"we have only to read the daily paper to see the results of ungoverned jealousy in adult life." For the emotional personality was set by around age twelve, correctable only by professional therapists. Here was a huge responsibility for parents, not only in setting the right tone for their own family but in regulating an omnipresent emotion that could ruin their children as adults. Small wonder that specific handbooks on dealing with jealousy in children emerged by the 1940s, that almost all child-rearing manuals had long and carefully noted sections on sibling jealousy and its prevention, that the columns of *Parents' Magazine* were filled with tales of childhood jealousy and practical measures to combat it.[26]

In children and adults alike jealousy was bad because it attacked the very values for which the family existed and because it denoted a selfish possessiveness unsuitable not only in family settings but in life in general. "Jealousy flourishes in souls where affection and response are wanting." "Jealousy is more than a subversion of love; it is the dark face of love ingrained with fear. The person into whose character habitual emotional insecurity has bitten deep can be so persistently or intensely jealous as to bring constant turmoil into the most promising family life." "We talk about good anger and good fear, but there is no good jealousy." "Its technique is domination. Its method is to enhance one's status at the expense of another. It is not conducive to growth and development. It is productive of strife, disharmony and wasted energy." Jealousy, in sum, was held to be incompatible with real love and also, in a newer twentieth-century element, to suggest a kind of person incapable of meeting the standards of cooperativeness and ease with others now seen as essential even in ordinary relationships.[27]

The importance of the jealousy problem dictated a variety of tactical responses, normally listed in child-rearing manuals from the 1920s onward. These responses were viewed as feasible and productive but not, at least until the 1950s, automatic. They required effort and some careful planning, even some rethinking, by parents, in response to an emotional issue seen as vital, but one which was also new.

Beyond sheer effort—and Dr. Spock specifically urged that the problem of childhood jealousy was so acute and menacing that "a lot of effort" was essential,[28] in contradistinction to the easygoing tone of most of his child care manual—the treatment of childhood jealousy rested on two basic ingredients. First, parents must recognize that children could not handle jealousy themselves. Left unchecked the emotion might take on disguise but it would only fester and worsen. Second, the logical response to overt acts of jealousy, punishment of some sort, was directly counterproductive. For though jealousy subverted love, it must be answered, at some sacrifice to short-run parental ease, with still more love.

Jealousy was caused, of course, by the child's perception of a threat to his claim to parental, primarily maternal, love. "No one, not even the most enlightened adult, can accept without many pangs the idea of sharing a love relation with a rival. We must remember that the child has been in the possession of all his mother's love; now he is called on to share it with another. . . . If we succeed in getting him to accept the situation happily, we have done much towards making him grow into an adult who looks upon all love as a sharing with others, not as a possession which must be calculated and selfishly held against all comers."[29] Jealousy, in other words, though extremely undesirable was also supremely understandable, because it rested in a loving relationship.

Yet while handling sibling jealousy required massive doses of parental love, so that on the arrival of a new baby, the older child realized that the affection directed at him was in no way reduced, it also required recognition that sibling love could not be insisted upon. Parents must let their children articulate a dislike for new babies. "A child should know that he is entitled to feel any way he wants to about his brother or sister, and he is not to think that he is a bad child because of it." Avoidance of guilt was as crucial to the development of a secure, jealousy-free personality as was the attack on the emotion itself. Parents should tell the child that he "sometimes won't like the new baby at all. Sometimes you'll be mad at momma too. You'll want to tell her 'Stop loving that little red baby. Come and love me.' Of course momma will give you more loving whenever you want it. So, be sure to ask." "I know how you feel, dear. Come on over and I'll give you a hug and we'll see if that doesn't help." "I know how you feel; you wish there were no baby; I love you just as always." Here, obviously, was explicit recognition, as against some of the more optimistic nineteenth-century renderings, that family and love were not indissolubly linked in the child's eye, though the solution was still more insistence that love could conquer all.[30] Jealousy entered the twentieth-century American pattern of emotional repression in which undesirable feelings were to be circumvented, rendered largely passive, rather than directly attacked.

Specific tactics within this overall framework became increasingly standardized, after some vagueness in the 1920s. They are of interest particularly because, at least in the eyes of experts, they ran counter to common parental impulses in some instances. Children must be carefully told that a baby is coming, as against some modest tendencies to duck the subject lest awkward questions be asked. If a child had to be moved to make room for baby, the move should come well in advance of the newcomer's arrival. Sharing should be downplayed. If at all possible, children should be given separate rooms, furnishings, toys, and clothing. Where sharing was economically essential—and Spock and others urged that unexpected expenses were worthwhile in this endeavor, as in possibly hiring a nurse to take care of baby so that maternal attention could flow to the older child—it should be masked by repainting furniture or dyeing clothes. Grandparents and others should learn not to make a great fuss over babies, in favor of turning to the older child. Invidious comparisons should never be made among children, and an atmosphere of careful fairness must prevail from the outset. Babies should be brought home without fanfare—there was some disagreement over whether older children should be present or not—and attention should immediately turn to the older child, even at some expense to the infant. After all, babies sleep a lot and a bit of neglect would not hurt them. Fathers, those vestigial remnants of traditional family life, actually had a role as well, in helping to divert the older child when mother was inescapably preoccupied with baby. Feeding the infant, particularly breast-feeding, was seen as a traumatic act, best done when the older child was diverted (and it was better to let a baby squall a bit than to turn away from the older child's needs). Finally, older children should be given responsibility for helping with babies, as well as treated to confidential asides about what a nuisance babies could be. Children should be given evidence, as one *Parents' Magazine* contributor noted, that "the baby was his."[31]

Some authorities went farther still, in urging sensible spacing of children now that most parents were aware of birth control. There were some amusing disputes about the ages of greatest vulnerability to jealousy, with opinions ranging from 2–3 to 4–5 or even 7–10, but ultimately considerable consensus emerged that the greatest danger of jealousy's taking root came in very early years, before children had any outside interests. Sensible spacing thus dictated two- or three-year intervals.[32]

At an extreme, of course, parents had to guard against violence to babies. Some experts treated this as a dire problem indeed, urging that a child never be left alone with a baby, as though murder were an almost predictable result. Finally, persistent or deep jealousy should be turned over to expert counseling, for the emotional bomb simply had to be defused.

The goal, of course, was to stem serious jealousy before it could start. Some experts were optimistic that their recommendations could produce full family harmony, as well as a healthy personality in the older child. Others, while claiming that personality development could indeed be set aright, admitted that recurrent, if relatively minor, outbursts of jealousy would continue, as part of a family life that fell short of ideal.[33]

The burst of concern about attacking jealousy in young children involved a number of expert-urged approaches against more traditional methods of discipline. Parents should respond to jealousy-induced quarrels not with a heavy hand, but with fairness, empathy, and assurances of love. They should not push generosity to the point of counterproductively insisting on down-the-line sharing. They should not expect their own joy at having a priceless baby to be shared by their own children. They should guard against their own impulses, for sheer power could not permanently prevail against jealousy, and short-term repression simply made matters worse. They should take seriously newer approaches to housing, feeding, and even spacing children. Experts obviously seized on jealousy as an occasion to assert their authority over what they assumed to be widespread parental errors, and they moved generally in the direction of greater permissiveness. Yet the real innovations rested not on tactics alone, but on the very issue that occasioned them: jealousy in children was being redefined as at once inescapable and dire.

And parents responded, both to the recommended tactics and to the novel identification of the emotional problem. Guidance authorities of various sorts reported widespread parental concern over jealousy in their young children. Letters from parents to family magazines show a similar reaction, as parents readily seized on a new problem and often indicated their personal shock at the manifestations of jealousy in the bosom of the family. In a standard pattern, one woman wrote to *Parents' Magazine*, in 1955, that jealousy was "by far the most troublesome, the gravest issue I've met so far in my career as mother." Many of the interwar experts who included sections on sibling rivalry in their manuals specifically noted that their interest had first been piqued by the numbers of parents who brought the problem to their attention in requests for counseling and guidance.

With this background of parental concern, fed by the experts but possibly antedating widespread expert advice, it is hardly surprising that tactical recommendations seem to have found a receptive audience. Recommended tactics were widely adopted, and some experts noted such enthusiastic response that older children were actually lionized or made to feel wronged by the apologetic presence of a new baby.[34]

A poll taken in the mid-1940s drives the point home: middle-class parents agreed that jealousy was a major issue, and were ready to shape family strategies accordingly. In a survey of 544 families, 53 percent reported significant problems of jealousy among siblings, rating this the third most important issue in dealing with children and the most serious of all concerns about children's personality and temperament. For suburban parents, sibling problems stood in fact second on the overall list, compared to an eighth place ranking for urban poor, eleventh for urban wealthy, and fourteenth for urban blacks. The problem was most acute where only two children were involved, and declined (in all categories) by about 15 percent where more than two children were present. Boys and girls ranked roughly equally in their parentally judged susceptibility to jealousy, with girls leading by a small margin.[35] Jealousy among children had become one of the leading emotional concerns, indeed emotional annoyances, of family life, as parents joined expert standard-setters in their readiness to identify and condemn this common impulse.

Jealousy among young siblings came close to being a twentieth-century invention. Before the 1890s experts had failed to mark the phenomenon or had treated it only in passing. Parents—though here we must argue, on the pre-1920s side, from indirection, through the absence of explicit comment and rebuke—had also failed to pinpoint jealousy as an emotional issue, at least before later childhood. Of course tensions among young siblings must have existed—Bronson Alcott among others hinted at this—and obviously some problems later hauled out for explicit comment were subsumed under more general categories of obedience, generosity, or quarrelsomeness. Yet there was change, both in the ability to label a specific emotional characteristic and the behavior resulting, and in the intensity with which many adults now defined their concern. The nature of the change can be further explored by turning to its explanation.

The most obvious explanatory path would see parental attention to sibling jealousy as an anxiety created by experts, a specific instance of the larger pattern of professional child-guidance types muscling in on parental, and childhood, autonomy. And, while this is not the whole story, it is without much question part of it. Spurred by the dissemination of Freudian theory, child psychologists unquestionably became more attuned to childish jealousy on the basis of theoretical preconceptions and to childhood generally as the source of adult personality. These predilections were in turn confirmed by a raft of studies from the mid-1920s through the 1930s that investigated actual incidence of jealousy symptoms among various groups of children in both institutional and family settings. The studies differed in some particulars, arguing over whether jealousy varied with children's age and the family's social background. Particularly important was dispute as to whether extended family settings heightened or diminished the chance of jealousy, and whether strict discipline favored or discouraged the emotion in young children. But the studies almost uniformly claimed a high rate of jealousy, usually in over half the sibling groups studied, and normally claimed as well that the emotion was most commonly experienced among girls. The results of these studies routinely found their way into general treatises on child psychology, which were in turn utilized (and sometimes even given credit) by the popularizing authors of child-rearing manuals and periodicals.[36]

So the experts found or invented a problem, often using research methods that would today be questioned, but finding what they expected to find. Their message battered at parents through the child-rearing literature—not surprisingly, reaching suburban middle-class parents most readily—until parents, too, came to see a problem where none had existed before. One could add to this picture the increasing conversion of American families to an emotion-based view of children[37] and to emotional rather than strictly economic functions more generally, a conversion which helped parents see what had previously been judged normal quarrelsomeness in more dire terms.

Expert opinion surely helps explain the timing of the rise of the childish jealousy problem and the precise vocabulary it acquired, including the standard use of the term sibling rivalry itself. But persuasive experts do not alone account for the popularity of the issue, or its widespread acceptance among parents themselves. Thus many experts also pushed the idea of basic Oedipal conflicts, and resultant jealousy between child and parent, which did not win nearly so much parental attention. To be sure, parents may have artificially turned away from this aspect of jealousy because it struck too close to home and involved a frank recognition of childish sexuality for which many were still unprepared. Or, as one French observer claimed (imaginatively, but with no effort at proof) Oedipal conflicts may have been muted in American families because of the sexlessness of parents themselves (in contrast of course to la belle France).[38] The main point is that expert findings on childish jealousy were not uniformly embraced by American parents. It was sibling jealousy that hit home, because it was sibling jealousy that merged expert recommendations with what American parents themselves were experiencing. Indeed it is possible that experts turned to sibling jealousy in part because parent-clients were telling them, in counseling sessions, that it was a problem.

The fact was that jealousy among young children almost certainly increased in the later nineteenth and early twentieth centuries, for the simple reason that family conditions became increasingly favorable to it. Obviously, jealousy among young children had existed before and equally obviously changes in incidence cannot be precisely measured. Nevertheless, it is highly probable that the absence of much explicit comment on jealous reception of new babies before the turn of the century resulted not only from distinctive adult vocabulary and expectations, including the ideal of a conflict-free family, but also from a distinctive actual experience. By the later nineteenth century the framework that had conduced to low-level jealousy among young children was beginning to change.

Jealousy most frequently arises when mothers are intensely affectionate. According to most findings it is most common when discipline is not severe (for harsh discipline helps unite siblings against parents). By 1900 maternal intensity was definitely on the rise, and discipline was probably moderating. Jealousy among young children may also have been heightened by the increasing practice of using hospitals for delivery of infants, which could exacerbate the tension, the apparent threat to maternal affection, experienced by an older child. Above all, sibling jealousy is most common in small families, where children do not see themselves as part of a larger group with mutual responsibilities for their own maintenance.[39] And smaller families were becoming increasingly common, particularly in those middle-class circles that most readily reported jealousy as a problem.[40] The various criteria commonly used to distinguish among family types, in terms of susceptibility to jealousy by young children, thus also operated over time. American families by the 1920s normally involved small sibling sets, enmeshed in abundant maternal affection whose disruption could be therefore more easily perceived, with children seeing themselves as rivals (sometimes, given encouragements to competition, prodded to do so)[41] instead of primarily as companions. Widespread parental reluctance to prepare a child for the arrival of a new baby, lest embarrassing sexual questions be raised, in favor of claiming that storks or doctors suddenly produced the new intruder, added to the mix.[42] Early-twentieth-century families were different from those of the midnineteenth century, and heightened jealousy was a key product of this change. It is no accident that several features prominent in nineteenth-century discussions of sibling affection figured among the changes, including smaller family size and a milder discipline that presented less target for sibling unity. The growing concern about sibling jealousy, and particularly its identification among young children rather than, nineteenth-century fashion, among older children preparing to dispute a partrimony or dowry, responded to fact. Expert prompting thus corresponded to a real emotional change, and the resultant clamor, though of course most easily perceived through the recommendations of authorities, was no mere artifact. Indeed, expert attention itself almost surely resulted in part from the novel childhood experiences of the experts themselves—including Freud, a jealous first child par excellence—whose own emotional context reflected the shifting conditions of family life. Though impossible to prove without some circularity, then, the greatest single factor in the heightened concern about sibling jealousy was heightened sibling jealousy. Expert advice was to a great extent directed, as in urging that children be given some responsibility for babies, at modifying some of the changes that had produced more jealousy, though few experts more than dimly perceived this historical perspective.

Further, while parents responded to new facts, as well as to child guidance pressure, they also reflected a final set of ingredients that colored their perceptions, sometimes beyond what the facts warranted. By the 1930s and 1940s middle-class parents were beginning to redefine the kinds of personalities they wished to raise, in response to alterations in business climate that stressed bureaucratic and service skills over entrepreneurship. They heightened their emphasis on social skills and became increasingly ambivalent about emotions that supported competitiveness. This tendency showed in a reevaluation of anger, and it also generated still greater sensitivity to jealousy. Here too, expert guidance picked up cues from the audience, in stressing that childhood jealousy might unfit an adult personality not only for familial love but for work relationships as well. Furthermore, in their zeal to ferret out childhood jealousy—and particularly perhaps in their own shock at the signs of such jealousy, as if no sibling squabbles had clouded their own early years—parents may have been projecting onto children the tension they felt in dealing with jealous emotions in a culture that attacked their validity. The declining gender rigidities, the wider socializing, and the looser sexual tone that described middle-class life from the early twentieth century onward may well have stimulated new pangs of jealousy that the culture refused to countenance. One recourse may have been to attack childhood symptoms with unprecedented zeal, buoyed by the belief that children would grow up freer from emotional strain as a result. Here was yet another intersection between the startling new emphasis on childhood jealousy and the wider experience of the emotion in twentieth-century American life.

The war on childish jealousy responded to a variety of interlocking factors, from expert prodding to a significant shift in the emotional experience of many children. The war reflected a growing need to answer change with change, to restrain jealousy even as it threatened to burst into more vigorous bloom.

The specific pattern of causation for the shocked awareness of childhood jealousy ran as follows: middle-class Americans were conscious by the 1890s of an emotionology that strongly urged a contrast between jealousy and real love, and even if they had not actively integrated this contrast into their own emotional perceptions they were certainly attuned to an equation of family and love. Then, through an interlacing series of shifts including new demography, they increasingly confronted a family situation where sibling jealousy was likely. Some resultant manifestations, such as threatened violence to babies, might have been inherently disturbing, but the pattern was particularly distressing in light of existing expectations about family life. Signs of new tensions over childhood jealousy began to surface in the 1890s and may

well have troubled many parents before they gained widespread public articulation. Experts then aided this articulation, developing a more elaborate set
of emotional standards regarding jealousy. Parental interest in developing
more cooperative personalities, for a corporate world, and possibly anxieties
about combatting their own jealousies encouraged an exaggeration of the
actual problems of sibling jealousy, and the sheer novelty of the issue worked
to the same effect. Nevertheless, in contrast to most known cases, where
emotionological change normally precedes shifts in actual emotional experience—as with anger or love in modern Western history—the rise of the
sibling jealousy issue moved more from actual emotional change to a heightened specification of standards.

One further chapter was yet to come. The expert and parental campaign
against childhood jealousy entered a new phase by the 1960s, in large part
because the hardest battles had been won. The emotionology established
during the previous half century remained largely intact, but the sense of
urgency and the impression of novelty both subsided.

Advice manuals, though varied, on average dramatically reduced their
treatment of sibling rivalry. A few dropped the standard section altogether.[43]
As early as 1956 Stanley and Janice Berenstain derided conventional expert
treatment. "There is so much talk about this phase of childrearing than even
fond grammas and misty-eyed aunts generally understand that it's not cricket
to chirp at baby while Big Brother is around." The Berenstains argued that
children normally liked each other and grew jealous only if parents fouled
the nest. They then, despite their amusing counterpoint, carefully repeated
all the standard tactics, but without any sense of crisis.[44]

Clearer measurements of the new tone come from Dr. Spock and *Parents'
Magazine*. Spock in his later editions pulled back, though slightly, from his
earlier warnings. The phrase about jealousy meriting a "lot of effort" was
dropped, and instead of threatening a permanently distorted personality
Spock opined that childhood jealousy "may sour his outlook on life for quite
a while." Successful management, while it would not eliminate jealousy, can
help children grow up and foster more "constructive" feelings. Again the
recommended tactics were unchanged, but the setting was less apocalyptic.[45]
Parents' Magazine continued high-frequency coverage on jealousy through
the 1950s, though with increasing emphasis on trusting children by 1959.
But the early 1960s carried some articles venturing to deny the inevitability
of sibling rivalry, along with columns citing the delight that children could
take in a new baby. One parent wrote about the attention she lavished on her
older child, to compensate for a new birth, "even though she didn't seem to
need it." And a 1961 poll on problem behavior (admittedly not comparable
to Jersild's 1940s poll because it did not focus on common issues between

parents and children) saw no reference to jealousy at all, with quar-relsomeness, the nearest candidate, ranking only twenty-sixth. Clearly, parents as well as experts were redefining urgency.[46]

To be sure, there were some treatments reminiscent of the earlier wars. Frank Caplan, who ignored jealousy in one 1977 manual, in another wrote that "Nothing so greedily consumes a child's inner emotional reserves than feelings of jealousy" and even advanced the age of peak openness to the monstrous emotion to six.[47] Sibling advice books remained popular, and some stressed the negative, unless balanced by careful parental strategies. "Whenever a child feels down, shaky, envious or threatened, jealousy crops up again." Parents must be extremely careful to be impartial and to offer demonstrative love.[48]

But the impression of imminent disaster eased overall. Earlier experts were derided, including Spock for his anxiety about breast-feeding in front of an older child. Parents who frantically overcompensated for a sibling birth were ridiculed: "they tended to fall over backwards trying to avoid it."[49] The 1930s social science studies were criticized, as experts more than halved the previous figures of likelihood of significant jealousy, from 44–60 percent to 20 percent.[50] Indeed scientific sibling jealousy studies themselves dropped from fashion, in favor of careful inquiries into the cognitive impact of birth order. Specific tactics were modified in light of the reduction of tension. Duplicating presents and avoiding any fuss over a new baby were counter-manded, as unnecessary and indeed detrimental to the older child's adjust-ment to reality. A bit of jealousy was still to be expected, but it could be corrected. "It is usually possible for you to change his emotionalized state with a changed situation."[51] "Youngsters with a sturdy sense of trust can handle these momentary feelings and even benefit." A few authorities re-turned to the invocation of useful spurs to ambition, while others disclaimed any necessary connection between child jealousy and the adult emotion. "Children are usually resilient. If one approach doesn't work and sibling rivalry gets out of hand, this doesn't mean the children will be permanently damaged."[52]

While treatments of childhood jealousy shifted in emphasis, with less space devoted to the subject and more attention directed to other problems such as low self-esteem, most of the earlier recommendations remained in force. There was simply more confidence that the problem could be managed. "Jealousy is rarely preventable but it need not be extreme."[53] Reading designed for fairly young children carried the same message, thus amplifying the range of signals available to siblings themselves while avoiding high anxiety. Beverly Cleary, for example, used the stubborn jealousy between her protagonist, Ramona, and an older sister as a central theme, treating "sib-lingitis" as a fact of life while making it clear that mother love would ultimately reduce the strain and growing maturity would take it from there: "[Ramona] was working at growing up."[54]

What accounted for this limited change in the assessment of children's propensity for jealousy? Expert fads, including the endless delight in selling books by modifying last year's advice, surely played some role. By the 1960s, a decline in maternal intensity, given new trends of outside-the-home employment, may actually have reduced the context for jealousy among young children, as a wider range of adult figures—baby-sitters, even fathers—helped distribute the emotional load while reducing insecurity about any single deprivation. The rise of a peer culture, reaching into grade school years, may have diverted some jealousy-producing intensity as well. The further decline in the birth rate after 1963 reduced sibling problems automatically in many families, by preventing siblings, while wider birth spacing may have had similar effect, as the number of only children increased, though new patterns of step- and half-relationships could induce serious jealousy still. At the same time, ongoing concern about jealousy shifted more directly to adults themselves, given the antijealousy experiments of the counterculture of the 1960s and widespread, though not entirely novel, attempts—complete by the 1970s with "jealousy workshops"—to dissociate love and sex from the green-eyed passion. For a variety of reasons, the focus of attacks on jealousy empirically widened, and while jealous adults were still accused of insecure childhoods they, and not children alone, had jealousy issues to work on.

Most important, however, was the routinization of the emotionology of the midcentury decades as applied to children themselves. The parents likely to be concerned about jealousy understood now what to expect, if only from their own childhoods. They were no longer shocked by a bit of sibling rivalry, and they knew the appropriate tactics by heart. They prepared children for new babies, they avoided overt favoritism, they had a much more elaborate overall policy than their forebears of the 1930s.[55] Their awareness eased their own anxiety and may actually have accounted for much of the reduction in jealousy reported, including a noteworthy diminution of serious jealousy among sisters. It is thus likely that new research findings that stipulated a lower incidence of jealousy reflected not only better methods and assumptions, but also a genuinely altered experience among children. The emotionology concerning childish jealousy changed to an extent, but basic goals were maintained as the socialization policies established earlier entered a more mature phase.

What was happening, from the 1960s onward, was a limited modification of the framework that had occasioned the increase of sibling jealousy in the first place, starting with the kind of attention mothers provided and the number and spacing of sibling pairs. More substantial changes resulted from the widespread use of jealousy-defusing tactics, which parents now found normal and unsurprising even without loud expert guidance. Less childhood jealousy existed, even allowing for some of the exaggeration of shocked reports in the interwar and baby boom years. Basic emotionology, however, remained unchanged: the hostility to jealousy that had been enhanced by the sibling crisis was intact, applied to adult and childish behaviors alike.

The United States in the twentieth-century witnessed a significant rise in childhood jealousy, matched, within a preexisting context of hostility to the emotion, by adult concern and some partially successful counterstrategies. Children's jealousy remained a greater family issue, by the 1980s, than it had been a century earlier, but it no longer seemed to be running amok. The development of a new focus on sibling jealousy, and particularly the attention given to early childhood, did not constitute simply an episode in parent-child relations, even as some of the most acute tensions eased. The three intertwined strands of the twentieth-century pattern—the increase in jealousy itself, the adult concern, and the nature of the suppression attempted—all had wider repercussions on the larger role of jealousy in personal and public life. This essay's emphasis on children's emotion and adult response cannot pretend a full statement of jealousy's recent course, and some questions raised about the broader impact of the shifts in the sibling context must remain open-ended. Nevertheless, just as the twentieth-century history of children's jealousy reflected changes in the larger society, including expert role, business personality, and basic demography, so it promoted change.

The implications of the rise in sibling jealousy itself are the most difficult to draw out, in absence of an appropriate theory of the relationship between childhood and adult emotion. Whatever the significance of some primal jealousy, inherent in the human animal or inevitably arising, it seems clear that the link between children's jealousy and adult personality is complex, and not merely because of the intermediary of socialization—too complex, certainly, to posit an increase in adult jealousy on grounds of heightened sibling tension in early childhood. In past time relatively harmonious sibling relations could turn bitter in youth, while the promptings of honor could pull a jealously protective adult from a child not marked by obvious rivalries. Some observers, though mainly non-American, given the national urge to downplay jealousy's value, continue to see a link between jealous children and competitively achieving adults, which would have interesting implications for twentieth-century American behavior both before and after the partially successful efforts to damp down new sibling tension.[56]

Certainly, at a simpler level, the rise in children's jealousy came at a difficult time in American emotional history, given the increasing dependence of families on positive emotional experience—defined as excluding serious jealousy—juxtaposed with the increasing opportunities for jealousy in adult life. One result, as we have seen, was a deepening of the disapproval with which jealousy was viewed. While the emotion had earlier been recast as negative, the intensity of the condemnation rose in response to the heightened threat from childhood. While the inevitability of some childhood jealousy was reluctantly granted, many adults could not easily accept its normality. As one authority recently put it, the emotion is too awful to be normal. It must be moderated, for its persistence becomes a sign of a "rotten moral fiber." And so the beast must be tamed, rather than put to any use.[57]

The resultant campaign must be seen as a significant part of twentieth-century American family and children's history, in which obvious changes in sibling relations, and their impact on parent-child contacts, have been too long neglected.[58] Many Americans took the charge of defusing jealousy quite seriously, and made a number of adjustments to this end. Some even talked about decisions over child spacing and family size—the idea of curtailing jealousy by having more than two children fit into the middle-class baby boom enthusiasm—in terms of these emotional goals.[59] Without question the anxious monitoring of jealousy, particularly in the decades when strategies were newly developed, complicated the evaluation of children themselves, seen as bearing new seeds of discord that must be controlled even as other impulses were given freer play. More general policies toward children, such as attempts to modify school settings to reduce jealous competition in favor of greater cooperativeness, reflected the new sense that prior practice must be reevaluated in light of new emotional problems and goals. Here, however, as in dealing with anger, the school environment moved more slowly than that of the family, setting up for children a new version of the public-private emotional dichotomy, with somewhat different emotional rules to be learned for each.

Even at home, however, the rules to be learned for jealousy were not exactly simple. Jealousy was bad, to be sure. Yet it should be greeted not with harshness or punishment, but with love and with tactics, such as fairness and gift giving, that reflected love. Jealousy might in this sense seem rewarded, its repression somewhat tentative and contingent. Yet, finally, jealousy was distinctly childish, its compensations temporary. This feature of the new emotionology remained in full force after 1960, as it had when the emotion seemed to threaten a crisis in childhood.

Important parts of this message were clearly assimilated. Expressions of childish jealousy did diminish after a few decades of the new approach. Teenagers frequently weighed the advantages of using jealousy in their dating behavior against the drawbacks of displaying a clearly juvenile emotion. "The further up the ladder we go, the less childish jealousies come back to haunt us."[60] At the height of the antijealousy campaign, right after World War II, many teenagers turned to steady dating as an institutional means of reducing an emotion that roused tension within them. In the longer run, as socialization became more complete, this approach tended to be jettisoned in favor of links with a larger peer group in which jealous interactions were distinctly frowned upon.

Jealousy remained active after childhood. Childhood experience may have taught many Americans to expect quick redress when the emotion was encountered—a loving reassurance—that in fact heightened the disruptive effects of jealousy within marriage.[61] Yet childhood also taught Americans to defend their maturity against accusations of jealousy. They sought to construct a complex personality in which clear identification of self and self-interest, the "me" impulse, was not sharpened by overt jealous possessiveness. Jealousy, as one 1960s observer put it, "is well on the way to becoming the New Sin of the liberated generation."[62] And when the emotion arose, it created discomfort and also prompted concealment. In one comparative study of the late 1970s, based on polling responses, Americans were rated far more likely to feel uncomfortable when jealous than any of the other nationalities surveyed (57 percent to the next closest—West Indian—40 percent), and considerably more likely than most to try to hide jealous feelings.[63] Discomfort and concealment reflected in turn the evolution that jealousy had undergone in twentieth-century America. The emotion existed; it would not yield to direct discipline; but it was harmful and unpleasant, a badge of emotional immaturity. So, though it still might goad action in personal relationships, it should largely be denied, even tested against an increasing array of situations that in other cultures would readily provoke a jealous response. The battle set up in childhood continued within many an American adult.

Notes

A note on sources: This article is based extensively on American child-rearing manuals from the nineteenth and twentieth centuries, from which evidence is taken about the emotionology applied to childhood jealousy and also about parental concerns and responses. A large sample of advice literature was studied. The most widely used and representative manuals for the nineteenth century have been identified by other historians (e.g., Bernard Wishy, *The Child and the Republic* [Philadelphia, 1968]), and my selections were made accordingly. For the twentieth century, particularly for the crucial decades from 1920 to 1960, a wider range of materials is available and was utilized, but always in reference to the most widely read authors (Fisher, Gruenberg, Spock) and to the popular *Parents' Magazine*. See Leone Kell and Jean Aldous, "Trends in Child Care over Three Generations," *Marriage and Family Living* 22 (1960): 176–77, and Celia B. Stendler, "Sixty Years of Child Training Practices," *Journal of Pediatrics* 36 (1950): 122–34. Representativeness was

218 *Peter N. Stearns*

also tested by using materials issued by major child-guidance groups and through analysis of internal consistency on key points within each period, as well as juxtaposition with some children's literature. As disputes over jealousy were quite limited within each period, a summary of principal approaches requires no liberties with the evidence. Claims about parental response to this expert emotionology are somewhat more speculative, and without question variations among subgroups are downplayed; but polling data and other signs of interest allow some statements of high probability about at least the middle class.

A number of people have assisted in this research, part of a larger project on the history of jealousy. For advice and suggestions, my thanks to John Modell, Linda Rosenzweig, Carol Stearns, Julie Wiener, Deborah Stearns, and Clio Stearns. I am particularly indebted to the thoughtful labor of my research assistant, Steve Tripp.

1. Arnold Gesell, "Jealousy," *American Journal of Psychology* 17 (1906): 484.

2. Ruth Fedder, *A Girl Grows Up* (New York, 1939), p. 180.

3. Gesell, "Jealousy," p. 438. For a more balanced statement, see Th. Ribot, *The Psychology of Emotions* (London, 1897).

4. Melanie Klein, *Envy, Gratitude and Other Works* (New York, 1977); on jealousy in thirty-month-olds across cultures, L. A. Stroufe, "Socioemotional Development," in J. Osofsky, ed., *Handbook of Infant Development* (New York, 1979).

5. Madeline Chapsal, *La Jalousie* (Paris, 1977).

6. Edmund Leites, *The Puritan Conscience and Modern Sexuality* (New Haven, 1985), pp. 109–10.

7. The same absence seems to hold for eighteenth-century parents. At least, secondary treatments have not picked up on any explicit attention to jealousy, whether the emphasis is on strict discipline or a more tolerant enjoyment of childish foibles. Philip J. Greven, Jr., *The Protestant Temperament: Patterns of Child-Rearing, Religious Experience and the Self in Early America* (New York, 1977); Dickson Bruce, Jr., *Violence and Culture in the Antebellum South* (New York, 1979), pp. 44–67; Daniel Blake Smith, *Inside the Great House: Planter Family Life in Eighteenth Century Chesapeake Society* (Ithaca, 1980).

8. Hills family papers, Amherst College, letters by Mary to her mother, 6 Mar. and 23 Mar. 1887, 20 Jan. 9 Feb., and 20 Feb. 1888, concerning her younger sister. I am very grateful to Prof. Linda Rosenzweig for calling this material to my attention. For comparison to twentieth-century teenagers, Arnold Gesell, Francis Ilg, and Laura Ames, *Youth: The Ages from Ten to Sixteen* (New York, 1956), passim.

9. John S. C. Abbott, *The Mother at Home* (London, 1834); Marion Harland, *Eve's Daughter, or Common Sense for Maid, Wife and Mother* (New York, 1882), p. 59; Jacob Abbott, *Gentle Measures in the Management and Training of the Young* (New York, 1871), pp. 100ff.

10. Hugh Hartsham, *Childhood and Character* (New York, 1919); see also H. Clay Trumbull, *Hints on Child Training* (Philadelphia, 1925).

11. Catharine Sedgwick, *Home* (Boston, 1841), pp. 48, 131; Lydia Sigourney, *The Book for Girls* (New York, 1844), p. 72, and *The Book for Boys* (New York, 1839), pp. 39ff.; T. S. Arthur, *The Mother's Rule* (Philadelphia, 1856), pp. 20, 25; Lydia

Sigourney, *Letters to Mothers* (Hartford, 1838), p. 58; T. S. Arthur, *Advice to Young Ladies* (Boston, 1848), p. 108, and *Advice to Young Men* (Boston, 1848).

12. Horace Bushnell, *Views of Christian Nurture* (Hartford, 1847); Lydia Child, *The Mother's Book* (Boston, 1831), p. 25; Bronson Alcott, *Record of Conversations on the Gospels* (Boston, 1837), 2:254–55.

13. Wishy, *The Child and the Republic*, p. 47. The treatment of jealousy in *Little Women* seems archetypical. With strong emphasis on family harmony, there is little mention of jealousy or rivalry; the sisters take pride in each other's accomplishments and strengths. Jealousy only emerged concerning lovers, intruders into sisterly affection; even this young adult jealousy is not phrased in terms of sibling rivalry. Romance, then, but not emotional relationships with parents, could stimulate thoughts of jealousy.

14. Mrs. Theodore Birney, *Childhood* (New York, 1904).

15. Michael Ryan, *The Philosophy of Marriage in Its Social, Moral and Physical Relations* (London, 1839). On the condemnation of adult jealousy see also Mrs. E. B. Duffy, *What Women Should Know* (Philadelphia, 1873), p. 64, and Max Lazarus, *Love vs. Marriage* (New York, 1854), p. 24.

16. G. Stanley Hall, *Adolescence* (New York, 1931), 1:357ff.

17. Felix Adler, *The Moral Instruction of Children* (New York, 1893), pp. 213–14.

18. Gesell, "Jealousy," p. 452.

19. D. A. Thom, *Child Management* (Washington, 1925), pp. 9–12; see also U.S. Department of Labor, Children's Bureau, *Are You Training Your Child to Be Happy?* (Washington, 1930), p. 31.

20. Child Study Association of America, *Guidance of Childhood and Youth* (New York, 1926), pp. 100–101. This approach was repeated verbatim in a number of other manuals, though without attribution, perhaps in case other, uncited authors might be jealous. Ada Arlitt, *The Child from One to Twelve* (New York, 1928).

21. Dorothy Canfield Fisher and Sidonie Gruenberg, *Our Children: A Handbook for Parents* (New York, 1932).

22. John B. Watson, *Psychological Care of Infant and Child* (New York, 1928).

23. Sidonie Gruenberg, ed., *Encyclopedia of Child Guidance* (New York, 1951); B. Harlock, *Child Development* (New York, 1954); Herman Vollmer, "Jealousy in Children," *American Journal of Orthopsychiatry* 16 (1946): 187.

24. Allan Fromme, *The Parents' Handbook* (New York, 1956), p. 93; Sidonie Gruenberg, *We the Parents* (New York, 1939), p. 90; Dorothy Baruch, *New Ways in Discipline* (New York, 1949), p. 124 and *Understanding Young Children* (New York, 1949), p. 41; John C. Montgomery and Margaret Suydam, *America's Baby Book* (New York, 1951), p. 123; Daniel M. Levy, *Maternal Overprotection* (New York, 1943), pp. 22–23.

25. Montgomery and Suydam, *Baby Book*, p. 123; Haim Ginnott, *Between Parent and Child* (New York, 1965).

26. Luella Cole and John J. B. Morgan, *Psychology of Childhood and Adolescence* (New York, 1947); Edmund Zilmer, *Jealousy in Children: A Guide for Parents* (New York, 1949); Mary M. Thomson, *Talk It Out with Your Child* (New York,

1953), p. 112; Sybil Foster, "A Study of the Personality Makeup and Social Setting of Fifty Jealous Children," *Mental Hygiene* 11 (1927): 53–77; Ruth Fedder, *You, the Person You Want to Be* (New York, 1957), p. 69.

27. Harold C. Anderson, *Children in the Family* (New York, 1941), p. 112; Mollie Smart and Russell Smart, *Living and Learning with Children* (New York, 1949), p. 209; Dorothy Baruch, *Parents Can Be People* (New York, 1944), p. 103; Gladys H. Groves, *Marriage and Family Life* (New York, 1942).

28. Benjamin Spock, *The Common Sense Book of Baby and Child Care* (New York, 1945), p. 272.

29. Winnifred de Kok, *Guiding Your Child through the Formative Years* (New York, 1935), p. 176.

30. Zilmer, *Jealousy in Children*, p. 85; Baruch, *New Ways*, pp. 122, 123; Joseph Teich, *Your Child and His Problems* (Boston, 1953), p. 101.

31. Montgomery and Suydam, *Baby Book*, pp. 123–25; "Family Clinic," *Parents' Magazine* (June 1955), p. 26, and passim, 1954–59; Spock, *Common Sense,* pp. 272–79; Fromme, *Parents' Handbook*, p. 251.

32. de Kok, *Guiding Your Child*, p. 172.

33. Groves, *Marriage and Family Life;* Leslie B. Hohman, *As The Twig Is Bent* (New York, 1944).

34. Teich, *Your Child*, p. 98; Margaret McFarland, *Relationships between Young Sisters* (New York, 1938), p. 67.

35. Arthur T. Jersild et al., *Joys and Problems of Childrearing* (New York, 1949), pp. 28–30, 87, 94.

36. Foster, "Personality Makeup," pp. 533–71; Mabel Sewall, "Some Causes of Jealousy in Young Children," *Smith College Studies in Social Work* 1 (1930–31): 6–22; Ruth E. Smalley, "The Influence of Differences in Age, Sex and Intelligence in Determining the Attitudes of Siblings toward Each Other," *Smith College Studies in Social Work* 1 (1930–31): 23–44; D. M. Levy, "Studies in Sibling Rivalry," *American Orthopsychiatry Research Monograph #2* (1937); D. M. Levy, "Rivalry Between Children of the Same Family," *Child Study* 22 (1934): 233–61; A. Adler, "Characteristics of the First, Second and Third Child," *Children* 3, no. 5 (1938). Only one of these studies, but an interesting one, ran counter to the pessimistic findings about jealousy, noting the diversity of reactions among children and the frequency of intense affection. See M. B. MacFarland, "Relationship between Young Sisters as Revealed in Their Overt Responses," *Journal of Experimental Education* 6 (1937): 73–79. But the MacFarland conclusions were ignored amid the welter of findings that jealousy was a major problem and that its resolution depended on careful parental policy, in what was almost certainly an exaggerated perception of a nevertheless common (though decidedly not uniform) childhood response. See Judy Dunn and Carl Kendrick, *Siblings: Love, Envy and Understanding* (Cambridge, Mass., 1982), passim.

37. Viviana Zelizer, *Pricing the Priceless Child* (New York, 1986).

38. Margaret Mead and Martha Wolfenstein, eds., *Childhood in Contemporary Culture* (Chicago, 1955), pp. 150ff.

39. Judy Dunn, *Sisters and Brothers* (Cambridge, Mass., 1985), pp. 98–99; Jane S. Brossard and E. S. Boll, *The Large Family System: An Original Study in the*

Sociology of Family Behavior (Philadelphia, 1956), pp. 186–87. This is not to claim that all small families are more likely to engender jealousy, but that this correlation with the new demography operated in the Western context where it was combined with intense maternal affection. Not surprisingly, there are signs of a similar correlation in other Western nations such as Great Britain, where childish jealousy won growing recognition in the twentieth century. For jealousy in actual nineteenth-century families, perhaps increasing toward the century's end, see various studies on the James or Adams clans. The correspondence in timing between new middle-class anxieties about jealousy and the decline of live-in maids and coresident grandparents should also be explored as part of the focus on newly intense child-mother bonds and the resultant change in the actual emotional experience of early childhood.

40. Note that black family manuals still do not treat sibling jealousy. Phyllis Harrison-Ross and Barbara Wyden, *The Black Child—A Parent's Guide* (New York, 1973).

41. Mollie S. Smart and Russell C. Smart, *Children: Development and Relationships* (New York, 1969).

42. Claudia Lewis, *Children of the Cumberland* (New York, 1946), p. 69, on efforts to avoid discussing pregnancy with children.

43. See for example Frank Caplan, ed., *The Parent Advisor* (New York, 1977); Dodi Schwartz, ed., *The Toddler Years* (New York, 1986), pp. 216–17; Seymour Fischer and Rhoda Fischer, *What We Really Know about Child Rearing* (New York, 1976).

44. Stanley Berenstain and Janice Berenstain, *Baby Makes Four* (New York, 1956), p. 8.

45. Benjamin Spock and Michael Rothenburg, *The Common Sense Book of Baby and Child Care* (New York, 1985), pp. 409ff.

46. *Parents' Magazine,* 1954–85. See particularly Jan. 1961, Sept. 1961, July 1962, July 1985.

47. Frank Caplan and Theresa Caplan, *The Second Twelve Months of Life* (New York, 1977).

48. Carole Calladine and Andrew Calladine, *Raising Siblings* (New York, 1979), p. 31 and passim.

49. Anna W. M. Wolf and Suzanne Szasz, *Helping Your Child's Emotional Growth* (New York, 1954), p. 255.

50. Stephen P. Bank and Michael Kahn, *The Sibling Bond* (New York, 1982), pp. 206–7.

51. Dunn and Kendrick, *Siblings;* Brian Sutton-Smith and B. G. Rosenberg, *The Sibling* (New York, 1979), pp. 6, 155, and passim; Lester D. Crow and Alice Crow, *Being a Good Parent* (Boston, 1966), p. 136; *Better Homes and Gardens, New Baby Book* (New York, 1979), pp. 138–39.

52. James Hymes, *The Child Under Six* (Englewood Cliffs, N.J., 1964), p. 81; Podolsky, *Jealous Child,* pp. 125ff.; Stella Chess et al., *Your Child as a Person* (New York, 1965), p. 145; T. Berry Brazelton, *Toddlers and Parents* (New York, 1974), pp. 51ff.

53. Eleanor Verville, *Behavior Problems of Children* (Philadelphia, 1967).

54. Beverly Cleary, *Ramona Forever* (New York, 1984), pp. 176, 182. I am grateful to Clio Stearns and Julie Wiener for guidance in this literature.

55. Sutton-Smith and Rosenberg, *Sibling*, p. 260.

56. Leila Tova Ruack, "Jealousy, Anxiety and Loss," in Amelia O. Rortz, ed., *Exploring Emotions* (Berkeley and Los Angeles, 1980), p. 469.

57. Carroll Izard, *Human Emotions* (New York, 1977), p. 200; see also pp. 194–202.

58. But see Richard Sennett, *Families against the City* (Cambridge, Mass., 1984), for some general remarks about the decreased resiliency of Americans, given a shift toward more intense, and smaller, nuclear families.

59. This is a link still to be explored. See John Modell and John Campbell, *Family Ideology and Family Values in the "Baby Boom"* (Minneapolis, 1984).

60. Oliver M. Butterfield, *Love Problems of Adolescence* (New York, 1941), p. 77; Rhoda C. Lorand, *Love, Sex and the Teenager* (New York, 1965), pp. 109–10; Evelyn Duvall, *Facts of Life and Love for Teenagers* (New York, 1950), p. 210.

61. For a comment on how parental responses to jealousy via reassurance might heighten a dependency which might be expressed in adult jealousy, see Bram Buunk, "Anticipated Sexual Jealousy: Its Relationship to Self-Esteem, Dependency, and Reciprocity," *Personality and Social Psychology Bulletin* 8 (1982): 310–16.

62. Gordon Clanton and Lynn G. Smith, eds., *Jealousy* (Englewood Cliffs, N.J., 1977), p. 35.

63. Shula Sommers, "Adults Evaluating Their Emotions: A Cross-Cultural Perspective," in Carol Malatesta and Carroll Izard, eds., *Emotion in Adult Development* (Beverly Hills, Calif., 1984), p. 324.

Bibliography

On early modern emotion and the transformation of the family, classic works are Lawrence Stone, *The Family, Sex and Marriage in England, 1500–1800* (New York, 1977); David Hunt, *Parents and Children in History: The Psychology of Family Life in Early Modern France* (New York, 1970); Edward Shorter, *The Making of the Modern Family* (New York, 1975); Jean Flandrin, *Families in Former Times* (Cambridge, Eng., 1976); and Randolph Trumbach, *The Rise of the Egalitarian Family: Aristocratic Kinship and Domestic Relations in 18th Century England* (New York, 1978). See also Norbert Elias, *The History of Manners* (New York, 1982).

Complementary works of great merit include John Demos, *A Little Commonwealth: Family Life in Plymouth Colony* (New York, 1970); Philip J. Greven, Jr., ed., *Childrearing Concepts, 1628–1861* (Itasca, Ill., 1973); David Sabean, *Power in the Blood: Popular Culture and Village Discourse in Early Modern Germany* (New York, 1984); and Rhys Isaac, *The Transformation of Virginia, 1740–1790* (Chapel Hill, 1982). More revisionist approaches to early modern emotion are Philip J. Greven, Jr., *The Protestant Temperament: Patterns of Childrearing, Religious Experience and the Self in Early America* (New York, 1977); Linda Pollock, *Forgotten Children: Parent-Child Relations from 1500 to 1900* (Cambridge, Eng., 1983); Keith Wrightson, *English Society 1580–1680* (New Brunswick, N.J., 1982); Steven Ozment, *When Fathers Ruled: Family Life in Reformation Europe* (Cambridge, Mass., 1983); Alan MacFarlane, *Marriage and Love in England: Modes of Reproduction, 1300–1540* (New York, 1986).

A more intermediate position, arguing for change but not an absolute modern-traditional contrast, can be found in John R. Gillis, *For Better, for Worse: British Marriages 1600 to the Present* (New York, 1985); Herman W. Roodenburg, "The Autobiography of Isabella de Moerloose: Sex, Childrearing and Popular Belief in Seventeenth-Century Holland," *Journal of Social History* 18 (1985): 517–40.

Other important approaches to early modern emotion, including social control, include John Demos, *Entertaining Satan: Witchcraft and the Culture of Early New England* (Oxford, 1982); Michael MacDonald, *Mystical Bedlam: Madness, Anxiety and Healing in Seventeenth-Century England* (Cambridge, Eng., 1981); Lloyd deMause, ed., *History of Childhood* (New York, 1974); Edmund Leites, *The Puritan Conscience and Modern Sexuality* (New Haven, 1985); Robert Muchembled, *Popular Culture and Elite Culture in France, 1400–1750* (Baton Rouge, 1985); Arthur Mitzman, "The Civilizing Offensive: Mentalities, High Culture and Individual Psyches," *Journal of Social History* 20 (1987): 663–88.

On individual emotions, Carol Z. Stearns and Peter N. Stearns, *Anger:*

The Struggle for Emotional Control in America's History (Chicago, 1986); Jean Delumeau, *La peur en Occident, XIVe–XVIIIe siècles: Une cité assiégée* (Paris, 1978); Jacques LeBrun, *La Peur* (Paris, 1979); Philippe Ariès, *The Hour of Our Death* (New York, 1981); Paul C. Rosenblatt, *Bitter, Bitter Tears: Nineteenth-Century Diarists and Twentieth-Century Grief Theories* (Minneapolis, 1983); Lynn Lofland, "The Social Shaping of Emotion: The Case of Grief," *Symbolic Interaction* 9 (1985): 171–90; Alain Corbin, *The Foul and the Fragrant: Odor and the French Imagination* (Cambridge, Mass., 1986); William Goode "The Theoretical Importance of Love," *American Sociological Review* 24 (1959): 35–49.

Treatments of emotional change in the nineteenth and twentieth centuries, ranging somewhat more widely, include Jan Lewis, *The Pursuit of Happiness: Family and Values in Jefferson's Virginia* (New York, 1983); Ellen Rothman, *Hands and Hearts: A History of Courtship in America* (New York, 1984); Viviana Zelizer, *Pricing the Priceless Child: The Changing Social Value of Children* (New York, 1985); Michael Barton, *Goodmen: The Character of Civil War Soldiers* (University Park, Pa., 1981); Steven Stowe, *Intimacy and Power in the Old South* (New York, 1987); Abram de Swaan, "The Politics of Agoraphobia: On Changes in Emotional and Relational Management," *Theory and Society* 10 (1981): 359–85; Theodore Zeldin, *France 1848–1945,* vol. 1, *Ambition, Love and Politics* (Oxford, 1972), and vol. 2, *Intellect, Taste and Anxiety* (Oxford, 1977); Peter Gay, *The Bourgeois Experience: Victoria to Freud,* vol. 1, *Education of the Senses* (New York, 1984), and vol. 2, *The Tender Passions* (New York, 1986); Christopher Lasch, *Haven in a Heartless World: The Family Besieged* (New York, 1975); Arlie Russell Hochschild, *The Managed Heart: Commercialization of Human Feeling* (Berkeley and Los Angeles, 1983).

For relevant theory, Carol Z. Malatesta and Carroll E. Izard, eds., *Emotion in Adult Development* (New York, 1982); James R. Averill, "A Constructivist View of Emotion," in Robert A. Plutchik and Henry Kellerman, eds., *Emotion: Theory, Research, and Experience* (New York, 1980); Richard A. Shweder and Robert A. LeVine, eds., *Culture Theory: Essays on Mind, Self, and Emotion* (Cambridge, Eng., 1984); Peter N. Stearns with Carol Z. Stearns, "Emotionology: Clarifying the History of Emotions and Emotional Standards," *American Historical Review* 90 (1985): 813–36; Stuart Clark, "French Historians and Early Modern Popular Culture," *Past and Present* 100 (August 1983): 62–99; Robert I. Levy, *Tahitians: Mind and Experience in the Society Islands* (Chicago, 1973); Steven C. Gordon, "The Sociology of Sentimentality and Emotion," in Morris Rosenberg and R. H. Turner, eds., *Social Psychology* (New York, 1981); Arthur Kleinman and Byron Good, *Culture and Depression: Studies in the Anthropology and Cross-Cultural Psychiatry of Affect and Disorder* (Berkeley and Los Angeles, 1985).

Notes on Contributors

John Demos, Professor of History at Yale University, has worked widely in American colonial social history and the history of family and childhood. His book *Little Commonwealth,* on Plymouth, was a pioneering effort in the "new" social history; more recently his study of witchcraft, *Entertaining Satan,* explored various facets of emotional expression.

John Gillis is Professor of History at Rutgers University. His most recent book is *For Better, for Worse: British Marriages, 1600 to the Present* (Oxford, 1985), and he is currently working on the ritualization of British family life in the nineteenth and twentieth centuries.

Judith Modell is an Assistant Professor of Anthropology at Carnegie-Mellon University. Her current research is on interpretations of parenthood in American society, and she has been pursuing this through an intensive, fieldwork-based study of adoption—including the current "search" movement that has prompted changes in laws and customs regarding adoption. Recently, she has added a comparative component and is looking at the relationship between customary practices and a legal system of adoption in Hawaii. The two projects will be published in separate monographs. Publications include a biography of Ruth Fulton Benedict (1983), articles on parenthood, and on the uses of personal testimony in social science research.

Shula Sommers is in the Psychology Department of the University of Massachusetts, Boston. She has published widely on the subject of comparative evaluations of emotion in a number of contemporary cultures, and many of her articles have been reproduced in anthologies in the field. She is currently engaged in a study of envy.

Carol Z. Stearns, M.D., has a private practice in psychiatry and is Clinical Instructor at the University of Pittsburgh School of Medicine. She holds a Ph.D. in history, and has been Visiting Assistant Professor in History at Carnegie-Mellon University. She has published articles on cultural history as well as co-authored *Anger: The Struggle for Emotional Control in America's History* (1986) with Peter N. Stearns.

Peter N. Stearns is Heinz Professor and Head, Department of History, Carnegie-Mellon University, and editor in chief of the *Journal of Social History.* He has published on a variety of topics in social and applied history, including gender, old age, and comparative civilizations. His current research focuses on the identification and repression of "unpleasant" emotions in modern American history.

Index

Abbott, Jacob, 197
Abbott, John, 197
Abolitionists, 81
Absenteeism, 138
Accidents, 56–7
Adams, William, 76
Adler, Felix, 200–1
Adolescence, 90ff, 124, 200
Adoption, 7, 32, 151ff; adoption experts, 161–62; adoption outcomes, 178–80; adoption qualifications, 164–65; adoption "telling," 181–182
Adoption manuals, 151ff
Alcott, Bronson, 198, 208
Alger, Horatio, 126
Ambition, 32, 213
Americanization, 129
Androgyny, 141
Anger, 2, 14, 30–31, 41ff, 79, 92, 123ff, 194, 197, 200; anger and democracy, 50, 142; and family, 45–46, 128, 140; and gender, 141; and neighbors, 43; and religion, 46–48; and work, 48; 124ff
Anthropology, 11, 30, 69, 89
Apprenticeship, 124
Ariès, Philippe, 4, 87
Arthur, T.S., 198
Asians, 141, 179
Averill, James, 14, 24

Baby and Child Care. See Spock
Baby boom, 216
Baldwin, Temperance, 72
Banks, Joseph, 34
Banns, 100, 104
Basic emotions, 10
Baxter, Richard, 92
Bedale (Yorkshire), 104–05
Bedford, Errol, 25–26
Behaviorism, 202

Benedict, Ruth, 69
Berenstain, Stanley and Janice, 212
Betrothals, 94ff
Biology, 8, 10, 15, 25, 161ff, 182
Birney, Mrs. Theodore, 199
Birth spacing, 206, 214, 216
Blood, 33–34, 43, 91, 93
Body functions, 43, 55, 91–93, 102
Bradstreet, Anne 73, 75
Breastfeeding, 158–59, 168, 206, 213
Briggs, Jean, 30
Burney, Fanny, 104
Byrd, William, 50, 54
Byron, John, 51

Calverly, Walter, 53
Calvert, George, 95
Cancian, Francesca, 88, 105
capitalism, 124, 142
Caplan, Frank, 213
Carnegie, Dale, 129, 130
Cheerfulness, 34, 51ff, 59, 124, 128ff
Child, Lydia, 198–99
Child Study Association of America, 202
Child Welfare League of America, 176
Childrearing, 8, 31, 48, 56, 59, 78–79, 139, 149, 151ff, 200ff
Children's Bureau, 202
Chinese, 282–29, 141
Christianity, 32–34. See also God, Puritanism
Church, 72
Civil War (England), 48
Civil War (United States), 126
Clark, Stuart, 11
Cleary, Beverly, 213
Clifford, Anne, 42
Clothing, 96, 102, 112, 206
Cognition, 29, 40, 44
Cohen, Charles, 11, 47
Commercialization, 13, 193, 195

Community, 13, 50, 57, 93–94, 105, 109
Conjuring, 94
Consideration, 133
Constructivism, 4
Courtship, 5, 17, 90ff, 194
Cunning men, 93, 96, 111

Darwin, 17, 193
Dating, 216
Declension, 76
Defamation, 73ff
DeMause, Lloyd, 4
Dee, John, 42
Degler, Carl, 59
Demography, 13
Depression, 55–56
Diaries, 39–40, 54, 89
Douglas, Mary, 93, 108
Duelling, 43
Duffy, Mrs. E.B., 196

Edwards, William, 73
Ego. *See* Self
Elliot, Emory, 53
Emotionology, 7–8, 25, 26–27, 40, 60, 91, 106, 136, 195ff
Emotions theory, 23ff
Enlightenment, 13, 48, 57
Enthusiasm, 28
Ethnography, 90ff
Evangelicals, 60, 82
Excrement, 93
Exit interviews, 132
Eyre, Adam, 49; 50

Family, 3ff, 12, 123ff, 161ff, 194ff; families and adoption, 101ff; families and work, 123–33
Fathers, 70ff, 156ff, 206, 214
Fear, 2
Feminization of love, 88, 105–06
Finney, Charles G., 82
Fisher, Dorothy Canfield, 202, 203
Flandrin, Jean, 4, 6

Folklore. *See* Ethnography
Forby, Robert, 111
Foremen, 126, 127, 128, 131–35, 137, 138, 139
Franklin, Benjamin, 124–25
Freke, Elizabeth, 42, 48
Freudian theory, 4, 17, 193, 208, 210

Garrison, William Lloyd, 81
Garters, 102, 104
Gay, Peter, 10, 59
Geertz, Clifford, 56, 152
Gender, 14, 33, 58, 88, 93ff, 141, 161, 177, 193ff; gender and love, 93ff, 193ff; and sadness, 58; and socialization, 193ff
General Electric, 128
Gesell, Arnold, 197
God, 46–48, 75, 81
Gouge, William, 99
Grandparents, 206
Greeks, 28
Greven, Philip, 5, 10, 59–60
Grief, 2, 5, 32ff, 79, 194
Groves, Gladys, 203
Guilt, 1, 57, 70ff, 93, 205

Hall, G. Stanley, 200
Haltunen, Karen, 106, 109
Hardwicke Marriage Act, 103
Harland, Marion, 197
Hate, 28–29
Hawthrone works, 128, 136
Hawthrone, Nathaniel, 71
Heywood, Oliver, 43, 44, 45, 52
Hierarchy, 13, 48, 54, 57, 123–24, 129, 130, 135–36, 142
Hochschild, Arlie, 24, 138, 142
Honeymoon, 104, 109, 168
Honor, 195, 200, 215
Huinzinga, Johann, 2
Humility, 32ff
Humm, Doncaster, 131
Hunt, David, 2, 49

Ifaluk, 25
Industrial psychology, 124, 128ff
Industrialization, 125–26
Insanity, 49, 153
Instinct, 89, 155, 193, 202
Insults, 3, 73ff

James, William, 193
Jealousy, 1, 103, 193ff; jealousy and causation, 208–212; and romance, 217; and siblings, 201ff; and violence, 206–07
Josselin, Ralph, 41, 43, 47, 51, 52, 53

Kaluli, 30–1, 52
Kinship, 151ff
Kissing, 91, 99, 108–09, 111, 113
Keller, Helen, 201
Kemper, Theodore, 24
Klein, Melanie, 193
Knives, 98

Law, 40, 71, 72–73
Leeper, R.W., 24
Levy, Robert, 24, 31–32, 56
Literacy, 91ff
Little Women, 199
Locke, John, 200
London, 46, 104, 112
Louis XIII, 49
Love, 1–2, 7, 10, 28, 39, 87ff, 151ff, 194ff; elite and popular definitions, 103–05; parental love, 151ff, 204–05. *See also* Courtship, Jealousy
Lowe, Roger, 41, 42, 44, 45, 47, 48, 52, 53
Lutz, Catherine, 25

MacDonald, Michael, 11, 87
Macfarlane, Alan, 87, 88
Magic, 92ff
Male liberation, 141
Manhood, 88, 111, 141, 178
Marriage, 94ff, 166, 217
Mather, Cotton, 44, 53, 76–77, 78

Mather, Increase, 76
Mayo, Elton, 128–29
Melancholy, 51
Mentalities, 8
Middle class, 9, 79, 88ff, 124ff, 184ff
Mills, C. Wright, 138, 142
Modernization, 4, 6, 39, 60, 87
Moore, Barrington, 140
Moral indignation, 140
Motherhood, 155ff, 202ff
Mourning, 32ff, 109
Muchembled, Robert, 56
Music, 100, 103, 198

Napier, Richard, 87, 93, 96
Narcissistic injury, 74–75
Narcissistic insult, 11, 73ff
Nature, 8, 157ff
Newcome, Henry, 45, 47–48, 51, 54
New England, 10, 43, 69ff, 95
New Guinea, 30–31, 52
Norwood, Richard, 44, 47, 49, 51–52, 56
Novel, 55

Oedipal conflict, 194, 209
Oglander, John, 43, 45, 48, 51

Parents' Magazine, 204, 206, 207, 212
Parkman, Ebenezer, 43, 45, 51, 53
Peasantry, 3
Penitentiary, 79–80
Periodization, 4ff
Photography, 112
Plummer, Ken, 90
Pollock, Linda, 5, 59, 87
Prayer, 51–52
Pregnancy, 162, 206
Pride, 28, 49, 75
Psychology, 11, 22ff, 89, 109, 128ff, 208; industrial psychology, 128–131
Psychoanalytic theory, 70, 76
Puritans, 11, 40, 41, 44, 45, 48, 49, 53, 69ff, 92, 99, 100, 109

Quarrels, 43, 93, 207, 208, 213

Rage, 28, 42
Religion, 75, 131
Repression, 134, 205
Rings, 98–99
Ritual, 90ff
Rollo books, 199
Romance. *See* Love
Romanticism, 108ff
Rousseau, Jean-Jacques, 172
Ryder, Dudley, 45, 46, 47, 48–49, 50, 51, 53

Sabean, David, 7
Sadness, 1, 41ff; sadness and sense of control, 55–58
Salespeople, 129, 135, 139
Saliva, 91, 93
Satan, 52
Schachter, Stanley, 24
Schneider, David, 153
Scientific management, 126, 128
Secretaries, 131, 135, 136–37
Sedgwick, Catherine, 198
Self, 31, 46, 54, 58, 59, 78, 96–97, 107, 142, 217
Self-alienation, 142
Sensitivity training. *See* T-groups
Sentimentality. *See* Romanticism
Servants, 43, 46, 48, 54, 124, 125, 127–28, 136
Service economy, 13, 131, 140
Sewall, Samuel, 42–43, 44, 51
Sexism, 177, 197
Sexuality, 6, 8, 10, 39, 71, 90, 99, 106, 111, 168, 193, 200, 209, 214; sex and courtship, 90, 99, 106, 111; sex and Puritanism, 71–72; sexual jealousy, 200, 209, 214
Shame, 1–2, 11, 57, 70ff
Shephard, Thomas, 75, 76
Shieffeln, Edward, 31, 52
Shorter, Edward, 4, 87, 88
Sibling rivalry. *See* Jealousy

Siblings, 102, 194ff
Sigourney, L.H., 198
Slander, 73
Social class, 9, 87, 88ff
Social history, 1–16
Solomon, Robert C., 39, 30
South (United States), 199
Spiro, Melford, 11
Spock, Benjamin, 140, 151ff, 204–05, 206, 212, 213
Spoiling, 175–76
Spontaneity, 6, 59
St. Agnes eve, 94, 95
Stewardess, 138
Stocks, 71
Stone, Lawrence, 2, 4, 87, 88
Stout, William, 52
Stowe, Harriet Beecher, 81
Strikes, 139–40
Symbolic interactionism, 89–90, 102

T-groups, 133–34, 139
Tahiti, 31, 33–34
Tahitians, 31–32, 56
Tantrum, 125, 132
Taylor, Frederick, 128
Tears, 51
Temperance, 80
Terkel Studs, 137
Terror, 28–29
Testing, 131
Textual analysis, 153
Thom, D.A., 201–02
Thomas, Keith, 56–57
Timidity, 32
Toilet training, 174
Tomkins, Sylvan, 10
Trade unions, 129, 138, 139
Trumbach, Randolph, 4
Turner, Victor, 102

Urine, 91, 92, 93, 102
Utku Eskimos, 30

Vahine, Tavana, 33

Valentine's Day, 94
Venice, 95
Victorianism, 8, 14, 58, 108, 110

Wales, 92, 96, 102
War Industries Board, 131
Watsonians, 202
Weber, Max, 13
Weddings, 97ff
West Indians, 28, 217
Wheeler, Anna, 110
Whipping, 49, 71
White collar work, 124ff
Wigglesworth, Michael, 76

Winthrop, John, 76, 77
Witchcraft, 60, 94, 95, 96, 102, 112
Witherspoon, John, 48
Wollstonecraft, Mary, 110
Women, 14, 33, 58, 88, 93ff, 127ff, 151ff, 193ff
Wood, Anthony, 43, 48
Work, 123ff, 193, 211
Working class, 88ff; 123ff
Wrightson, Keith, 87

Yorkshire, 95, 96, 100, 101, 104, 105

Zeal, 48, 50, 54, 195
Zeldin, Theodore, 14

DATE DUE

MAR 2 5 2002			